THE EMERGING NATIONS

AND

THE AMERICAN REVOLUTION

A 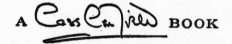 BOOK

BOOKS BY *Richard B. Morris*

The Emerging Nations and the American Revolution (*1970*)
The American Revolution Reconsidered (*1967*)
The Peacemakers (*1965*)
Great Presidential Decisions (*1960*)
The Spirit of 'Seventy-Six (*1958, 1967*)
(WITH HENRY STEELE COMMAGER)
Alexander Hamilton and the Founding of the Nation (*1957*)
The American Revolution: A Brief History (*1955*)
Encyclopedia of American History (First Edition, *1953*)
Fair Trial (*1953*)
A Treasury of Great Reporting (*1949*)
(WITH LOUIS L. SNYDER)
Government and Labor in Early America (*1946*)
The Era of the American Revolution (Editor, *1939*)
Studies in the History of American Law (*1930*)
A Guide to the Principal Sources for Early American History (*1929*)
(WITH EVARTS BOUTELL GREENE)
Volumes I and II of
The LIFE History of the United States:
The New World (*1963*)
The Making of the Nation (*1963*)

THE

EMERGING

NATIONS

AND THE

AMERICAN

REVOLUTION

Richard B. Morris

1817

HARPER & ROW, PUBLISHERS

New York, Evanston, and London

FIRST EDITION

LIBRARY OF CONGRESS CATALOG CARD NUMBER: 77–105233

CONTENTS

Preface · ix

I. THE AMERICAN REVOLUTION: MODEL FOR
EMERGING NATIONS? · 1

II. THE AMERICAN REVOLUTION IN THE AGE OF
DEMOCRATIC REVOLUTIONS · 36

III. THE AMERICAN REVOLUTION AND THE
LIBERATION OF EUROPE · 74

IV. THE AMERICAN REVOLUTION AND THE EMERGING
NATIONS OF THE WESTERN HEMISPHERE · 129

V. THE AMERICAN REVOLUTION AND THE EMERGING
NATIONS OF AFRICA AND ASIA · 178

Index · 225

To
Donald Morris
and
Donald Robinson

PREFACE

It is almost two hundred years since John Hancock affixed his oversize signature to a bold promulgation, some of whose promises have still not been fulfilled. Yet the Declaration of Independence, which invested a people's revolution with both moral content and legitimacy, possesses a quality of universality which transcends time and place.

To suggest that a revolution which formally began in 1776 and still has not run its course has a genuine relevance to the Nuclear Space Age may, at first glance, seem as incongruous as to compare the United States of today with the young nations now emerging out of that revolutionary process of decolonization which has transfigured the face of the globe.

It is the argument of this book that the American Revolution has meaning and message for our own age, not only for the enduring political and constitutional changes that it effected but also because the profound transformation of American society that it sparked has touched the lives of all peoples everywhere. One could write a multivolume encyclopedia documenting the contrasts between the United

States and emerging nations like Burma, Kenya, or Swazi-
land, to choose at random. To do so would be to belabor the
obvious. What may come as something of a surprise, if not a
shock, are the numerous analogies that can be demonstrated
between the circumstances of America during her revolution, along with her professions and practices, and the experiences and dogmas which govern the emerging states of
today.

For too long have Americans been content to view their
revolution as a central experience in *their* national life and to
ignore the libertarian currents that the event set off throughout the world. If Americans themselves have held so parochial a view of the primary event in their history as a nation,
they have been encouraged in their misconceptions by historians of revolutions who have rather consistently down-
graded the American and hailed the French or the Russian
or the Chinese as the transforming event of the modern
world. The facts, as they are adduced in this book, do not
support this assessment. Contrariwise, they demonstrate that
it was the American War for Independence that inaugurated
the Age of Revolutions which has still not come to an end,
and in a good many cases it has been the American Revolution which has been the model preferred by various nations
disenchanted with the social violence of the French Revolution as well as by its imperialist aftermath.

One may argue, and certainly many critics do, that the
Americans have paid lip service to the American Revolution
while behaving in ways quite contrary to its central libertarian message. In every schoolboy declamation, in every
Fourth of July oration, the slaveholding South invoked the
"Spirit of 'Seventy-Six," equality of rights, and the rights of
man, while seeing no inconsistency in confining that equality
to the people of one race and in denying the applicability of
the Declaration of Independence to the people held in

bondage. Admittedly, there is another and a less attractive side of the shield, one exemplified by the screech-eagle expansionist sentiments of the 1840's and by the imperialist ideology of the turn of the century. It is this paradoxical note in the American story that has heartened those who choose to regard America as a counterrevolutionary force that has disavowed her own libertarian traditions. Those— and this author is of their company—who feel that the values derived from the American Revolutionary experience are still central to the American way of life and the American purpose as a nation, regard such accusations as an egregious distortion both of the American spirit and the American sense of national interest.

In the rhetoric characteristic of his generation, Louis Kossuth, the Hungarian patriot, speaking at Lexington, Massachusetts, in May, 1852, predicted that it was America's destiny "to become the cornerstone of Liberty on earth." He coupled this eulogy with a warning. "Should the Republic of America ever lose the consciousness of this destiny," he declared, "that moment would be just so surely the beginning of America's decline, as the 19th of April, 1775, was the beginning of the Republic of America."

Recent involvements have given an ironic pertinence to Kossuth's warning. If America's position as the pre-eminent exemplar of a successful and lasting national revolution, as the first modern nation to achieve decolonization, is no longer as secure as it was when Kossuth visited this country, then Americans should be in for some serious stock-taking. Which image do Americans prefer? Do they wish the world to regard them as a nation with a revolutionary tradition, sympathetic to colonies in their struggles against their imperial rulers, tolerant of change and progress, and dedicated to the principle of equality? Or do they prefer that other image which America's adversaries depict, that of a counterrevolutionary America, everywhere on the side of urban elites seeking to stamp out the ardor for change on the part of the peasantry, against all national movements which seem to have a socialist orientation, as a white supremacist power determined everywhere to put down wars of liberation started by the colored races?

No doubt the alternatives are unfairly oversimplified. Nonetheless, the approach of the bicentenary of the American Revolution provides this nation with a timely occasion to reassess its basic values and confront its moment of truth.

In preparing this book the writer has incurred a heavy debt to numerous scholars both here and abroad. Columbia University's resources have been extensively tapped, and helpful leads and criticisms have been obtained from Professors Carrington Goodrich, Henry F. Graff, Graham Irwin, Otakar Odlozilik, and David Rothman, among others. Professor Bailey W. Diffie of the University of Washington furnished valued criticisms of the Latin American section, while Professor Aleine Austin of the University of Maryland, Baltimore, proved especially constructive in the initial phases of the project. Other scholars whose generous counsel has proved suggestive include Professors Yehoshua Arieli and Yaakob L. Talmon of the Hebrew University of Jerusalem; a number of Yugoslav scholars, including Prof. Dr. Fran Zwitter, University of Ljubljana, Prof. Dr. Jovan Kovačević, Faculty of Philosophy, University of Belgrade, Dr. Dragan R. Zvivojinović of that University's History Faculty, and Dr. Theodore V. Gjurgjevic, Andrija Stampar School of Public Health, Zagreb; Prof. Dr. Gerald Stourzh, History Faculty, University of Vienna, and the writer's associates at the John F. Kennedy–Institut für Amerikastudien, Free University of Berlin; and Mr. Norman Jacobs, Foreign Policy Association. Special acknowledgment must be made to Prof. Dr. Erich Angermann and his stimulating group of American specialists at the University of Cologne, to Margaret Butterfield for invaluable editorial advice, and to Ene Sirvet for the preparation of the index. Finally, the author has benefited by the critical judgment and sage advice of his son Jeffrey B. Morris of the New York Bar. His wife, Berenice R. Morris, patiently endured a long journey to nations, some long emerged, some still in their infancy, and throughout provided fertile suggestions and constant encouragement.

RICHARD B. MORRIS

I

THE AMERICAN REVOLUTION:
MODEL FOR EMERGING NATIONS?

In RITUAL or in substance, all the emerging nations of our time have paid obeisance to the American Revolution. As the first successful decolonization movement of the modern world, it serves as an object lesson even for emerging nations who have obtained their independence not through overt rebellion, as did the Americans, but through that piecemeal liquidation of empires by which the Great Powers have in most cases abdicated colonial rule since the Second World War.

If the American Revolution had done nothing more than to pioneer that historic movement of peoples from colonialism to national independence, it would still have enormous relevance for the emerging nations. The fact is, however, that the Revolution provided more than a set of guidelines for revolutionary tactics and strategy; it led to a total transformation of American society, and thus it has special pertinence in an age of revolutionary social change.

At first glance it might seem incredible that there should be any affinity in spirit between a superpower like the

United States and the young nations rising phoenix-like from the ashes of colonialism, handicapped by poverty, illiteracy, overpopulation, and landlordism. Many striking analogies may be demonstrated, however. At Independence the United States was both young and relatively weak. The Chinese called the youthful United States "The New People,"[1] while Europe's tradition-bound statesmen considered America not only young, but crude, undeveloped, and even primitive. Few if any of Europe's statesmen had faith in the lasting powers of a republic which extended its sway over so vast a territory as did the Thirteen States. Instead, they confidently expected that the centrifugal forces of sectionalism would soon rip it asunder. Even if America managed to survive as a political entity, Englishmen assumed that economic imperatives would once again attach the erstwhile insurgents to the mother country, and that the Thirteen States would resume a subordinate and dependent commercial role in the temporarily aborted relationship of Metropolis and Colony.

How like the posture assumed today by the Great Powers toward the young nations that have just emerged or are in the process of emerging from colonialism. Because so many Americans are not heedful of their revolutionary past it may come as a shock to many of them to have so powerful and affluent a nation as their own compared with Nigeria or Kenya, with Burma or Indonesia. Striking dissimilarities there are, to be sure, and they seem too obvious to need spelling out, but it is the appropriateness of the analogy in certain areas which should command our attention.

All of the devices to which the emerging nations have resorted in achieving independence for themselves can be discovered in that first anticolonial revolution waged by

1. Samuel Shaw to John Jay, May 19, 1785. The Papers of John Jay, Special Collections, Columbia University Libraries.

Thirteen Colonies against a powerful world empire. In that revolutionary process the Americans, like latter-day revolutionaries, utilized the weapons of noncooperation, civil disorder, provisional congresses, and finally war itself, even before issuing their declaration of independence. The Patriot or Revolutionary forces drew unity and inspiration from a charismatic leadership and fought a long and bitter war to a successful conclusion against seemingly hopeless odds.

First of all, though, the American Revolution determined the ritual observed by most later revolutions. Virtually all of the nations recently emerging from colonial status have felt obliged to justify their revolutions by declarations couched in language very similar to that utilized by the Americans in 1776. Even the Democratic Republic of Vietnam in its proclamation of September 2, 1945, made an open and intended levy on Jefferson's Great Declaration.

Secondly, in the use of sustained guerrilla operations over a period of years the American Revolution bears comparison with recent so-called "wars of national liberation." Except for climactic battles like Saratoga and Yorktown, the Patriot operation depended on maintaining a fighting force in being through mobility, withdrawal, and surprise counterattack. Operating with lightning speed from inaccessible bases which they changed frequently, Marion, Pickens, and Sumter, leaders of irregular forces, struck blows in rapid succession at isolated British and Tory camps, garrisons, and convoys in the lower South. Theirs indeed was a tactic of terror, which William Cullen Bryant has captured in his "Song of Marion's Men." The same kind of tactic has been exploited by such modern revolutionaries as Mao Tse-tung and the late Che Guevara.[2]

2. See Mao Tse-tung, *On Guerrilla Warfare,* translated by Samuel B. Griffith (New York, 1961), pp. 9, 58. See also Jesse Lemisch, "The American Revolution From the Bottom Up," in Barton J. Bernstein, *Toward a New Past: Dissenting Essays in American History* (New York, 1968), p. 26.

If so many of the emerging nations have capitalized on peasant unrest, it should be remembered that despite the elitist character of its leadership, the American Revolution was a mass movement that drew support from farmers and workers, and that originated in mass meetings and demonstrations, escalating to town riots, mobbism, tarring and feathering, and vigilantism. Even before mobbism came to focus upon antiministerial grievances, mobs during the early 1760's had erupted on the frontiers of Pennsylvania and the Carolinas, exploiting violence and intimidation to redress a variety of grievances when the colonial governments proved weak and unresponsive.[3] By the year 1765, however, demonstrations had as their objective the redress of imperial grievances.[4] The nucleus of pre-Revolutionary radical mob action was, originally, the Sons of Liberty—groups making their appearance in New York and New England, but soon springing up in virtually every colonial town. In New York, a center of such agitation, the leadership of such groups was quickly assumed by affluent merchants like Isaac Sears, John Lamb, and Alexander McDougall. Significantly, all three were shipowners as well as traders and thus had close relations with the seamen, who nursed long-standing grievances against the British government. Similarly connected were shippers like the Browns of Providence and John Hancock of Boston.

The grievances of the maritime workers sprang principally from the inequitable and irresponsible impressment practices of the Royal Navy. Indeed, of all working-class groups, the seamen felt perhaps the most oppressed and exploited.

3. See Brooke Hindle, "The March of the Paxton Boys," *William and Mary Quarterly*, 3rd ser., III (1946), 461–486; Richard M. Brown, *The South Carolina Regulators* (Cambridge, Mass., 1963).

4. See E. S. and H. M. Morgan, *Stamp Act Crisis* (New Haven, 1953), Ch. VIII.

Rootless, they had the least stake in the status quo. Accustomed to settling matters by brawn rather than brain, they proved the hard core of the "muscular radicals" so cleverly manipulated by affluent merchants and shrewd lawyers.

Joining the seamen in dissent were the "mechanics," a catchall term covering master employers along with their journeymen wage workers, both sharing a common economic resentment against the new tax measures of the British government and a common desire to have a larger voice in domestic politics. The mass demonstrations conducted by these groups carried either a symbolic purport, as with the raising of the liberty pole, or a design to implant terror in the breasts of those charged with the enforcement of the law. They had precise targets on which to mete out retribution. In Boston they burned the home of the collector of customs and sacked the residence of Lieutenant Governor Hutchinson, a symbol of royal authority. In Albany they pulled down the house of the stamp collector, and in New York City a crowd knocked down the residence of a British officer, who had provocatively announced that he would "cram the stamps down" the people's "throats with the end of my sword." Without romanticizing these mass demonstrations, it seems fair to assert that in their beginnings they were subject to purposeful discipline, and, with some exceptions, not given to looting or committing arson indiscriminately. When the "Mohawk braves" hurled the 342 chests of tea into Boston Harbor in the action that triggered the Revolution, they made sure that none of their company stole any of the tea for himself. Generally speaking, the leadership and discipline of the rioting mobs were so effective that they could be utilized as vigilante groups to enforce the nonimportation agreements which the town merchants adopted.

In short, the demonstrations cannot be dismissed as meaningless acts of a mischief-bent riffraff, but must be viewed as purposeful protest designed to articulate a political position or to intimidate the authorities responsible for the enforcement of detested parliamentary laws. And nobody can deny that they achieved their aim. Like the activists of our own day, the radical leaders revealed themselves to be extremely touchy about preserving undiminished their own civil liberties while remaining disgracefully indifferent to the civil rights of their opponents. There is perhaps no better example than the raid that "King" Sears staged on the newspaper office of his archenemy, the Royalist and later secret turncoat Rivington, whose printing press Sears and his cohorts seized. It should be noted that Patriots of sounder judgment like Alexander Hamilton and John Jay made no secret of their disavowal of Sears' rash action. What concerned these young New York Patriots was that, when the "multitude" acted with unrestrained passion to punish a detestable character, they might be naturally led to "a contempt and disregard of all authority." John Jay was equally concerned that the provisional revolutionary machinery set up by the state of New York would exert its powers with vigor to suppress "licentiousness," and he remarked that "the tenderness shown to some wild people on account of their supposed attachment to the cause" not only was of disservice to that cause but diminished the dignity and authority of provisional governments.[5]

In the main the elite who directed the Revolution kept the checkrein on mob violence. Even the attack of a Philadelphia mob in the fall of 1779 against the residence of the Patriot lawyer James Wilson, in whose house a number of profiteering merchants and speculators had taken refuge,

5. Alexander Hamilton to John Jay, November 26, 1775. R. B. Morris, ed., *Alexander Hamilton and the Founding of the Nation* (New York, 1957), pp. 475–477; Jay to Colonel Alexander McDougall, March 23, 1776. Jay Papers, Special Collections, Columbia University Libraries.

could be put down to a purposeful, if dangerously unruly, effort to discipline businessmen who refused to abide by the schedule of prices set by a price-fixing committee acting under the authorization of a mass meeting in the Statehouse yard.[6] If anything, this incident highlights the tendency of popularly chosen conventions, associations, and committees to usurp or encroach upon the governmental functions of constituted bodies. This phenomenon had its origins in the pre-Revolutionary agitation, burgeoned notably in the price- and wage-fixing conventions of Revolutionary years, and was continually utilized in the post-Revolutionary years as an institution for channeling a wide variety of socioeconomic and legal grievances, which may be said to have climaxed with Shays' Rebellion.[7] What diverted the American Revolution from the path of tumult and even anarchy was the evolution of governmental mechanisms to express the will of the people.

A recent scholar has referred to the "crisis of legitimacy" that confronts all post-revolutionary societies, the need to create new bonds of loyalty to replace the old.[8] The Americans resolved that crisis with great facility. They insisted upon the legality of their revolution, and fought for the rights of Englishmen as they believed them to be guaranteed by the British Constitution, and for the rights of man as they understood them to be guaranteed by Nature and Nature's God. Step by step they trimmed down Parliament's author-

6. William B. Reed, *Life and Correspondence of Joseph Reed* (Philadelphia, 1847), II, 423–426; Allen McLane, Ms. Journal, New-York Historical Society.

7. This point is developed in R. B. Morris, *Government and Labor in Early America* (New York, 1946), pp. 117, 118. See also Gordon S. Wood, *The Creation of the American Republic* (Chapel Hill, N.C., 1969), pp. 312–328.

8. Seymour Martin Lipset, *The First New Nation* (New York, 1967), pp. 19–26.

ity over the colonies until the King was the sole remaining tie. This, too, they deftly sundered. The Declaration cites "a long train of abuses" suffered by the colonies, and, taking a leaf from Tom Paine's *Common Sense,* presents the "history of the present King of Great Britain" as a "history of repeated injuries and usurpation." Denouncing as "unfit to be the ruler of a free people," "a prince whose character is thus marked by every act which may define a tyrant," the Great Declaration goes on to declare "these United Colonies" to be "free and independent states" and then to absolve them from "all political connection" with Great Britain. Thus the "crisis of legitimacy" was ingeniously resolved.

In the conduct of its diplomacy the American Revolutionaries were perhaps no more scrupulous than the leaders of emerging nations today. To win its fight for freedom America appealed to England's traditional enemies and counted on foreign aid to sustain the cause. Thus the American Revolution inevitably became part of a burgeoning world war, fought not only at Trenton, Saratoga, and Cowpens, but waged within the sight of the cliffs of Dover, at Gibraltar, off the Cape of Good Hope, in Caribbean waters, and along India's Coromandel Coast. In this larger involvement the Americans were reluctant participants. Their courtship in Europe had as its primary purpose military aid in the form of supplies and money and, secondly, commercial alliances. They were disinclined to get involved in balance-of-power politics, and resisted being dragged into wars which they felt were no concern of theirs. In short, they were neutralists or proto-isolationists like so many leaders of the new states of today who quite cynically exploit the Cold War to their own advantage but want no part in a conflict between the rival Great Powers. That capacity for ingratitude which recent nations have manifested on so many occasions may well be matched by President Washington's Proclamation of Neutrality, wherein he gave classic formulation to the Great

Rule of Non-entanglement in words that might have been voiced by a Nehru of India or a U Nu of Burma. America then waged a quasi-war against France to bring to an end an uneasy military alliance which no longer served America's interest.

Not only in its disposition toward nonalignment was Revolutionary America akin to the emerging nations of Asia and Africa today, but also in its adherence to a one-party system. Since most Americans regard a multi-party system as a hallmark of a democratic state, they might profit by the reminder that, despite factionalism, there was only one party in America for some fifteen or sixteen years at the least, and that was the party of the Revolution.[9] Antifederalism could hardly be elevated to the level of a nationally organized and structured party. The opposition provided by the Tory party the virtuous Revolutionaries proceeded to smash, hunting down or forcing its active members into exile. Those Loyalists who were sufficiently chameleon-like to escape patriotic censorship stayed and made their peace with the party of the Revolution. In time they became good Federalists. In short, there were factions but no parties in America. Before the country could afford the luxury of party divisions a national consensus had to be built. Thus, the Constitution takes no account of parties, and the first President denounced the substituting "for the delegated will of the nation the will of a party." Out of the power struggle between Jefferson and Hamilton, exacerbated by the divisions in America touched off by the French Revolution, a two-party system did emerge. But it was still necessary in 1804 to

9. An exception was Pennsylvania, where the "Constitutionalists" and "Republicans" were polarized over both the state Constitution of 1776, which the former favored, and the federal Constitution whose ratification they opposed. See William N. Chambers, *Political Parties in a New Nation* (New York, 1963), pp. 19, 20; and most recently, Owen S. Ireland, "The Ratification of the Federal Constitution in Pennsylvania," unpublished dissertation, University of Pittsburgh (1967).

adopt the Twelfth Amendment to the Constitution providing for the separate designation on the ballot of a President and a Vice President to prevent the embarrassment of having a Vice President elected from a party opposed to the President-elect as had occurred in the 1790's.

If nationalism is the yeast which produces the revolutionary ferment of emerging nations, the analogy from the world of the present to young America is by no means strained. The American nation was born of revolution, and from its infancy it possessed characteristics which set it apart from the nations of the Old World. Goethe caught that essential difference in his *Poems of Wisdom* when he wrote:

> America, you fare much better
> Than this old continent of ours
> No basalt rocks your land enfetters
> No ruined towers . . .

In its emergence America was destined to fix the character of much of modern nationalism. Leaders like Washington and John Jay were concerned about establishing a national character. To start, the common tongue, the English language, had to be Americanized—Noah Webster saw to that. Even before Webster the process was going forward. "You speak American well," the French traveler Chastellux reported to be a common remark as early as 1782. Education had to be made more available and pragmatic, the divisive force of religious intolerance mitigated, and the penal code modernized to fit a more humane society. The statesman John Jay did more than coin a phrase when he observed in 1797, "I wish to see our people more Americanized, if I may use that expression; until we feel and act as an independent nation, we shall always suffer from foreign intrigue."[10]

10. H. P. Johnston, ed., *Correspondence and Public Papers of John Jay* (New York, 1893), IV, 232. Yehoshua Arieli persuasively argues that Amer-

Accordingly, when the Irish Free State compels its children to study Gaelic, when Israel adopts Hebrew as its official language, when the Vietnamese require all foreign signs removed and replaced by those in the Vietnamese language, and when fanatical Indian patriots riot to make Hindi, not English, the language of instruction, we must bear in mind that they are taking the same basic steps in building national character that Americans themselves assumed without a venerated national tradition, with but few national myths, and with heroes chosen from an immediate past.

There is a dynamic of revolution which pervades all societies that have undergone a revolutionary experience, not least the American. If China has been in fierce competition with the Soviet Union in exporting its brand of Marxist-Leninism to the underdeveloped nations, and if Fidel Castro wants Latin America to bear the stamp of Fidelismo, the sense of revolutionary mission has not been confined to the Marxist-Leninist nations of the twentieth century. That sense of mission inspired the French Revolutionary leaders, and perhaps in a perverted sense the values and institutions of their revolution were transplanted to adjacent lands by a bold and imaginative Corsican adventurer. But even earlier that sense of revolutionary mission gripped America's Founding Fathers. In a closing *Crisis* letter Tom Paine voiced it with naive candor. "To see it in our power to make a world happy," he observed, "to teach mankind the art of being so—to exhibit on the theatre of the universe a character hitherto unknown, and to have, as it were, a new creation intrusted to our hands, are honors that command reflection

ican nationalism rested on a political consensus rather than on folk tradition or on ethnic, religious, or cultural unity. *Individualism and Nationalism in American Ideology* (Baltimore, Md., 1964), pp. 22, 23.

and can neither be too highly estimated nor too gratefully received."

From its inception the American Revolution was pitched on a moral and even evangelical plane. The didactic character of the American Revolution has for better or worse permanently stamped itself upon American diplomacy. Stripped of its sense of mission the American Revolution would have lost much of its world significance, while America's intervention in world affairs in the twentieth century would have assumed the character of a naked power grab. That America now ventures to shoulder global responsibilities of awesome dimension is attributable in no small part to the rearing of the American people during the infancy of the Republic.

Having considered various analogies between the emerging nation of '76 and the new nations of our own time, it would seem pertinent, if the American Revolution deserves consideration as a model for transforming societies, to inquire what distinctive and durable notions of the relationship of men to government came out of the American Revolution and in what ways American society was radically transformed.

First, it should be remarked that in the invention of the mechanisms of government the American Founding Fathers proved both innovative and profound. Much has been said about the origins of these remarkable constitutional principles. Years of ideological preparation served to lay the foundation for the acceptance of the notion of a republic and its innate superiority to monarchy,[11] of government by consent

11. Prior to the American Revolution, especially after the failure of the Puritan commonwealth, "republicanism" had been used in a derogatory sense. See Willi Paul Adams, *Republikanismus und die ersten amerikanischen Einzelstaatsverfassungen zur idee geschichtlichen under verfassungsgeshichtlichen Komponente der amerikanischen Revolution, 1775–1780* (Berlin, 1968).

of the governed, and of fundamental law and constitutionalism. That classical influences shaped the Revolutionary
mind can be quickly demonstrated by perusing the debates
of the Constitutional Convention with its stream of references to the governmental innovations and ideas of the
ancients. From Locke to Rousseau, various Revolutionary
ideologists levied heavily upon the Age of the Enlightenment. England's legal history, as the Revolutionary pamphleteers chose to misconstrue it, provided further arguments
for their revolutionary program of government. Nor did
some American pamphleteers neglect the English radical
thinkers of the early eighteenth century, notably John
Trenchard and Thomas Gordon. The radical Whig tradition,
with its paranoiac mistrust of power, provided some of the
rhetoric used in expounding the novel American principles
of republicanism. Finally, the entire operation was imbued
with a sense of moral purpose and uplift derived from the
covenant theology of New England Puritanism.[12]

The American Revolution culminated almost two generations of ideological opposition to monarchy, although attachment to the Crown remained the one tie to empire that
most Patriots abandoned with greatest reluctance. Supplanting monarchy, the American Revolution ushered in an era of
republican governments. Emerging America was threatened
by, but did not succumb to, the specter of dictatorship, in
which respect most of its imitators have been far less successful.

Predisposed in favor of notions of fundamental law and
popular sovereignty, it seems to have been an almost instinctive process for the colonists to resort to democratic means
to create their new revolutionary governments. If, in most

12. For the most recent and fullest exposition, see Bernard Bailyn, *Ideological Origins of the American Revolution* (Cambridge, Mass., 1967).

instances, the leadership in that constitutional process was retained by the Revolutionary elite, they felt a certain propriety, even confidence, in resting their governments upon the consent of the governed. Richard Henderson, the founder of the Transylvania Colony in what is now Kentucky, pointed out to a Glasgow correspondent as early as July 30, 1774, that the Revolutionary squirearchy "have always hitherto been, as King Alfred said the English ought to be, *free as their own thoughts.*" He also had some perceptive comments to make about the common man. "Even our commonality," he pointed out,

> have never been used to stand in awe of rank and station. They are a well-informed, reasoning commonality too, perhaps the most of any on earth, because of the free intercourse between man and man that prevails in America: their free access to courts of law, as parties and jurors, where they hear the rights of the subject nobly debated; their frequent and free elections, which give occasion for candidates to scan each other's principles and conduct before the tribunal of the people, together with the freedom and general circulation of newspapers, and the eagerness and leisure of the people to read them or to listen to those who do.[13]

In May, 1775, Henderson called a convention of representatives from four minuscule settlements in Kentucky, at which he praised the English Constitution but reminded the delegates that "all power is originally in the people." The delegates listened to Henderson's eloquent advice and accepted the constitution which he had written vesting authority largely in the Transylvania Company. Even when these and other newcomers revolted against the Company, the next year they followed in their revolt the democratic procedure which Henderson had advised.[14]

13. Force, *American Archives,* 4th ser., III, 54–55.

14. William L. Saunders, ed., *Colonial Records of North Carolina* (Raleigh, 1886–90), IX, 1268–1271.

Persuasive and contagious was the notion that government of necessity derives its authority from the consent of the governed. The people were quick to raise that issue in deciding how to delegate the authority to draft a constitution. In New York City the mechanics asserted in June of 1776 that the authority to create a constitution had to come from "the inhabitants at large." The freemen in one Connecticut town argued that the town should elect its delegates to the Continental Congress directly. The frontier town of Hanover, New Hampshire—rent by the rival claims of New Hampshire and Vermont—argued the absurdity of maintaining a legislature which held over from before Independence.

The classic example of a creative commitment to the democratic principle of constitution-making was the Massachusetts Constitution of 1780. On September 17, 1776, the Massachusetts House called upon the towns to vote whether they would authorize it to draw up a new constitution. Various towns took it upon themselves to instruct the General Court in constitutional theory and practice. Ashfield, for example, favored abolishing the "Old Tiranical Laws" under the British Constitution and taking instead "the Law of God for the foundation of the forme of our Government." That town's fear of executive power, a fear shared by most Americans, was expressed in the vote "that it is our Opinniun that we Do not want any Goviner but the Goviner of the univarse, and under him a States Ginaral to Consult with the wrest of the united States for the good of the whole."[15] The committee chosen by the House to draw up a constitution shared with the townsfolk of Ashfield their deep republican principles, but was a good deal more sophisticated in its approach. Its draft, reported in December, 1777, was accepted by a convention meeting the next year, and then

15. October 4, 1776. Massachusetts Archives, CLXI, f. 131.

submitted to the towns. Lacking a Bill of Rights and other features deemed essential by the voters, it was defeated by a resounding vote of almost five to one.

In a chastened mood the General Court took up once again the next year the task of constitution-making. Again it called upon the people to authorize a convention, which was done. As evidence of the fact that the Revolutionary period perceptibly enlarged the basis of popular consent it may be noted that all freemen over twenty-one years of age were entitled to vote on this issue. Happily, John Adams had just returned from France for a brief stay in between diplomatic assignments. He guided the convention's deliberations and drafted the constitution. This second try was submitted to the towns and ratified. As Adams, not one to deprecate his own achievement, saw it, Massachusetts had in so doing "realized the theories of the wisest writers." The innovating aspect of the constitutional convention and ratification by the voters was hailed by others as well. "The people of Massachusetts," commented Thomas Dawes, "have reduced to practice a wonderful theory. A numerous people have convened in a state of nature, and like our ideas of the patriarchs, have deputed a few fathers of the land to draw up for them a glorious covenant." Sam Adams, a foremost advocate of popular sovereignty, considered that the new constitution had been "proposed and agreed to in the most legitimate manner of which there is any legitimate example since the days of Lycurgus."

It was not only the participants who recognized that a revolutionary constitution-making process had been innovated. New Hampshire, whose voters had rejected an earlier constitution, submitted a new one based on the Massachusetts model, and, after additional rejections and delays, an acceptable constitution was ratified by the people in 1783.[16]

16. R. F. Upton, *Revolutionary New Hampshire* (Hanover, 1936), pp. 180–186. See also Wood, *American Republic,* pp. 259–291, 328–343.

The process by which the federal Constitution was adopted served to invest the constitutional and ratifying conventions which Massachusetts had innovated with all the trappings of republican, if not revolutionary orthodoxy, and the device, beginning with the French Revolution, has since spread throughout the globe.

The men of the American Revolutionary era decided the question of how men make government. Fearing government in varying degrees, they were equally concerned with the issue of how government can be limited. Some might agree with Tom Paine that "government, like dress, is the badge of lost innocence." Others were prepared to apply Jefferson's aphorism that government was best that governed least. If government was not to be trusted, certainly not kingly governments, then a republic must strictly limit the executive powers, and through notions of division of powers and checks and balances, build in guarantees that no one branch of the government might act tyrannically. Even the bicameral legislature, which all the Revolutionary state constitutions save those of Pennsylvania, Georgia, and Vermont instituted, accorded with the American consensus about the virtues of a mixed or balanced government to protect the commonwealth from the unbridled power of any one group or interest in society.

Convinced that all men had certain inherent rights upon which government could not trespass and long familiar with the bills of rights which formed a part of English fundamental law, the Revolutionary statesmen, beginning with George Mason in Virginia, had these rights spelled out in the state constitutions. Yielding to public pressure, the Founding Fathers incorporated them in the Federal Constitution in the form of the first Ten Amendments. Anticipating by weeks Jefferson's Great Declaration, the Virginia Declaration of Rights begins by asserting that all men are by nature equally free and independent, and have certain inherent rights, of which, when they enter into a state of society, they cannot by any compact deprive or divest their posterity; namely, the enjoyment of life and liberty, with the means of acquiring and possessing property, and pursuing and obtaining happiness and safety.[17]

These bills of rights have had momentous consequences in the shaping of American constitutional history. Their rigorous and courageous interpretation by the recent courts have served to press America forward in its continuing search for a more equal and more democratic society. They raised a standard to which revolutionary France and other nations have felt impelled to repair, a standard of respect for individual liberties which, more than any other single criterion, distinguishes the free world from totalitarian societies. Civil libertarian values were basic to the American Revolutionary tradition. The American colonists had, notably in the Zenger Case, eloquently contended for the broadest freedom of speech against governors and judges. Still, while demanding the unrestricted right to criticize royal officials, the colonists saw no inconsistency in condemning seditious libels against the representatives of the people in their colonial assemblies.[18] Here, too, one could analogize to the tight controls on the press exercised by the magistrates of the people in the emerging nations.

If the constitution-making process and the incorporation of bills of rights were to become the hallmarks of revolutionary virtue, the renunciation of the trappings of colonialism proved another distinguishing characteristic of American republicanism. That anticolonial spirit was exemplified in

17. B. P. Poore, ed., *The Federal and State Constitutions* (rev. ed., Washington, 1878), II, 1908–1909.

18. See Leonard W. Levy, "Did the Zenger Case Really Matter?," *William and Mary Quarterly*, 3rd ser., XVII (1960), 35–50.

a unique way by Congress in its provisions for the government of newly acquired territories. In his territorial plan of 1784 Jefferson would have allowed the entire West the fullest possible measure of self-government, with provisions for adult male suffrage and the eventual admission of the territories into the Union. Even though some of its more liberal provisions (notably the barring of slavery in all the territories, both North and South)[19] were watered down in the justly celebrated Ordinance of 1787, that statesmanlike measure constituted a repudiation of colonial imperialism. While, as a concession to Eastern conservatives, it introduced a "first stage" of tutelary government by officials appointed by the federal government, the Ordinance also set up the machinery for admission of territories to statehood on the basis of absolute equality. This innovating concept assured prospective settlers that, regardless of where they settled on the continental domain, theirs was not to be a permanent colonial subordination; they could look forward to participating in the Union of the states on equal terms with the Original Thirteen. Indubitably, this fair and even generous guarantee contributed to a climate that proved hospitable to Western settlement.[20]

Finally, one cannot conclude the consideration of the innovating and durable constitutional concepts that emerged from the American Revolution without paying tribute to the concept of federalism. In adapting the erstwhile colonial relationship within the empire to a new concept of federalism, one that refused to sacrifice effective national power while conceding the reserved powers of the states and the people, the American Revolution demonstrated extraor-

19. See Staughton Lynd, *Class Conflict, Slavery, and the United States Constitution* (Indianapolis, 1967), pp. 186–213.

20. See the illuminating analysis in Francis S. Philbrick, *The Rise of the West, 1754–1830* (New York, 1965), pp. 125–133.

dinary ingenuity and originality. Balancing the claims of central and state authorities proved a delicate feat, and even James Madison, in the Thirty-ninth *Federalist,* is not transparently clear about how much and in what areas the government is "national" and not "federal." Indeed, each generation since Madison has been obliged to reassess the relative roles of the federal and state governments. Since the New Deal the United States has enormously expanded the role of the federal government in the fields of taxation, finance, business regulation, and social welfare, activities undreamed of when the nation was in its infancy. If, then, federalism today has more of a Hamiltonian cast than a Jeffersonian, it is because the ends of government have ranged far beyond the vision of the Founding Fathers. A welfare state in the Nuclear Space Age simply must possess effective powers if it wishes to remain as a functioning entity. Still, federalism in the United States is by no means moribund. Its continued operation serves as an example to emerging nations torn by ethnic, linguistic, religious, tribal, and regional divisions. The six republics that compose Yugoslavia might find it to their profit to explore its potentialities before they permit separatist tendencies to fragment their society. Where federalism has broken down, as in Nigeria, the results have been catastrophic.

Revolutionary as the constitutional, legal, and political relationships established in the course of America's War for Independence may have proven, they were inextricably bound up with that profound transformation of American society initiated under the aegis of republicanism. Most transforming of all the republican doctrines spelled out by the philosopher-statesmen of the American Revolution was the notion of equality.[21] The Virginia Bill of Rights affirmed

21. See, most recently, Gordon S. Wood, *The Creation of the American Republic, 1776–1787* (Chapel Hill, N.C., 1969), pp. 70–75.

that "all men are by nature equally free and independent"; the Declaration of Independence, "that all men are created equal."

When the Founding Fathers talked about equality, it should be borne in mind, they did not mean social leveling, for one and all affirmed the superior position which men of virtue and talents should hold in the state. As the Massachusetts jurist Theophilus Parsons argued in the *Essex Result*, a pamphlet written in 1778 to oppose the draft of the Massachusetts State Constitution of that year, the aim of a political society was not to secure equality of property, but to maintain equality of rights. Parsons, and the committee of the ratifying convention whose views he formulated, even went so far as to insist that laws affecting property had to be approved by those who had "a majority of the property"; otherwise the right of property "is vanished."[22] Committed as they were to the notion of equal rights rather than equality of wealth, the Founding Fathers were also committed to the doctrine of equality of opportunity, and were firmly opposed to setting up in America an hereditary aristocracy.

By its vigilant concern over any move which might encourage special privilege, the American Revolutionary generation proved the sincerity of its dedication to the creation of an egalitarian society. When, at the end of the war, the promise of half pay for life to Revolutionary War officers was commuted by Congress to full pay for five years, a storm

22. Theophilus Parsons, Jr., *Memoir of Theophilus Parsons* (Boston, 1859), pp. 359–402. Parsons' views are in contrast with the returns of Lenox (Berkshire County, May 20, 1778), protesting the exclusion of nonproperty owners from voting for higher officials in the state, a protest that Sutton (Worcester County) had already registered (May 18, 1778). Massachusetts Archives CLVI, fols. 347–354, 375–381. For the Whiggish nature of Parsons' arguments, see J. R. Pole, *Political Representation in England and the Origins of the American Republic* (London, 1966), pp. 186, 187.

of dissent arose. New Englanders were especially prone to indict the proposal as laying the seeds of an aristocracy. Then, when the Society of Cincinnati was founded at the conclusion of the war, many Americans deemed this action corroborative evidence that the military was planning to set itself up as a force uncontrolled by the civil power. The most obnoxious feature of the Society was its provision making membership hereditary. Despite Washington's nominal presidency of the Society, many leading Americans joined the popular opposition in assailing the Order. Some of the heaviest broadsides were fired by Judge Aedanus Burke of South Carolina, who warned that, if unchecked, the Society would divide the country into two classes, the patricians and the rabble. Even in remote New England Burke's attack aroused a furor. Town meetings and county conventions, joined by one state legislature after another, proceeded to denounce the Society. In France, Benjamin Franklin, who scoffed at the Cincinnati as "hereditary knights," turned Burke's pamphlet over to Mirabeau to translate into French. Soon to be a Revolutionary protagonist in his own land, Mirabeau issued his own adaptation and amplification of Burke's indictment. Therein he warned that, while monarchies might need an aristocracy, such a "body" was antipathetical to the republican spirit and to the American constitutions and bills of rights which asserted the equality of all citizens.[23] Retrospectively, the anxieties aroused both in France and America over the Order of the Cincinnati seem all out of scale with that society's aims and capacities. Bowing to the almost universal clamor, the Society promptly abolished its hereditary

23. (Aedanus Burke), *Considerations on the Society or Order of Cincinnati* (Charleston, 1783); H. G. R. de Mirabeau, *Considerations sur l'ordre de Cincinnatus, ou imitation d'un pamphlet Anglo-Américain* (London, 1784); Wallace E. Davies, "The Society of the Cincinnati in New England, 1783–1800," *William and Mary Quarterly*, 3rd ser., V (1948), 3–25; Merrill Jensen, *The New Nation* (New York, 1950), pp. 261–265.

character and placed the funds of the state societies in the keeping of the state legislatures.

It has been the fashion of commentators to consider the American Revolution as legalistic and as exhibiting a tender concern for property unlike such twentieth-century revolutions as those of Mexico and Cuba, for example. Like all oversimplifications, this one fails to take into account the complex currents which swept the American Revolutionary movement and the wide range of socioeconomic ideas which the leaders espoused. Time after time minority groups sought to move their states in leveling directions not acceptable to the majority. By way of example, the preliminary draft of Pennsylvania's Declaration of Rights contained an article stating "that an enormous Proportion of Property vested in a few Individuals is dangerous to the Rights, and destructive of the Common Happiness of Mankind," and should accordingly be discouraged by the laws of the state.[24] Many of the states fixed price and wage ceilings during the Revolution, along with regulations against profiteering and monopolizing, and various legislatures in post-Revolutionary years enacted paper money and stay laws. They provide documentation attesting to the widespread conviction that property values should not be elevated above human values, and that the property owner and creditor should not on all occasions be awarded their pound of flesh.

In one way or another reformers devoted considerable attention to the ownership of property and sought to bring about its redistribution. While great landlords could be found both on the Patriot and the Tory side of the Revolutionary controversy, the Patriots soon recognized the dangers of an emerging land monopoly. As a result of the confisca-

24. *Pennsylvania Packet*, Nov. 26, 1778.

tion of immense Tory estates and the opening up of the Crown lands of the West obtained by the Patriots at the peacemaking in Paris, a magnificent opportunity presented itself to create a new society of relatively small freeholders. However, unless quick action were taken the land jobbers and monopolizers were likely to take over. So prescient a statesman as Thomas Jefferson anticipated the problem. He sought unsuccessfully to incorporate curbs on the ownership of unappropriated lands in the various drafts he formulated for the Virginia Constitution of 1776; his Land Office Act of 1779, which speculators managed to evade, had a similar purport. Jefferson was not alone in his concern. So voracious a land speculator and engrosser as Robert Morris warned Congress in 1782 that "a large proportion of America is the property of great landholders," who "monopolize without cultivation."[25]

Thwarted in his efforts to curb land speculation and engrossment, Jefferson proceeded to draft legislation in Virginia to end primogeniture (descent to the first-born) and entailed estates. The enactment of Jefferson's proposals in 1776 crowned his efforts to supplant "an aristocracy of wealth" by an "aristocracy of virtue and talent."[26] Emulating Virginia's example, the other states abolished primogeniture and most of them ended or transformed the character of entails, thereby paying tribute to the pervasive notion that legal devices for the descent and distribution of land must, so far as possible, guarantee and perpetuate an egalitarian society. These sweeping reforms in real property law, so far in advance of the mother country, constituted telling blows both against land monopoly and the notion of a class-struc-

25. *Journals of the Continental Congress, 1774–1789*, XX, 429–447.

26. Jefferson, *Writings* (H. W. Washington, ed., 1853), I, 36, 37; Hening, *Statutes at Large of Virginia*, IX, 226.

tured society.[27] It might prove instructive to contrast the
land reform experiences of the new North American nation
with those of Latin America. In Chile, when O'Higgins
attempted to abolish the entail, it was not the entail that
disappeared but O'Higgins, and the great estate holders
managed to put off ending this legal device until the 1850's.[28]
Indeed, in Chile, as in most of Latin America, the political
revolutions which secured independence from Spain did not
bring about anything comparable to the root-and-branch
land reforms that were instituted in North America in the
Revolutionary years and that were buttressed by further reforms of real property law in the first half of the nineteenth
century.

   In disputes with underdeveloped nations over such issues
as the confiscation of American and other foreign-owned
property and the honoring of debts, the United States has
invariably, if not inflexibly, applied long-accepted Hamiltonian standards generally observed in the more stable democracies of the Free World. As a Revolutionary nation the
United States honored these standards in the breach. The
American states during and after the Revolution confiscated
the estates of the Loyalists. The initial purpose of such
confiscatory measures was not to universalize freeholding,
since a very broad class of freeholders already existed, but to
punish notorious dissidents and raise funds desperately
needed to carry on the war. However, the confiscated estates
either at the beginning, as in cases where manor tenants
were allowed to exercise pre-emption rights and thus trans-

27. See R. B. Morris, *Studies in the History of American Law* (New York,
1930), pp. 69–125; *The American Revolution Reconsidered* (New York,
1967), pp. 79–81; and, most recently, W. P. Adams, *Republikanismus*, pp.
392, 393.

28. See R. A. Humphreys, *Tradition and Revolt in Latin America* (London,
1969), p. 11.

formed into freeholders, were broken up, or in the long run they were sold by insiders and speculators to small holders. Either way, the long-range effect was egalitarian. In some cases the objective was clearly the breaking up of land monopoly. Thus the estates of the Penn family in Pennsylvania were taken over, as one correspondent reminded Lady Juliana Penn in the summer of 1782, "not in a way of confiscation, but upon principles of policy and expedience." They thought the estate "two [sic] large for a subject to possess, supposing it dangerous to the public that so much property should rest in the hands of one family."[29]

If the Soviet Union refuses to honor the Czarist debts, its actions are hardly unique among revolutionary states. For a generation Southern planters in the American states, buttressed by legal devices adopted by their state governments, refused to pay their prewar debts owing to English and Scottish merchants. The evidence of such indebtedness is massive and the devices employed to avoid payment provide some of the strongest arguments for considering the War for Independence a social revolution. Despite the provision of the Treaty of Peace that creditors on either side should meet with no lawful impediment to the recovery in full value of their debts, many Virginians remained adamant on the subject. George Mason remarked to Patrick Henry that the question most frequently raised in conversation was: "If we are now to pay the debts due to the British merchants, what have we been fighting for all this while?"[30]

29. James Tilghman to Lady Juliana Penn, Chester Town, Md., August 14, 1782. Shelburne Papers, 72:311, William L. Clements Library, University of Michigan. Among the recent studies of this complex subject, see Catherine S. Crary, "Forfeited Loyalist Lands in the Western District of New York," *New York History*, XXXV (1954), 239–256; Beatrice G. Rubens, "Preemptive Rights in the Disposition of a Confiscated Estate," *William and Mary Quarterly*, XXII (1965), 435 *et seq.*

30. George Mason to Patrick Henry, May 6, 1783, in William W. Henry, *Patrick Henry: Life, Correspondence and Speeches* (New York, 1891), II, 187.

When the federal courts sought to carry out the provisions of the peace treaty and to enforce payment of such debts, violent feelings were aroused in debtor areas. A grand jury of the Federal Circuit of Virginia, for example, presented "as a *national* grievance the recovery of debts due to British subjects." Despite a cluster of affirmative decisions in both federal and state courts, the issue of the British debts was not lightly resolved. In dispatching Chief Justice John Jay to the Court of St. James, President Washington had in effect given public endorsement to the views of Jay which were highly critical of debtors who hid behind the protection of state laws to evade their obligations. At Jay's initiative the British agreed to set up a mixed commission to decide on these claims. Payments for all debts validated by the commission were to be assumed by the United States. Aside from Jay's notable innovation in international law of the principle of mixed commissions, so frequently employed thereafter by the United States and Great Britain in resolving other controversies, the effect of this treaty stipulation was to impose upon the United States an obligation to settle unpaid claims of private British citizens for sums owing by private American citizens. Such a settlement, on a compromise basis, was finally made, and thereby the American people repudiated their Revolutionary anti-creditor posture, and enshrined among their foremost principles the Hamiltonian doctrine that "every breach of the public engagements, whether from choice or necessity, is, in different degrees, hurtful to public credit."[31]

We are accustomed to associating recent revolutions, whether the Bolshevik Revolution of 1917 or the Cuban Rev-

31. Alexander Hamilton, *Report of the Secretary of the Treasury to the House of Representatives relative to a provision for the support of the Public Credit of the United States . . .* (New York, 1790). The issue of the debts is discussed at length in R. B. Morris, *John Jay, the Nation, and the Court* (Boston, 1967), pp. 71–97.

olution of 1959, with violent social upheaval. In contrast, the American Revolution, with its sober and affluent leadership and its emphasis on legitimacy and moderation, seemingly accomplished its social transformation in a less explosive fashion. To the Loyalists who were forced to emigrate and whose property was seized, the social revolution seemed violent enough, to be sure. The estimate of the emigré Loyalists who went to Canada or England during the American Revolution ranges as high as 100,000, with perhaps an equal number of black people joining the exodus. As one perceptive scholar of revolutions has pointed out, this represents a far higher percentage of displaced persons for the American than for the French Revolution.[32]

To fill the places of the Loyalists many new men came into business and government, and many new fortunes were created by the special opportunities afforded by the Revolution in such areas as privateering, war manufacturing and supplies, and by the establishment of new trade patterns and the speculative opportunities afforded by inflation. In addition, in most cases representation in the state legislatures was enlarged to the advantage of newly settled areas and men of less established families. In the Sixty-second *Federalist* James Madison stresses "the mutability in the public councils" which he attributed to "a rapid succession of new members," and asserts that "every new election in the States is found to change one half of the representatives." Madison's contention that within the American Revolutionary states the new governments were operated by new men, many of whom could hardly have expected to attain prominence had the colonies remained British, is sustained by a comparative study of the membership of colonial legislatures on the eve of independence and shortly after inde-

32. See R. R. Palmer, *The Age of the Democratic Revolution* (Princeton, 1959), I, 188.

pendence had been obtained. In three states the proportion of those in the lowest socioeconomic category, denominated as being in "moderate" circumstances, rose from 17 percent of the legislatures in 1770 to 62 percent in 1784, with a corresponding decline recorded in the ranks of the "wealthy" and the "well-to-do." Even in the South the "wealthy" lost their predominance in the legislatures. The proportion of merchants and lawyers in the state legislatures suffered a startling decline while the representation of the farmers doubled during these years. If, then, socioeconomic upthrust is an essential criteria of a true revolution, one headed in a democratic direction, the American Revolution, with its partial, if not total, displacement of the colonial "upper" or "aristocratic" class, must be considered a social revolution.[33]

From the perceptive French emigrant Crèvecoeur to the South Carolina aristocrat Charles Pinckney, observers painted an idyllic landscape of American Revolutionary society. Crèvecoeur saw the American as being "free as he ought to be," and dwelling in a climate of "pleasing equality." Barbé-Marbois, first secretary to the French mission in Philadelphia, found in America a freedom and equality "united to the real advantages which the older societies of Europe enjoy, without any of the maladies which afflict some of those exhausted and decrepit social structures."[34] Other Frenchmen found proof of the existence of an egalitarian society in America a rather painful experience. For example, the Baron de Vioménil might have felt that as an aristocrat he was entitled to hunting rights, but a Rhode Island peasant who caught him hunting on his land threat-

---

33. Jackson Turner Main, "Government by the People: The American Revolution and the Democratization of the Legislatures," *William and Mary Quarterly*, 3rd ser., XXIII (1966), 391–407; *The Upper House in Revolutionary America, 1763–1788* (Madison, Wis., 1968).

34. F. Barbé-Marbois, *Our Revolutionary Forefathers*, trans. by E. P. Chase (New York, 1929), pp. 85–89.

ened to beat him over the head with a stick.[35] Speaking at
the Federal Convention of 1787, Pinckney pronounced as
"the most singular" characteristic of American life its equality, an equality surpassing that achieved among the people
of any other country, and one which he predicted would be
"more likely to continue." According to other observers, in
no area of American life were these new principles manifest
more strikingly than among the working class, which
quickly repudiated the notion as well as the term "servant"
to describe their relations to their employers, erstwhile
"masters." True, as Martin Chuzzlewit later found out,
there were no "masters" in America—only "owners"! For
white society, however, one would be compelled to agree
with Crèvecoeur's conclusion that the American of the Revolutionary Age who enjoyed both individual freedom and
equality "was a new man who acts upon new principles."[36]
This egalitarianism proved to be the most profound as well
as the most pervasive transformation of American Revolutionary society.

Remarkable as was the transformation of American white
society, nevertheless the American Revolution tragically
failed to confront the issue of black inequality fairly and
squarely. The wealthy South Carolinian Henry Laurens, a
former slave-trader himself and later president of the Continental Congress, declared that the principles enunciated
by the Declaration of Independence must have relevance to

35. Durand Echevarria, *Mirage in the West* (Princeton, 1957), p. 80.
"Nabobs" like the Rutledges of South Carolina found the aspiration for
social equality of occasional cantankerous "Republicans" quite insufferable.
See *Gazette of the State of South Carolina*, April 29, 1784.

36. Michel Guillaume Jean de Crèvecoeur, *Letters from an American
Farmer* (London, 1782), Letter III; C. C. Tansill, ed., *Documents Illus-
trative of the Formation of the Union of the American States* (Washington,
1927), pp. 267–273; Abbé Charles César Robin, *Nouveau Voyage* (Paris,
1782). See also Elkanah Watson, *Men and Times of the Revolution* (New
York, 1957), pp. 169–170; Thomas Cooper, *Some Information Concerning
America* (Dublin, 1794); Albert Mathews, "Hired Man and Help," Col.
Soc. of Mass., *Transactions* (1897–98), pp. 225–254.

the Negro as well as the white man. In August of 1776 he asserted his readiness to manumit his slaves, despite the formidable opposition of "the laws and customs of my country, my own and the avarice of my countrymen." Laurens scorned the hypocrisy of "those who dare trust in Providence for defence and security of their own liberty while they enslave and wish to continue in slavery thousands who are as well entitled to freedom as themselves."[37] On the other hand, a fellow Southerner, Aedanus Burke, recognized no inconsistency in opposing the establishment of an hereditary aristocracy while remaining a firm proponent of the institution of slavery.

Serious moves to end slavery were in fact put in motion. Into the 1776 Virginia Constitution Jefferson tried unsuccessfully to write a provision that "no person hereafter coming into the state would be held in slavery." When he included the slave trade as one of the evils ascribed to George III in the Declaration, his fellow delegates had the reference stricken out. Even before the Great Declaration the North took steps to end slavery, a process which the war accelerated. In 1774 Rhode Island provided that all slaves brought into the colony should be free henceforth. After 1776, states like Massachusetts[38] and Vermont abolished slavery outright, while others, like Pennsylvania in 1780 and Connecticut and Rhode Island in 1784, began to make provisions for gradual emancipation. Indeed, the 1780's saw the burgeoning of manumission societies, as well as widespread manumissions of slaves in some of the Southern states.

The harsh fact is that the Patriot side numbered most of

37. See R. B. Morris, ed., *A Letter from Henry Laurens to His Son John Laurens, August 14, 1776* (New York, 1964).

38. From Worcester County, Massachusetts, the towns of Westminster and Sutton protested article V of the draft Constitution of 1778 which disqualified Negroes, mulattoes, and Indians from voting as contrary to natural rights and the law of God, and as wearing "a very gross complexion of slavery." Massachusetts Archives, CLVI, fols. 347–351.

the big slaveowners of the South, who were intensely provoked by various offers of freedom held out by royal officials
to the Negro slave in exchange for loyalty to the Crown.[39]
To men with strong antislavery convictions like the New
York statesman John Jay, the failure of the American Revolution to end slavery and discrimination against the Negro
made the Declaration of Independence a continuing commitment. Having failed to come to grips with the subject of
black inequality in the Revolution and managing to evade
the issue during the federal Convention, the Founding Fathers postponed to some remote time the implementation of
the principles and promises embodied in the Declaration of
Independence. The long history of the antislavery and civil
rights movements in the United States provides continuous
and abundant proof that men of conscience in America considered Negro inequality the great unfulfilled commitment
of the American Revolution. That was what Abraham Lincoln meant when, in speaking of Jefferson's generation, he
remarked in 1857: "They meant to set up a standard maxim
for free society, which should be . . . constantly looked to,
constantly labored for, and even though never perfectly
attained, constantly approximated, and thereby constantly
spreading and deepening its influence and augmenting the
happiness and value of life to all people of all colors everywhere."[40]

Although America stands as the classic example of a
nation which enjoyed a phenomenal degree of economic
growth since its establishment, it is seldom realized how
great a spur to development the casting off of the shackles of
colonialism proved. On balance, the entire mercantilist pro-

39. For a consideration of the paradox of the slaveholding South's devotion
to "liberty," see Charles G. Sellers, Jr., *The Southerner as American* (Chapel
Hill, N.C., 1960), pp. 40–45.

40. See also R. B. Morris, *The American Revolution Reconsidered*, pp. 73–
77.

gram of external control of trade embraced under the rubric of Parliament's Navigation Laws was disadvantageous to the economy of the mainland. Yet some historians play down the trade laws as an issue between colonies and mother country and would minimize the hardships imposed upon the colonial economy by the trade laws. If the colonists complained comparatively little about the Navigation Laws before 1763, it may well have been because they were so loosely administered. Powerful and articulate segments of the colonial population considered the strict enforcement of the acts after 1763, along with the revenue measures, as a serious grievance.[41]

The anticolonial stance of the Americans represented a protest against the permanent debtor status assigned the colonies in the imperial economic scheme. In that respect it is not unlike the anticolonialism of emerging nations seeking to free themselves from economic dependency upon one or another of the Great Powers. What Jefferson felicitously called "the pursuit of happiness" was a concept embracing a variety of freedoms, including social mobility, freedom of occupational choice, freedom from monopolistic restraints, security, and a more abundant life, including a fair sharing of the nation's resources.

That America has achieved these goals for most of its citizens cannot be denied, nor can one controvert the fact that in some measure these achievements stem from the liberative effect of the American Revolution on the economy.

41. See L. A. Harper, "The Effects of the Navigation Acts on the Thirteen Colonies," in R. B. Morris, ed., *The Era of the American Revolution* (New York, 1939), pp. 1–39; "Mercantilism and the American Revolution," *Canadian Historical Review,* XXIII (1942), 24–34; Curtis P. Nettels, "British Mercantilism and the Economic Development of the Thirteen Colonies," *Journal of Economic History,* XII (1952), 105–114. Cf. Oliver M. Dickerson, *The Navigation Acts and the American Revolution* (Philadelphia, 1951); Robert P. Thomas, "A Quantitative Approach to the Study of the Effects of British Imperial Policy Upon Colonial Welfare: Some Preliminary Findings," *Journal of Economic History,* XXV (1965), 615–638.

The federal principle in the new Constitution gave America an instant common market, still unmatched in the world to date. Emulated by the Common Market nations of Europe, it serves as an example to Latin America and to the new states of East Africa now engaged in setting up their own common market. The sound fiscal policies inaugurated by Alexander Hamilton made abundant credit available to business, while the government's land programs encouraged the farmer just as the innovative and inventive climate of America spurred the manufacturer.

Whether one would date the take-off into a self-sustained economic growth with the adoption of the Constitution, or with the 1840's, or perhaps with even a later period, America did manage to win economic as well as political independence. Without the former the latter would have proven a hollow gain indeed. That sustained rate of growth and that degree of affluence which America did achieve still makes the United States the envy of the older nations whose economies it has surpassed. And if it may be said that the revolutions which have swept the underdeveloped world are a response to rising expectations, then the United States through the image of affluence it has projected is as much responsible for these insurgent movements as are dread subversives reared on the gospels of Marx, Lenin, and Mao.

To sum up the durable contribution of the American Revolution and its relevance to today's revolutionary world, it should be acknowledged at the start that the American War for Independence was a revolution of enormous consequences for the world. On the occasion of Great Britain's recognition of American independence, Edmund Burke declared:

> A great revolution has happened—a revolution made, not by chopping and changing of power in any of the existing states, but by the appearance of a *new state*, of a *new species*,

in a *new part of the globe.* It has made as great a change in all relations, and balances, and gravitations of power, as the appearance of a new planet would in the system of the solar world.

The Founding Fathers shared Burke's opinion of the uniqueness of their revolution which, to them, culminated in the adoption of the Constitution. In the Fourteenth *Federalist* James Madison paid tribute to the drafters of the Constitution who "accomplished a revolution which has no parallel in the annals of human society. They reared the fabrics of government which have no model on the face of the globe."

As the first great revolution of modern times, the American Revolution was both a war of decolonization and a movement of broad social change and reform. Waged to establish an independent nation, sovereign and equal with all the nations of the earth, it constituted at the same time a movement to support the rights of man, of all men, and women too. And, in that wider sense, the American Revolution, with its egalitarian overtones, has enormous relevance to the revolutions of the emerging nations of later times and, not least of all, to our own time.

General Washington was indulging in no mere rhetorical effusion when, in his notable Circular to the States issued from his headquarters at Newburgh on June 8, 1783, he observed that, "according to the system of policy the States shall adopt at this moment, they will stand or fall, and by their confirmation or lapse, it is yet to be decided, whether the Revolution must ultimately be considered as a blessing or a curse; a blessing or a curse, not to the present age alone, for with our fate will the destiny of unborn millions be involved."[42]

42. John C. Fitzpatrick, ed., *The Writings of George Washington* (Washington, 1931–44), XXVI, 483–486.

II

THE AMERICAN REVOLUTION
IN THE AGE OF
DEMOCRATIC REVOLUTIONS

IT IS HARDLY a coincidence that on the day the Bastille was stormed Thomas Jefferson, the American minister to Bourbon France, was a guest at the residence of Ethis de Corny, the pro-American spokesman for the populace in pressing their demands on the governor of that detested prison. It was from de Corny that Jefferson heard firsthand an account of the storming. How the fortress that had stood a number of military sieges fell so easily, how the enraged mob proceeded to cut off the head of Bernard Jordan de Launay, the governor, and to display it throughout the city were all recorded by Jefferson.

So, too, Jefferson describes how the news was conveyed to the King, who "went to bed fearfully impressed," and how the account of de Launay's decapitation threw the aristocratic party into a paroxysm of fright. Thus it was necessary for the King to make his peace with the Revolutionary movement in Paris. Accordingly, a procession took off from Versailles, with the King's carriage in the center. Riding on horseback at its head as commander-in-chief was none other than that darling of an earlier Revolution, the Marquis de Lafayette.[1] Thus did two ideologues who participated in the American Revolution in such different but conspicuous ways play their respective parts when the opening guns announced the start of France's great and terrible Revolution.

It was equally appropriate to the ritual of the day that a key to the Bastille should have been transmitted by Lafayette to Washington, then considered the world's premier revolutionary. Perhaps, as has been alleged, the key which now graces Mount Vernon's collection of memorabilia may have been duplicated to fill mounting requests, but the symbolic significance of the gift was duly recognized by the Marquis. Writing in March, 1790, Lafayette informed Washington that, despite counterrevolutionary plots on the one hand and extremism on the other, "the reports of our anarchy . . . are greatly exaggerated." Transmitting to Washington the key of "that fortress of despotism" constituted in Lafayette's view proper tribute which he owed "as a son to my adopted father, as an aide-de-camp to my general, and as a missionary of liberty to its patriarch." In acknowledgment Washington sent the Marquis a pair of shoe buckles manufactured in New York City (evidence no doubt of the technical progress already achieved by a nation so recently emerging from its own revolution), while hastening to reassure Lafayette that the American people would "never" forget the "conspicuous part" he had played in an event which proved a "triumph for the new world, and for humanity in general."[2]

The presence in Paris of the veteran revolutionary

1. *Papers of Thomas Jefferson,* ed. by J. P. Boyd (Princeton, 1950–), XV, 245–247.

2. *Mémoires, correspondance, et manuscrits du Général Lafayette* (Paris, 1837), II, 446, 447; W. C. Ford, ed., *Writings of Washington* (New York, 1891), XI, 493–498.

Thomas Jefferson quickly made itself felt. Although a foreign diplomat he was not content to be a mere bystander. He sat down with the Girondist leaders, the moderate antimonarchists, and proceeded to draft a bill of rights to end arbitrary rule and to transform the absolute Bourbon monarchy into a limited one. That indeed was the American notion of how to start a Revolution—set limits on the powers of the governors and secure guarantees of the rights of the people. Looking back, many years later and when he had confused his own role and attitude at the time, Jefferson, who had been far from unsympathetic to those revolutionaries like Lafayette who would have preserved the monarchy, remarked:

> . . . I should have shut up the Queen in a Convent, putting harm out of her power, and placed the king in his station, investing him with limited powers, which I verily believe he would have honestly exercised, according to the measure of his understanding. In this way no void would have been created, courting the usurpation of a military adventurer [Bonaparte] nor occasion given for those enormities which demoralized the nations of the world, and destroyed, and is yet to destroy, millions and millions of its inhabitants.[3]

Speaking of France on another occasion Jefferson said that the American Revolution appeared "to have awakened the thinking part of this nation from the sleep of despotism in which they were sunk." He could have pointed to at least five concrete ways in which the American Revolution influenced the course of events in France in the years following Yorktown. In the first place, the American Revolution provided both warning and example of how to put an end to monarchical rule and to replace it by a republic based on the

3. P. O. Ford, ed., *Autobiography of Jefferson*, I, 141.

consent of the governed. Secondly, it afforded to that army of Frenchmen and other Europeans who saw military service in America an education in the values of a republic, even a democratic society. Thirdly, the Revolutionary Congress dispatched as its emissaries abroad some of its most astute publicists, among whom were men typifying those simple republican virtues that European intellectuals were prone to idealize. Fourthly, the diplomacy of Congress constituted a revolutionary weapon whose impact abroad was incalculable. Lastly, the two billion dollars that France expended in the War of the Revolution contributed directly to that nation's bankruptcy and thus to the immediate onset of the French Revolution. The uncontrolled fiscal blaze rather than long smoldering social grievances set off the terrible conflagration.

In short, whether as indirect cause or contagious example, the American Revolution provoked the French upheaval. As a rural Virginian put it to James Madison, "America may rejoice, and plume herself in the idea of having made the Rent in the great curtain that withheld the light from human nature—by her exertions she let the day and the Rights of Man become legible and intelligible to a Shakled World."[4]

At its inception the American Revolution had been greeted in France in quite different ways by quite different interests. To France's foreign minister, the Comte de Vergennes, the American insurrection offered France an opportunity, perhaps even without overt war, of redressing the balance of power that had been so grievously upset in England's favor by the Seven Years' War. In line with Vergennes' and his monarch's thinking, court circles favoring support for the American cause conceived of the American Revolu-

4. George de Turberville to James Madison, January 28, 1793. Madison Papers, Lib. 15, Library of Congress.

tion as a limited war for limited objectives. For official France, American independence was merely a means to an end, and not a positive good of itself. Others, like Turgot and Necker who held the purse strings, warned that active intervention would be ruinous to France's fiscal position. The King threw his weight on the side of the hawks, and, much like the Americans in Vietnam, the French were soon involved in a mugh bigger commitment than they had originally anticipated.

Outside court circles, especially among intellectuals, the American Revolution assumed a larger dimension. Robert R. Palmer has felicitously captured the mood of the time in his observation that "the first and greatest effect of the American Revolution in Europe was to make Europeans believe, or rather feel, often in a highly emotional way, that they lived in a rare era of momentous change." What he has called "a kind of drama of the continents" was exemplified by such writings as Raynal's *Philosophical History of European Institutions,* published in Paris in 1770, with its long recital of the alleged evils brought upon the world by European greed and colonialism. Other intellectuals observed it was no mere coincidence that the American Revolution coincided with the Age of the Enlightenment. America appeared to be the one place in the world where the utopian notions of Rousseau's *Social Contract* were put to work. Social contract, written constitutions, popular sovereignty, religious freedom, freedom of thought and speech, and separation of powers— these were all Enlightenment ideas. That the American states in practice departed widely from the clumsy and complicated system of representation that Rousseau had urged seemed beside the point.

Here indeed was a new mystique of world revolution, and the Americans were by no means innocent of responsibility for launching it. Turn to the reverse side of any dollar bill, and you will find engraved thereon the Great Seal of the United States, an everlasting pyramid carrying the date 1776, and underneath, the Latin motto: *Novus Ordo Seclorum* ("A New Order of the Ages [Is Born]"). Every dollar that we spend abroad, carrying this adaptation of an inspired phrase of Vergil, conveys this subversive message.

Europeans were made conscious of the American Revolution in many ways, through the press, through discussion in reading clubs or Masonic lodges, through the reports of returned soldiers, and through deliberate propaganda by Americans. That these notions enjoyed so favorable a reception was as much due to the fact that Enlightenment thinking had prepared the ground as to the merit of the ideas themselves. Robert Palmer lists some thirteen titles of works on America written abroad which appeared in three or more languages mainly between 1760 and 1790, and still another eight volumes produced in America and republished in English, French, German, Dutch, or Italian editions. Significantly, only Raynal's *Two Indies* and a book by an Italian writer on Chile were issued in Spanish translations prior to 1790. Of all countries, the Spaniards most feared the subversive influence on their own colonies of the ideas of the American Revolution.[5] The French government, which had no more use for revolutions than the Spanish, proved more venturesome, and sponsored a propaganda journal known as the *Affaires de l'Angleterre et de l'Amérique,* which began publication in 1776 and printed such subversive documents as the Declaration of Independence and the state constitutions, along with American propaganda. If Benjamin Franklin could report that the separate state constitutions were read "with rapture," it might also be noted that French

5. R. R. Palmer, *The Age of the Democratic Revolution* (Princeton, 1959), I, 244. For the debate which Raynal touched off, see Henry Steele Commager and Elmo Giordanetti, *Was America a Mistake?* (New York, 1967).

intellectuals of the standing of Turgot, Démeunier, and the Abbé Mably subjected them to objective scrutiny and raised doubts about such aspects of these new constitutions as the system of checks and balances, for example. In turn, John Adams, William Livingston, and other leading American constitutional expositors replied at length.[6]

Much has been said about the liberalization of Lafayette's views as a result of his experience in America. In fact, that conventional-minded aristocrat caught fire from his close relations with Patriots like Washington and Hamilton, and came to espouse in France the constitutional and egalitarian notions that he had imbibed in his stay in America. A citizen of the United States by Act of Congress, Lafayette expected that the peace commissioners could utilize his services when he returned to France, and later, when he was imprisoned, counted on America to extricate him from his difficulties.[7]

Among French officers Lafayette did not stand alone. The extensive correspondence of Chastellux, Rouerie, and Ségur with Washington, and between Noailles and Hamilton, reveals how frequently the thoughts of these young officers reverted to their moments of glory. That the war had politicized the French officers in a republican direction was widely conceded. The American war might not have created great generals, the turncoat Charles François Dumouriez conceded, "but the young men who had fought in its campaigns had seen at close range a new people governed by a wise constitution. Their heads were turned. They brought back badly digested ideas."[8]

6. See Henry E. Bourne, "Constitutional Precedents in the French National Assembly," *American Historical Review*, VIII (1902–03), 466–490.

7. The ideological transformation of Lafayette is perceptibly examined in Louis Gottschalk's multivolume biography, notably in *Lafayette and the Close of the American Revolution* (Chicago, 1942) and *Lafayette between the American and the French Revolution* (Chicago, 1950).

8. Cited by Lewis Rosenthal, *America and France* (New York, 1882), p. 141.

It is intriguing to speculate on the possible impact of the American Revolution on the European enlisted man who fought in this country. A recent scholar has shown that of the seven thousand soldiers in Rochambeau's army a high proportion came from those parts of France in which agrarian insurrection and peasant revolution were most in evidence in 1789. This would suggest that the prosperity of the American farmers, their holding of freehold estates devoid of manorial or feudal payments and restrictions, left a lasting impression on the returning veterans, although the case is not conclusive.[9] It is not improbable that a higher percentage of soldiers came from regions where poor economic conditions prevailed, and that for the very same reason, such regions would be more prone to revolt. (As for the thirty thousand German troops who went to America, some twelve thousand liked it so much that they settled down here and never returned.)

There is no reason to question the continuing impact of the American Revolution on the intellectuals of France. When the French Revolution broke out, a group of *américanistes*, as they were sometimes called, looked to the American model. Among them were old-line pro-Americans like Lafayette, Mirabeau, Condorcet, the Duc de la Rochefoucauld, and Pierre Samuel Du Pont. Just as they had been once a part of the Franklin circle so now they became fast friends with Jefferson and his young secretary William Short. The Florentine Philip Mazzei, author of a four-volume study of the new American nation, served as a further link between French intellectuals and their American friends. What the *américanistes* wanted was an American program, including the eradication of the special privileges

9. See F. McDonald, "The Relation of French Peasant Veterans of the American Revolution to the Fall of Feudalism in France," *Agricultural History*, XXV (1951), 151–161.

of Church and aristocracy, the setting up of a constitutional monarchy, and a popular national assembly. They definitely preferred the American constitutional models to the British example, while *anglomanes* like Jean De Lolme publicized the English constitutional system, praising the virtues of balanced government. Indeed, John Adams' *A Defence of the Constitutions of Government of the United States*, first published abroad in February, 1787, with its rather anti-democratic temper and its pro-English orientation, proved an embarrassment to the *américanistes*, who were particularly unhappy at the re-eligibility of the President, fearing it would lead to a dynasty.[10]

As the first revolution of modern times the American Revolution initiated a propaganda war both at home and abroad that set the example for all later revolutions and revolutionaries. Like later revolutions, too, the American Revolution had a distinctive propaganda style. It is instructive even to this day to recall old Benjamin Franklin in action in Paris at a session of the Academy of Sciences. There in the year 1778 the American commissioner to France was publicly introduced to the great Voltaire. The two world-famous intellectuals shook hands, but the audience was not so easily appeased. "They must embrace in the French manner," they shouted. Thereupon, so cynical John Adams reported, "the two aged actors upon this great theatre of philosophy and frivolity then embraced each other, by hugging one another in their arms, kissing each other's cheeks, and then the tumult subsided. And the cry immediately spread through the whole kingdom, and, I suppose,

10. Adams' work was not published in a French translation for a good five years. See Joyce Appleby, "The Jefferson-Adams Rupture and the First French Translation of John Adams' *Defence*," *American Historical Review*, LXXIII (April, 1968), 1084–1091.

over all Europe, How charming to behold Solon embracing Sophocles." For, as the *philosophe* Condorcet, the great disciple of the American Revolution, remarked, "The French Sophocles had demolished error and advanced the reign of reason, while the Solon of Philadelphia, resting the constitution of his country on the unshakable foundation of the rights of man, had no occasion to fear that he would see during his lifetime doubtful laws fashioning chains for his country and opening the door to tyranny."[11]

As a propagandist of revolution, Franklin still stands without a peer, towering above later rivals from Gracchus Babeuf to Fidel Castro. Here was a man who enjoyed a masquerade as much as anyone. From his beaver hat and Quaker garb, no one could readily discern that the costume which symbolized innocence abroad concealed a hard-boiled businessman-scientist, with a tremendous bump of curiosity about everything and an extraordinary range of talents as editor, politician, scientist, publicist, and humanitarian. At home as much with the courtiers of Versailles as with the courtesans, with the intelligentsia and the bankers, and with the proletariat of Paris and the peasantry of the countryside, Franklin was a phenomenon whose like this country has never sent abroad again. An inveterate literary prankster from his precocious teens until his death, the old doctor perpetrated one literary hoax after another, including the fictitious speech in court of Polly Baker, prosecuted for the fifth time for bearing a child, and his surreptitious "Advice to a Young Man on the Choice of a Mistress." In the midst of his peace negotiations with the British, Franklin fabricated a hoax about the scalping of Americans by Indians in the pay

11. C. F. Adams, ed., *Works of John Adams*, III, 147; Condorcet, "Vie de Voltaire," *Oeuvres de Voltaire*, I, 290.

of the British, and printed it in the guise of a *Supplement to the Boston Independent Chronicle.* Gruesome propaganda to be sure, but Franklin justified his deception by telling John Adams he believed the number of persons actually scalped "in this murdering war by the Indians to exceed what was mentioned in invoice."[12] Franklin did more. He arranged to have his *Poor Richard* translated, along with other writings.

Not only what the old Doctor wrote but even what he reputedly said spread by word of mouth like the pronouncements of an ancient oracle. When disturbing news reached France in the winter of 1777–78 of Washington's military setbacks and the desperate condition of his troops at Valley Forge, *américanistes* in Paris seemed prepared to give up the cause as lost. Not Franklin, however, who was quoted as having said: "*Cela est fâcheux, mais ça ira, ça ira.*" ("It's a pity, but it will pass.") Franklin's confident reaction reached the newspapers, and his words, still remembered by the French people during the darkest days of the French Revolution, were quoted over and over again. A popular singer of the day put the words into verses designed to fit the tune of a favorite *contredanse.* Thus "Ça Ira" was launched on its spectacular career.[13]

The short, stocky, and far less diplomatic John Adams performed in Holland a comparable propaganda role. In many respects Adams faced greater odds than did Franklin. The Dutch were not renowned as dreamy-eyed ideologues. Quite aptly did one foreign visitor speak of Holland as "a land, where the demon of gold, crowned with tobacco, sat on a throne of cheese." The Netherlands, Adams found, was permeated with material values. Even the Dutch businessmen who carried on a hugely profitable contraband trade with

12. A. H. Smyth, ed., *Writings of Franklin* (New York, 1905), VIII, 437–438.

13. *Moniteur Universel* (Paris), September 21, 1792.

rebellious America by way of the Dutch West Indian island of St. Eustatius were as conspicuously anxious to avoid an open breach with England as was the Anglophile stadholder. A few ideologues, like Joan Derk van der Capellen, combined hostility to the British with sympathy for American Revolutionary and republican ideals,[14] but these were the rare exceptions.

Adams, finding the Dutch astonishingly ill-informed about America and the cause for which it was fighting, placed his battle for the minds of the Hollanders ahead of his quest for a loan or a treaty. He had the new Massachusetts Constitution, of which he was a major author, published in the *Gazette de Leyde,* edited by Jean Luzac, a Leyden lawyer and university professor. In a group of twenty-six letters addressed to a Dutch jurist named Hendrick Calkoen, Adams stressed America's continued will to resist and support her political leaders. In his literary labors he drew upon the services of Charles William Frederic Dumas, an indefatigable man of letters and capable linguist, who from the start of the Revolution had been enlisted in the service of America as agent and correspondent at The Hague.

Men like Franklin, Adams, and Jefferson fired the imaginations of such publicists as the Abbé Morellet, a liberal-minded Frenchman who formed a part of the radical circle gathered about the Earl of Shelburne at Bowood, of Philip Mazzei, the Italian who seems to have persuaded the King of Poland to put up a bust of George Washington in his study, and of numerous other radical writers, who formed what Palmer calls "the beginnings of a group of international subversives."

What rendered the diplomacy of the American peace

14. See [Joan Derk van der Capellen], *Aan het volk Nederland* (Ostend, 1781), pp. 19–20, 42, 47–49, 53; *Brieven van en aan Joan Derck van der Capellen tot den Pol,* ed. by W. A. Beauford (Utrecht, 1879), pp. 88–89, 413.

commissioners at Paris so effectual in 1782–83 was the vision they had of a great and durable republic. That vision was shared by a few imaginative statesmen like Oswald and Hartley, who, oddly enough, represented the adversary power at the peacemaking. Franklin, Jay and company proved effective instruments of a new revolutionary society which confronted the Old Order. Even adversaries were bound together by ties of blood and caste in that Old Order, wherein men of lesser social rank would not be accepted as equals at the negotiating table. Governed by its balance-of-power politics, its pseudo-Machiavellian ethics, and its objectives of limited gains, the Old Order could not be expected to comprehend revolutionary ends.[15]

The Americans resolutely contended for the right of a sovereign people to choose their own form of government and insisted on the recognition of a revolutionary state as a precondition to entering into peace negotiations. In short, American independence inaugurated a new era of diplomacy in a way as abrasive to the Old Order as the North Koreans or the North Vietnamese may seem to their American counterparts at Panmunjon or Paris. The style of the Americans was candid. Their Revolution meant a break with the traditional politics of the balance of power. Under the latter notion a gain to one nation meant a loss to another. Under the "new diplomacy" obstacles to free commercial intercourse among nations would be removed, expansion would be replaced by friendship and cooperation, double-dealing by candor. We can almost see faint germs of Woodrow Wilson's idea of "open covenants, openly arrived at."

To liberals of the school of Shelburne, Franklin, Hartley, and others, free trade was a panacea for world conflict. In this new enlightened spirit, Franklin issued a passport for

15. See R. B. Morris, *The Peacemakers* (New York, 1965), pp. 458, 459.

the voyage of Captain Cook on the ground that it would promote, first, geographical knowledge which in its turn would facilitate communication between distant nations; second, exchange of useful products and manufactures; and third, extension of the arts, all of which, he said, would augment "the enjoyment of human life and redound to the benefit of mankind in general."[16]

The American commissioners showed a good deal of respect for the principles of international law which were then being hammered out by juristic scholars. Perhaps the most popular with the Americans were the writings of the liberal-minded Swiss jurist Emmerich von Vattel. One of the areas where Vattel provided ammunition for the Americans was in his argument supporting free navigation to the sea, even by nations who did not control the lands on either side of the river at its outlet. Thus, the arguments of the Americans on the free navigation of the Mississippi were comparable to the arguments raised in the empire to support the free navigation of the Scheldt. Of course, everybody did not read Vattel, and as Jay once pointed out, they did not even allow his book to circulate in Spain.

The Revolutionary diplomacy sparked a re-examination of the law of neutrality. There is no need here to review the findings of recent scholars about who originated the system of armed neutrality that Catherine the Great officially sponsored.[17] Without derogating one whit from the various European statesmen who are credited with this notion, one should note that the American "plan of treaties" of 1776 included the provision of "free ships, free goods" which was

16. Gerald Stourzh, *Benjamin Franklin and American Foreign Policy* (Chicago, 1954), pp. 217–218. This book provides a penetrating analysis of Franklin's ideas on international relations.

17. Most recently by Isabel de Madariaga, *Britain, Russia, and the Armed Neutrality* (New Haven, 1962).

also included in a treaty of amity and commerce with France in February of 1778. Franklin, who ran America's naval operations from his armchair in Passy, ordered American captains to stop seizing neutral ships on the ground that such prizes "occasion much litigation and create ill blood." Finally, Franklin sought to include in the peace treaty with Great Britain some recognition of the developing law of nations. Writing to Benjamin Vaughan on July 10, 1782, he reviewed the progress that had already been achieved in this direction. In the first place, the killing of prisoners had been replaced by slavery. Then slavery had been superseded by the exchange of prisoners. Franklin then went on:

Why should not this Law of Nations go on improving? Ages have interven'd between its several Steps; but as Knowledge of late increases rapidly, why should not those steps be quicken'd? Why should it not be agreed to as the future law of Nations that in any War hereafter the following Descriptions of Men should be undisturbed, have the Protections of both Sides, and be permitted to follow their Employments in Surety, viz

1. Cultivators of the Earth, because they Labour for the subsistence of Mankind.

2. Fishermen, for the same Reason.

3. Merchants and Traders, in unarm'd Ships, who accommodate different nations by communicating and exchanging the Necessaries and Conveniences of Life.

4. Artists and Mechanics, inhabiting and working in open towns.

It is hardly necessary to add that the Hospitals of Enemies should be unmolested; they ought to be assisted.

In short, It would have nobody fought with, but those who are paid for Fighting. . . .

This once Established, that Encouragement to War which arises from a Spirit of Rapine, would be taken away, and Peace therefore more likely to continue and be lasting.

It is interesting to note how durable Franklin's notion of a protective blanket of neutrality proved. Almost thirty years later, and under quite different circumstances, James Madison declared that the United States could have no special interest in the rule of "free ships, free goods," unless combined with another principle of which an example was found in Russia and probably in no other country, namely, that unarmed merchant vessels, "like waggons, or ploughs, the property of one belligerent, should be unmolested by the other." This principle might claim undisputed American paternity in the person of Dr. Franklin.

Underscoring the thinking and actions of the American diplomats at the time of the American Revolution was a moral approach to international politics. Franklin spoke of the Almighty favoring the American cause and prayed that God might "perfect his work, and establish freedom in the New World as an asylum for those of the old who deserve it." He was fond of alluding to the greatness of his cause and of asserting over and over again that "our Cause is the Cause of all Mankind and that we are fighting for their liberty in defending our own." From Franklin and Jay of 1782 to Woodrow Wilson of 1913 a continuity of thought might be traced. In his famous Mobile speech of that year, Wilson declared: "We deal in turn from the principle that morality and not expediency is the thing that must guide us and that we will never choose iniquity because it is most convenient to do so."

Finally, the new diplomacy introduced by the Americans heralds the peace movement of the nineteenth century. In a memoir drawn up in 1776 by Silas Deane, Franklin's fellow commissioner in France, the point is made that the Americans would be so content to secure and enjoy their own rights, that they would not contemplate invading those of other people. "From their local situation, the circumstances by which they are surrounded, their habits, interests, and dispositions, and above all from the immense extent of uncultivated territory which they possess, their attention must for a multitude of years necessarily be fixed upon agriculture, the most natural, beneficial, and inoffensive of all human employments." To obtain suitable markets and commodities, Deane argued, it would "ever be their interest to pursue an inviolable peace with the states of Europe." Thus the world would become peaceful because no new war-loving nation replaced the two powers, England and France, that had been expelled in whole or part from North America. John Adams reassured Europe that the Americans for a long time to come would be too much occupied with conquering land "from the trees and rocks and wild beasts," and during that time "we shall never go abroad to trouble other nations." As Tom Paine put it, America's trade would always be a protection, "and her barrenness of gold and silver [would] secure her from invaders." Franklin, who wanted to achieve expansion by peaceful means (he would have bought out the Spaniards, if necessary) echoed Deane, Adams, and Tom Paine. Just before the American commissioners put their signatures on the definitive treaty, Franklin wrote an English scientist expressing the fervent wish that peace would be "lasting, and that mankind will at length, as they call themselves reasonable creatures, have reason and sense enough to settle their differences without cutting throats; for, in my opinion, *there never was a good war or a bad peace.*"

No person argued more eloquently the case for considering the American Revolution as a guarantor of world peace than did that French apostle of the Enlightenment, the Marquis de Condorcet. In his prize essay, "The Influence of the American Revolution in Europe," Condorcet predicted that the American Revolution "would make wars less frequent in Europe." It would do so, first of all, by tilting the balance of naval power in the Americas to the advantage of whichever nation the Americans might favor. As a result, a war in the Caribbean waters on the part of a European power would involve such a nation in imprudent risks once the United States repaired the destruction it had suffered as the price of independence. Assuming that an aggressive posture would ill accord with America's own notion of liberty, Condorcet confidently assured the reader that America would not try to conquer the West Indian islands. More than that—and here the *philosophe* took a great big leap into the future—he predicted that "Americans will also help to maintain peace in Europe by the force of their example." Unlike Europe, where pacifism was confined to a few ideologues, such opinions were embraced in America, Condorcet asserted, "by a great people," who condemn "any idea of aggressive wars undertaken for aggrandizement or conquest."[18]

In perhaps a less creditable way did the American Revolution activate the French Revolution by seducing the French nation down the path of bankruptcy. Spotty though economic conditions may have been in France on the eve of the Revolution—and the issue of whether France was prosperous or in the throes of an economic crisis at the end of the *ancien régime* is still a hotly contested one—that nation's political crisis stemmed initially from fiscal difficulties rather than mass hunger. Elsewhere this writer has suggested that the crisis is by no means unfamiliar to us today.[19] In America's great urban centers we have an affluent society dwelling in and around cities which are periodically confronted by fiscal bankruptcy. Surely it is not proposed to bring back the ghost of M. Necker to solve America's urban

18. Condorcet, "The Influence of the American Revolution in Europe," trans. by Durand Echevarria, *William and Mary Quarterly*, XXV (1968), 99–100.

19. R. B. Morris, *The American Revolution Reconsidered*, p. 48.

problems, but it is submitted that the analogy is not as farfetched as it may seem at first glance.

The whole issue of French fiscal solvency in the decade before the French Revolution is one of those moot subjects that can perhaps never be settled. Thus, it is hard to reconcile the two Jacques Neckers. First, there is Necker the alarmist who warned the French cabinet in the summer of 1780 that a continuation of the war meant imminent bankruptcy and that he had discovered a serious discrepancy in the Treasury accounts as the result of a fresh audit. "A blow of a bomb," he called it, "as unexpected as it is believable." Since estimated tax returns would not make up this deficiency, it was clear that the only way to finance another military campaign would be by floating huge war loans, which would sit perilously atop the vast debt already accumulated. The only sensible course, Necker urged, was to come to terms with the enemy. It was indeed a close thing, but Vergennes had his way and the war hawks secured the funds for a final campaign in America.

Secondly, we see Necker the miracle-worker, who astonished the world by the publication in January, 1781, of his *Compte rendu*. That historic report, extravagantly praised and savagely denounced, revealed that, despite the enormous subventions to the court entourage, despite the deficit which Necker had inherited from his predecessors, despite the immense expense of the war and the heavy interest payments on loans, current revenues apparently exceeded expenditures by 10,200,000 livres. A successor, Calonne, was to charge the Franco-Swiss financier with legerdemain and to expose the grave deficit which Necker's report had in fact concealed. These deficits continued under Calonne's successors, and, with ironic justice, Necker inherited the entire bankrupt structure when he took over again in 1787.

What Necker requested was what Grenville and Townshend had earlier proposed—more taxation to pay for the deficits of a previous war. Thus both revolutions arose out of disputes over taxation. In America the initial dispute over Parliament's right to tax escalated into a repudiation of the monarchy and an assertion of independence from the British Empire. In France a movement of internal reform to deal with ominously rising national deficits soon mounted a foreign war, overthrew a monarchy, nationalized the Church and took over its property, broadened land distribution to the peasants, reformed the laws, and extended the suffrage. Constitutionalism, on which both revolutions were founded, was maintained in America and subverted in France, which succumbed to a military dictatorship.

However, a preoccupation with consequences has led many people to ignore the common starting points of the two revolutions. Initially, both were rooted in legality. The Declaration of Independence and the Constitution-making by the American states so widely publicized in France inspired the Tennis Court Oath which the Third Estate took, vowing that it would not disband before a constitution was drafted and accepted by the monarch. The legalistic and even conservative character of both revolutions at the start received further bolstering from their affirmations of the rights of man and the sacredness of private property. In proposing a declaration of rights for France, the constitutional committee of the French National Assembly paid tribute to the influence of the American state constitutions. The committee report alluded to "the noble idea, conceived in another hemisphere," and considered it fitting that it should "first be transferred to us," for "we assisted in the events which gave to North America her liberty; she shows to us upon what principles we should preserve ours."[20]

20. Henry E. Bourne, "American Constitutional Precedents in the French National Assembly," *American Historical Review*, VIII (1902–03), 473.

The Virginia statesman George Mason might well have instituted an action of plagiarism against the authors of the Declaration of the Rights of Man and the Citizen which the French National Assembly adopted on August 26, 1789. The resemblance to Mason's Bill of Rights which the Virginia Assembly had enacted back in June of 1776 is too close to be coincidental. Even the sequence in which the ideas are presented is almost identical. Both affirm the equality of man, the security of all men's rights to life, liberty, and property, and the doctrine of popular sovereignty. The differences between the two are more in tone than in substance, although in some cases they stem from different institutional developments. One does not find in the French Declaration the same stress on freedom and frequency of elections, on jury trial, the same caveats against excessive bail, general warrants, suspending of laws, and standing armies that we find in the Virginia Declaration of Rights. The French Declaration also displays a greater reserve than the Virginia model in defining liberty—in this case as the right to do what does not harm another. It also differs from Mason's Bill of Rights in relating freedom of thought and religion to law and order, in its less explicit reference to moral virtues, and in its adoption of a deistic rather than a Christian tone. However enthusiastic the ardent revolutionaries of '89 may have been about the American bills of rights, they were less responsive to those portions of the state and federal constitutions which evidence distrust of the popular will, notably the bicameral system. Nor were they prepared to engraft on France the American federal system which would have enlarged the scope of provincial home rule.

Students of both revolutions have frequently remarked

The constant allusion to the American models which recurs in the debates in the National Assembly on the Declaration of the Rights of Man is conveniently summarized in Rosenthal, *America and France*, pp. 182–187.

that, although the beginnings of the two revolutions were not dissimilar, they would pursue divergent paths, that the American would maintain a steady Whig-Girondin course, avoiding the traps which beset the Jacobins and eschewing both the Terror and Thermidor. Out of the American Revolution a durable constitution emerged while in France the Revolution soon dissolved into an avalanche of constitutions, discrediting the very notion of constitutionalism beyond recognition.

If in retrospect the American Revolution appears to have been much more moderate than the French, the differences in tone and substance cannot be facilely ascribed to one simple explanation, but a variety of clues at hand make the variances between the two events more comprehensible. It should be conceded, to begin with, that fiscal and social grievances were by no means as acute in America as in France, nor was class hatred rooted in centuries of exploitation as under the *ancien régime*. Hence, the revolution in France would, as Condorcet pointed out, have of necessity to embrace the whole of society and transform every social relationship.[21] In the second place, the extremism which marked the later stages of the French Revolution was in no small part a response to foreign intervention, to a counter-revolutionary threat far greater than anything the Loyalists were able to mount in the American Revolution. The monarch was far away, and the Tories were hardly expected to set him on a throne in Philadelphia.

That the revolutions pursued differing courses must be put down in no small part to the contrasting leadership of the respective movements, and perhaps even in larger measure to the contrasting collective characters of the masses who allowed themselves to be led down the road to revolu-

21. Condorcet, *Outline of an Historical View of the Progress of the Human Mind* (Philadelphia, 1796), pp. 212–213.

tion. The fact that in America the same elite that began the Revolution remained in control at the end has given to the American a deceptively conservative coloration which the French Revolution never adopted. From James Otis to Henry Laurens, the Patriot leadership counted men of standing and influence, hardly the dispossessed, constituting perhaps the most conservative leadership any revolution ever confessed. As Alexander Graydon remarked, "The opposition to the claim of Britain originated with the better sort. It was truly aristocratical in its commencement." In addition, it demonstrated an extraordinary continuity in direction from the Declaration of Independence to the framing of the Constitution. Contrariwise, as Chateaubriand remarked of the French Revolution, while the patricians began it in France, it was the plebeians who brought it to an end.

The patrician origins of both revolutions suggest a similarity in the character of the leadership which the facts do not support. True, the sociological composition of the leadership of both revolutions was not markedly variant. The leadership of the Sons of Liberty, of the membership of the Committees of Correspondence, of the Revolutionary state legislatures, and of the Second Continental Congress was heavily recruited from businessmen, lawyers, and the landowning gentry who were in fact entrepreneurial operators, to whom land offered a chance for speculative gains rather than a way of preserving or enhancing social status. In this respect the leadership of the French Revolution shared backgrounds similar to the American. As Crane Brinton's investigation has disclosed, above 60 percent of the membership of the Jacobin clubs, in both the moderate and the violent phases of the French Revolution, were recruited from the middle class, and a sizable number of the bourgeoisie managed to keep in good standing in both the Girondin and Montagnard phases of the Revolution.

It is not, then, in the sociological composition of the leadership that one is likely to uncover the roots of variance between the respective revolutions. Rather, it is their contrasting psychological aspects which in retrospect seem so fateful. The American Revolution achieved its reforms by gradualism and created a durable constitutional system. The French Revolutionary reforms, more thoroughgoing on paper than the American, were pressed at the price of anarchy, civil war, terror, and the heritage of a divided nation—a division which cuts across French society down to the present moment. Granted that conditions in the two nations at the time of their respective revolutions were very different, the contrast in the results of the movements may be imputed in no small part to the contrast in leadership and to a quite different revolutionary mentality both in the leaders and among the masses. Rousseau, rightly considered the father of the French Revolution, was deeply alienated from society. Convinced of his own virtue and of the dishonesty of those who surrounded him, he felt himself misunderstood, conspired against, and betrayed. By later standards of mental health Rousseau would have been a candidate for psychiatric treatment.

Now, it must be confessed that the Patriots had their own quota of unstable figures—the fiery James Otis who suffered a complete mental breakdown before the Revolution even began, the demagogic Samuel Adams, with his trembling hands and shaky voice, a Patriot who takes on a more respectable coloration in his later and more conventional years, and Arthur Lee, a born troublemaker, quarrelsome, and suspicious, with a sizable paranoidal bump. But neurotics such as these were accorded minor roles when the curtain went up on the great drama. Then more stable and responsible leadership took the center of the stage.

In France, the story was quite the reverse. The aristocrats, who may be said to have begun it, men like Lafayette and Mirabeau, were torn between loyalty to the King and a sincere desire for reform, and ended by being distrusted by both the Left and the Right. The indecisive Lafayette, by now a genuine liberal, lacked a positive program, while Mirabeau, an untamed spirit in constant and notorious rebellion against his own father, had a talent for intrigue and double-dealing which undercut his solid merit as a moderate constitutional reformer.[22] The men who succeeded them were far more doctrinaire and extreme and had extravagant defects of character for which the French nation has paid a fearful toll. The dynamic and eloquent Danton constantly sold himself to the highest bidder.[23] The enemy who supplanted him, the chaste and sober Robespierre, impelled by class hatred, intolerance, and self-righteousness in roughly equal amounts, was corrupted by his own enormous vanity; the man who believed that "Virtue is powerless without Fear" could shed blood without scruple. As for the eccentric and vengeful Marat, the apostle of virtue, he came to the Revolution with a violent dislike of the scientific establishment which had refused him an honored place and was consumed by a paranoiac conviction that he had been persecuted.[24]

That streak of demagoguery, that implacable spirit, that taste for bloodletting, that sublime confidence that one has a corner on virtue, and that propensity to scurrilous attacks on one's enemies—all these traits that characterized French Revolutionary leadership could not, fortunately, be matched by the more moderate, responsible, and less vindictive

22. Crane Brinton, *A Decade of Revolution, 1789–1799* (New York, 1934), pp. 11–12.

23. For a castigation of Danton, see M. Mathiez, *Girondins et Montagnards* (Paris, 1930) pp. 260–305.

24. Brinton, *A Decade of Revolution*, pp. 104–105.

spirit of the prime leaders of the American Revolution. There were demagogues and bloodletters to be sure, but they were condemned to play background roles as the war unfolded. One might justifiably conclude that the reason the French Revolution was transformed into a military dictatorship was that there was no leadership in France of the stature or selfless patriotism of Washington. No one was prepared to renounce power when the major goals of the Revolution had been achieved; no one dared to speak out as Washington did to the army officers in March, 1783, when at Newburgh he demanded that they give voice to their "horror and detestation" at the possibility of a military coup against the civil authorities.

The character of the two Revolutions was determined as much by the distinctive traits of the participating masses as by their leaders. In France, where literacy was far less widespread than in America, the populace was much more credible, readier to believe every idle rumor, to put down to conspiracies food shortages and other hardships. If, as one scholar has suggested, humor and revolutionary fervor are never congenial bedfellows, the lack of a sense of humor seemed to be a salient characteristic of the French revolutionary personality. Setting the credulous revolutionary masses in so humorless and conspiratorial a climate gives us some understanding of why Saint-Just's task was so easy.[25]

Parisians might relish the sinister, macabre humor of the foulmouthed Hébert, whose ever-recurring subject was "the little window, the *linotte,* the national razor, the republican head-shorteners, and the little basket." When the time came for Hébert to put his own head in "the republican window," the little people of Paris might be forgiven for laughing their heads off at the humorist who was shaved by "the national

25. Richard Cobb, "Quelques aspects de la mentalité révolutionnaire," *Revue d'histoire Moderne et Contemporaine,* VI (1959), 81–120.

razor." The macabre note underscored by venom was sounded in typical French Revolutionary cartoons. Consider the caricature called "The Present Time," which depicted the clergy reduced to a skeleton and standing humbly before the other two estates, or another showing a cleric in a press being flattened and forced to disgorge gold while a great fat priest is held fast, but is told, "Patience, sir, your turn will come next."[26] The humor is invariably biting, and the choicest shafts reserved for Marie Antoinette. At one moment she is portrayed as a vile harpy treading on the Constitution, at another lying on a sofa in the arms of the Comte d'Artois, and in numerous others in various stages of undress in the process of being guillotined. The flight to Varennes is caricatured under the caption, "The family of the pig is brought back to the pigsty," while still another cartoon likened Louis XVI to a piece of out-of-date money and recommended that he be melted up.[27] Even French Revolutionary songs, of which several thousand have been identified for the years 1789 to 1800, mirrored the psychological transformation of the French masses. For example, in its early version the catchy lyrics of "Ça ira," set to an irresistible dance tune, reflected the gay spirit which launched the Revolution, but as the French Revolution turned out to be a grim affair, the lyrics in turn became sanguinary.[28]

French revolutionary leaders became increasingly puritanical and touchy. Not only did they regard moral laxity as counterrevolutionary, but they would not even brook bawdy jokes or allow the representatives of the people to be made

26. See Ernest F. Henderson, *Symbol and Satire in the French Revolution* (New York, 1912), pp. 117, 119.

27. André Blum, *La Caricature Révolutionnaire*, 1789 à 1795 (Paris, n.d.), pp. 121, 178, 179, 212, 286.

28. Cornwell B. Rogers, "Songs—Colorful Propaganda of the French Revolution," *Public Opinion Quarterly*, XI (1947), 436–444.

the butt of humor. Even venturing to criticize the new costume worn by the people's representatives was considered a counterrevolutionary vilification, and the people of Lyons were prosecuted for carrying on their traditional practice of poking fun at the Parisians. In short, the Revolution, with its Patriot saints and martyrs of liberty, became a religious cult too sacred to be soiled by ridicule or profaned by humor.[29]

All revolutions possess a paranoid quality, and one must concede that it was not entirely absent from the American Revolution. The Patriots, with their constant allusions to conspiracy and tyranny, took on some of the coloration of Cromwellian protest.[30] Self-righteous Revolutionary figures employed inflated rhetoric to remind their listeners of the tyrannies by which they were oppressed. Indubitably the American Revolution has its moments of saber-rattling and tub-thumping. To secure ample confirmation, one has merely to read the annual Boston Massacre commemoration addresses or the lurid charges by which Patriot judges exhorted grand juries to do their duty. In fairness, one must add that the American Revolutionary appeal was addressed at least as much to reason as to the emotions, and that the level at which the American Revolutionary ideology was pitched was determined in large measure by the knowledge that a substantial audience had long been trained to follow closely reasoned political argument.

If Americans managed to keep their sanity during their revolution, they also managed to draw comfort from their sense of humor. There could be a macabre note, but it was

29. Albert Soboul, "Sentiment religieux et cultes populaires pendant la Révolution; Saintes patriotes et martyrs de la liberté," *Annales Historiques de la Révolution Française* (1957), pp. 195–213.

30. Bernard Bailyn, *Pamphlets of the American Revolution* (Cambridge, Massachusetts, 1965), I, 86–89.

far less vindictive than French Revolutionary humor and less spiced with sadism. The boy who went down to camp with his father "along with Captain Gooding," was scared out of his wits by the trench-diggers, who told them they were digging him a grave.

> It scared me so I hooked it off,
> Nor stopt as I remember
> Nor turned about till I got home
> Locked up in Mother's chamber.

In "What a Court Hath Old England" the ballad makers, to the tune of "Down Derry Down," captured in verse the grievances that led to revolution.

What a court hath old England of folly and sin,
Spite of Chatham and Camden, Barré, Burke, Wilkes, and Glynn!
Not content with the game act, they tax fish and sea,
And America drench with hot water and tea.

From Arundel to Savannah patriotic Americans acclaimed the action of the "Mohawk Indians" in jettisoning the cargo of tea into Boston harbor.

> We made a plaguey mess of tea
> In one of the biggest dishes,
> I mean we steeped it in the sea and treated all the fishes.

In one short Yankee ditty a revolutionary act of defiance had been transmuted into farce, and another patriotic legend with comic overtones had been conceived.

When the feared British war machine turned its guns upon the rebels, the Patriots gleefully celebrated in ballad and verse every setback for the Redcoats. Thus, when that Revolutionary Falstaff, Sir Peter Parker, came to grief off Charleston, the balladeers put in rhyme Parker's report to the Admiralty:

> De'il take 'em, their shot
> Came so swift and so hot,
> And the cowardly dogs stood so stiff, sirs,
> That I put ship about
> And was glad to get out,
> Or they would not have left me a skiff, sirs!

Saratoga, a far greater victory, was thus neatly epitomized in a ballad entitled "Our Commanders":

> Gage nothing did, and went to pot;
> Howe lost one town, another got;
> Guy nothing lost, and nothing won;
> Dunmore was homewards forced to run;
> Clinton was beat and got a garter;
> And bouncing Burgoyne catch'd a tartar;
> Thus all we gain for millions spent
> Is to be laughed at, and repent.

Even the occupation of Philadelphia by the enemy had its amusing side. Consider Francis Hopkinson's enjoyable "Battle of the Kegs," that satirical account of a skirmish for control of the Delaware, with the classic stanza:

> Sir William, he snug as a flea,
>   Lay all his time a-snoring;
> Nor dreamed of harm, as he lay warm
>   In bed with Mrs. (Loring).

Or sing along with the good-humored Whigs that wonderful parody on "The Banks of the Dee," the American words of which were composed by Oliver Arnold, a relative of the war hero turned traitor:

> 'Twas winter and blue Tory noses were freezing,
> As they marched o'er the land where they ought not to be;
> The valiants complained at the fifers' cursed wheezing
> And wished they'd remained on the banks of the Dee.[31]

31. See also Arthur Loesser, *Humor in American Song* (New York, 1942), pp. 64–77.

Humor helped the Patriots salvage their sanity in the face of terror. When the British fleet under Admiral Wallace pillaged the Narragansett shore and fired upon the town of Bristol, Rhode Island, the ballad makers, while not overlooking the terror that struck the townsfolk, found occasion to scoff at the poor marksmanship of Wallace's gunners.

> With all their firing and their skill
> They did not any person kill,
> Neither was any person hurt
> Except the Reverend Parson Burt.

> And he was not killed by a ball,
> As judged by jurors one and all,
> But being in a sickly state,
> He frightened fell, which proved his fate.

> And another truth to you I'll tell
> That you may see they levelled well,
> For aiming for to kill the people,
> They fired their shot into a steeple.

> They fired low, they fired high,
> The women scream, the children cry,
> And all their firing and their racket
> Shot off the topmast of a packet!

A colonial wit composed a jingle to a popular square-dance tune to epitomize Cornwallis' southern campaign with its climactic ending at Yorktown:

> Cornwallis led a country dance,
> The like was never seen, sir,
> Much retrograde, and much advance,
> And all with General Greene, sir.

> They rambled up, they rambled down,
> Joined hands and off they run, sir,
> Our General Greene to Charlestown,
> The Earl to Wilmington, sir.

And the denouement:

> His music soon forgets to play—
> His feet can move no more, sir,
> And all his bands now curse the day
> They jiggèd to our shore, sir.
>
> Now Tories all, what can ye say,
> Come, is not this a griper?
> That while your hopes are danced away
> 'Tis you must pay the piper.

If the Americans managed to derive considerable amusement out of the American Revolution, it is dubious whether the French extracted much from theirs. As revolutions have proliferated, the sense of humor has virtually vanished. Of the humorless breed of present-day revolutionaries it might be said in all charity that they start out in dead earnest and end up deadly bores.

It is indeed paradoxical that the French Revolution, shaped as it was in its early constitution-making phase by the American example, should in turn have contributed directly to the first political trauma of the new American nation. At its start the French Revolution was viewed in America as a necessary and constructive reform movement, but swift-moving events abroad quickly divided American opinion. The abolition of the monarchy, the execution of Louis XVI, the Reign of Terror, and the transformation of the French Revolution into a general European war proved a catalyst to the rise of two opposing parties in the United States. The followers of Jefferson opposed Washington's Neutrality Proclamation as a violation of America's alliance with France while at the same time they advocated a retaliatory boycott against England because of her actions interfering with neutral shipping. The Jay Treaty, with its many concessions to the English position and its sparse advantages on paper for the United States, exacerbated the differences. By then the American and French Revolutions seemed quite different and distinct. As Hamilton put it in an undated letter written around May, 1793:

> . . . The cause of France is compared with that of America during its late revolution. Would to Heaven that the comparison were just. Would to Heaven we could discern in the mirror of French affairs the same humanity, the same decorum, the same gravity, the same order, the same dignity, the same solemnity, which distinguished the cause of the American Revolution. Clouds and darkness would not then rest upon the issues as they now do. I own I do not like the comparison.[32]

What alarmed the Federalists perhaps most of all was the egalitarian tone of the unfolding revolution in France, with its evidence of social upheaval, and the fear that it might catch fire in America. "Our greatest danger is from the contagion of levelism," Chauncy Goodrich of Hartford wrote to Oliver Wolcott, Jr., adding, "What folly is it that has set the world agog to be all equal to French barbers."[33]

When Citizen Genêt, the French minister to the United States, was rebuked by President Washington for commissioning privateers in American ports, he reputedly threatened to appeal over the President's head to the people. The Federalist press launched a furious denunciation of Genêt's presumption, an attack touched off when Chief Justice John Jay and New York's Senator Rufus King joined in publicly disclosing Genêt's threat.[34]

That France interfered in American domestic policies to

32. Henry Cabot Lodge, ed., *Works* (New York, 1904), X, 45.

33. Oliver Wolcott, *Memoirs of the Administrations of Washington and Adams,* ed. by George Gibbs (New York, 1846), I, 88.

34. William Jay, *The Life of John Jay* (New York, 1833), I, 304.

secure a government sympathetic to its own aims is supported by considerable evidence. Delacroix, in charge of foreign affairs under the new Directory, insisted that Washington be overthrown by "the right kind of revolution." But if the French government hoped that the party of Jefferson and Madison would start a pro-French popular revolution, they were quickly disabused. This is not to imply that Jefferson did not remain basically sympathetic to the aims of the French Revolution. He demonstrated his sympathy as Secretary of State by laying down a principle for the recognition of a revolutionary government which was long followed. "It accords with our principles to acknowledge any government to be rightful which is formed by the will of the nation substantially declared," he informed Gouverneur Morris, the American minister to France in 1792. Morris, despite his revulsion toward the Revolution's excesses and his innate conservatism, had spelled out a similar principle in a letter written before Jefferson had composed his. "I am bound to suppose," Morris wrote, "that, if the great majority of the nation adhere to the new form, the United States will approve thereof, because, in the first place, we have no right to prescribe to this country the government they shall adopt, and next, because the basis of our own constitution is the indefeasible right of the people to establish it."[35] Enunciating what he called "the Catholic principle of republicanism," Jefferson wrote Pinckney in England later that year, "The only thing essential is the will of the nation. Taking this as your polar star, you can hardly err."[36] In its pure and simplistic form, this principle of recognition seemed in keep-

35. Jefferson to Morris, November 7, 1792. Ford, *Writings*, VI, 131; Morris to Jefferson, August 22, 1792, *American State Papers, Foreign Relations*, I, 336.

36. Jefferson to Thomas Pinckney, December 30, 1792. *Writings*, ed. by Lipscomb and Bergh (20 vols., Washington, 1905), IX, 7–8.

ing with the traditions of the American Revolution. It was to be sternly tested in the years ahead when governments were overthrown and replaced by others by no means clearly "formed by the will of the nation substantially declared." Such changes posed a dilemma not easily resolved for presidents and State Departments.

In other respects Jefferson has been criticized for permitting his sympathies for the cause of France to affect his judgment as Secretary of State. It was hardly to his credit that he failed to recognize the propriety of the Proclamation of Neutrality issued by President Washington or that he was dilatory in disabusing Genêt in the latter's euphoric expectations of the help for France he might obtain in America. The fact is that Jefferson displayed a tolerance for other people's revolutions which many of his American contemporaries failed to share. He seems to have been able to draw upon a limitless resource of revolutionary zest, a capacity which his correspondent, John Adams, for one, lacked. Perhaps with tongue in cheek Jefferson remarked that "the tree of liberty must be refreshed from time to time with the blood of patriots and tyrants. It is its natural manure." Concerned that America's reputation for republican reformation might be damaged by reason of such events as the crushing of Shays' Rebellion and the adoption of a centralizing Constitution bereft of a bill of rights, Jefferson could not fail to recognize how such acts in America would affect his own standing among the revolutionary ideologues of France. Thus, as Secretary of State he would not be budged from his pro-French course. He felt that the victory of the anti-French coalition would provide the "monocrats" of America with the example and perhaps the means of setting up a monarchy in the United States along the British model.[37]

37. Jefferson to Lafayette, June 16, 1792; to Joel Barlow, June 20, 1792. *Writings*, ed. by Lipscomb and Bergh (Washington, 1905), VIII, 380–383.

Yet even Jefferson was alarmed at the "furious republicans" who embraced Genêt after his warning to abandon him as "a sinking wreck." Indeed, many of Jefferson's followers were quite prepared to press for dramatic changes in America, providing substantiation for Jefferson's admission that "all the old spirit of 1776 is rekindling."[38] In the leading towns Jacobinism seemed endemic, and a mélange of libertarian currents, ominous portents to vigilant Federalists, were being stirred up. At the spring commencement of '93, Columbia College students, for example, delivered orations on such progressive, if not radical, themes as "the inhumanity of the slave trade," "the impropriety of capital punishment," and "the dignity of man."[39] Enlightenment issues dominated "literati" discussions, and even local politicians caught the fever. It seemed politic for the Common Council of New York City to change the names of King, Queen, Princess, and Duke Streets to Pine, Cedar, Beaver, and Stone respectively.[40] Working-class members of Jacobin clubs with red mobcaps on their heads paraded and demonstrated in the streets of New York and Philadelphia, singing "Ça ira." From his retirement at Quincy in 1813 John Adams still shuddered when he recalled those stormy days. Gently chiding that unreconstructed revolutionary Thomas Jefferson, he remarked, "You certainly never felt the terrorism excited by Genêt, in 1793, when ten thousand people in the streets of Philadelphia day after day, threatened to drag Washington out of his house, and effect a revolution in the government."

38. Thomas Jefferson to James Monroe, May 5, 1793, *Writings of Jefferson,* ed. by P. L. Ford, VI, 238–239.

39. "Commencement Scrapbook," Columbiana Collection, Columbia University.

40. See Alfred F. Young, *The Democratic Republicans of New York* (Chapel Hill, 1967), p. 363.

In so supercharged an atmosphere, Benjamin Carr, a British emigrant to Philadelphia, chose the occasion of the tenth anniversary of the withdrawal of British troops at the end of the American Revolution to appeal to Federalist and Antifederalist alike with a performance of his newly composed *Federal Overture*. It is with obvious design that the overture begins with an introduction based on "Yankee Doodle," then launches into the instantaneously popular "Marseillaise," and goes on to include both "Ça ira" and "La Carmagnole," along with the "President's March."[41]

Carr's long-forgotten *Federal Overture*, that potpourri of revolutionary airs of both continents, proved prophetic. The presidential system as well as the Constitution survived the French Revolution in America, but France's revolution in spirit if not in execution was never wholly repudiated by either the people or the statesmen of the United States. Whatever doubts Jefferson may have had about Bonapartism, they failed to swerve him. In a retrospective comment he remarked of France's revolution, "The liberty of the whole earth was depending on the issue of the contest, and was ever such a prize won with so little innocent blood."[42]

Even some of the severe critics of the course of the French Revolution among the Federalists, Jefferson's political adversaries, recognized, however grudgingly, that the dread upheaval in France had served a necessary purpose. As late as 1810 John Jay wrote to his English abolitionist friend, William Wilberforce, "The French Revolution has so discredited democracy, and it has so few influential advocates in Europe, that I doubt its giving you much more trouble. On the contrary, there seems to be a danger of its depreciat-

41. Irving Lowens, *Music and Musicians in Early America* (New York, 1964), pp. 89 *et seq*.

42. *Writings*, ed by P. L. Ford, VI, 154. See also Lawrence S. Kaplan, *Jefferson and France* (New Haven, 1967).

ing too much. Without a portion of it there can be no free government."[43] With the exception of a minority of die-hard Federalists, the American statesmen who had made a great revolution and shaped a Constitution built on revolutionary principles remained at heart convinced that inequality, the European caste system, and all the trappings of the *ancien régime* had no place in a New World. Perhaps they were never entirely reconciled to the French Revolution, but they were obliged to adjust themselves to the new political climate which the winds of change had brought to the American main. Jefferson, himself, continued in his later years to hold out to his liberal French correspondents the hope that in the long run the taste of freedom that Europeans had enjoyed would some day topple the autocratic regimes, and that once again France would lead Europe along the path of liberty.

43. John Jay to Wilberforce, October 25, 1810. Jay Papers, Special Collections, Columbia University Libraries.

III

THE AMERICAN REVOLUTION AND
THE LIBERATION OF EUROPE

On the fifth of May, 1969, hundreds of Pilsen residents
raised American flags in a demonstration defying the toning
down by their officials of the commemoration of their city's
liberation by the American army in 1945. As the undaunted
populace stepped past a line of policemen to place little
American flags next to a flower bed on Peace Square, they
were by these actions paying tribute not alone to America's
military role in freeing Czechoslovakia from Nazi rule but
also to America's important part a generation earlier in
creating the modern state of Czechoslovakia. By these acts,
one might say, they symbolically reaffirmed the recognition
of the historic role of the United States in the liberation of
Europe.

That America had such a role to play was implicitly
understood by America's Founding Fathers, although
Americans then and now have never been entirely in agreement on the shape and direction of that role. Writing in
1821, at the height of the reaction in Europe against revolutionary movements, the aged statesman Thomas Jefferson

74

commented to John Adams: "The flames kindled on the fourth of July, 1776, have spread over too much of the globe to be extinguished by the feeble engines of despotism."[1]

In giving primacy to the role of the American Revolution in touching off liberative currents, Jefferson's appraisal has been largely ignored by historians of revolutionary movements, for it is now the fashion to depict the American Revolution as a parochial movement and the French as ecumenical. To begin with, there is a long European tradition which regards the American Revolution as exceptional and not in the main stream. Goethe might well concede, *"Amerika, Du hast es besser."* Lacking feudal classes and internecine feuds, blessed with boundless resources, the American experiment seemed admirable but hardly a model for the Europe of the future. But if there was any conspiracy to deny to the American Revolution its revolutionary character, it may well have been hatched by Alexis de Tocqueville, if not by Condorcet before him. Conceding that American society "was shaken to its center" by the American Revolution and America's democratic tendencies aroused by that event, Tocqueville still insisted that America was reaping the fruits of a democratic revolution "without having had the revolution itself."[2]

Since so prescient an observer as Tocqueville should have ignored the revolutionary implications of the doctrines of popular sovereignty, individual liberties, constitutionalism, and federalism, or did not come fully to grips with the significance of the social transformation touched off by the American Revolution, it is easy to understand why more recent European writers have followed in his wake, have

1. *The Adams-Jefferson Letters,* ed. by Lester J. Cappon (Chapel Hill, 1959), II, 554.
2. Tocqueville, *Democracy in America,* ed. by Phillips Bradley (New York, 1945), I, 13, 47.

denied to the American Revolution an impact on Europe and the rest of the world, and have failed to perceive that the American Revolution, as distinct from the War for Independence, was a continuing process that has not yet run its course.

Typical of specialists of the European scene, Eric Hobsbawm, for example, concedes that the American Revolution remained "a crucial event in American history," while leaving "few major traces elsewhere." Contrariwise, he finds that the French Revolution stands as a "landmark in all countries" and "remains *the* revolution of its time."[3] Even Robert R. Palmer, who has fully recognized the place of the American Revolution in the "age of the democratic revolution," would deny to the American event its primacy. He would have the American Revolution preceded by civil turmoil such as occurred in the tiny republic of Geneva in the 1760's or by Chancellor Maupeou's "revolution" of the Parlement of Paris in 1771, or even by the monarchist *coup d'état* in Sweden of 1772. Admittedly, Palmer's examples are all manifestations of the mood of change and reform that swept the Western world in the Age of the Enlightenment, and in the two latter cases of the attempts of monarchs to deal with them. By the same token one might cite the reformism of the Enlightened Despots, of Joseph II, Frederick the Great and Catherine II, as well as of that absolutist ruler with reforming urges, Charles III of Spain. Manifestations of civil unrest and reform, to be sure, but none of the precedents deserve to be called revolutions.

The American Whigs on the eve of their Revolution were perfectly aware of the currents of unrest touching other

3. See Eric J. Hobsbawm, *The Age of Revolution, 1789–1848* (New York, 1962), pp. 76–77; also Hannah Arendt, *On Revolution* (New York, 1963), p. 87. Cf. also J. H. Plumb, "Introduction" to John R. Alden, *Pioneer America* (New York, 1966), pp. xxv, xxvi.

shores. They applauded dissenters and magnified their achievements and significance. They toasted Charles Lucas, the "Wilkes of Ireland," and endorsed his crusade for a greater role for the Irish Parliament. They sympathized with "the distressed Poles," facing the partition of their country at the hands of the Great Powers. They admired "the brave Dantzickers," and were heartened by the tenacity of that free city to resist being taken over by Frederick the Great. Hearing of the anti-Church reforms instituted by Charles III of Spain, the Patriots drank a toast to "Added Vigour to the Spark of Liberty Kindling in Spain."[4]

None of these movements could be classed as revolutions, or even revolutionary. The closest parallel to the American colonial struggle was offered by the people of Corsica. Back in 1757 Pasquale Paoli headed a rebellion of Corsicans against the city-state of Genoa, a war which carried overtones of a colonial revolt. He succeeded only in having the island attached to France, but continued the struggle against Corsica's new rulers, counting on English sympathy and support. "Paschal Paoli and his brave Corsicans" proved one of the most popular Whig toasts in America, and, of all the resistance movements abroad, little Corsica's stand evoked the most reports and comments in the pre-Revolutionary colonial press.[5]

Most of all, the American Whigs looked to the radical reformers of the mother country for inspiration. American pamphleteers owed a heavy debt to English radical writers of the early eighteenth century, notably to men like John Trenchard and Thomas Gordon, while Jefferson wove into the patterned texture of his ideology notions derived from

4. See Arthur M. Schlesinger, Jr., *Prelude to Independence: The Newspaper War on Britain, 1764–1776* (New York, 1958), pp. 35, 36.

5. G. P. Anderson, "Pascal Paoli, An Inspiration to the Sons of Liberty," Colonial Society of Massachusetts, *Publications,* XXVI (1924–26), 180–210.

Locke and borrowings from the Whig party line.[6] On the eve of the Revolution, London was experiencing a ferment of radicalism, with the demagogic Wilkes as its momentary darling. "Wilkes and Liberty" was a universal toast among American Whigs. Since issue No. 45 of the Wilkes' periodical, the *North Briton,* touched off the ferment in England with its criticism of a speech from the throne, that number took on special significance among colonial radicals. Typical of these celebrations was the gathering of forty-five New Yorkers on the forty-fifth day of the year 1770 to consume forty-five pounds of beefsteak cut from a bullock forty-five months old.[7]

Encouraging as these dissenting voices may have proved to the American radicals, it was the full-scale insurgency in America which offered the world the first example of a successful secession of colonies from empire, of the overthrow of a monarch, and of the formulation of states and nation on principles of constitutionalism and federalism. And how contagious that example proved! Aside from France, its impact was felt in the mother country, in Ireland, and throughout the European mainland, not to speak of Spain's possessions in the New World.

The libertarian protest movement in America evoked a cordial response in English radical circles. Of the more extreme radicals, the pro-American activities of Horne Tooke are perhaps typical. That erstwhile Wilkes enthusiast and veteran of legal warfare had the presumption to sponsor a resolution of the Constitutional Society of June 7, 1775, directing that a subscription be raised on behalf of "our beloved American fellow subjects" who had "preferred death to slavery" and "were for that reason only inhumanly mur-

6. See Bernard Bailyn, ed., *Pamphlets of the American Revolution, 1750–1776,* I (Cambridge, Mass., 1965), pp. 33, 34.

7. *Massachusetts Gazette and Boston News-Letter,* March 1, 1770.

dered by the king's troops" at Lexington a few months
before. The government was not amused. Horne Tooke was
tried before Lord Mansfield, fittingly on July 4, 1777, found
guilty, and sentenced to pay a fine and suffer a year's
imprisonment.[8]

More consequential in arousing liberal Britons to recognizing the merits of the American cause were the efforts of
the nonconforming minister and political philosopher, Dr.
Richard Price. In 1776 he published a pamphlet entitled
*Observations on Civil Liberty and the Justice and Policy of
the War with America,* in which he voiced his espousal of
America's side of the controversy, and other literary efforts
served to identify him with the cause of American independence. Crowded congregations hung on his words. Lord
Shelburne turned to him constantly for advice. Price rated
the American Revolution second only to the founding of
Christianity among world epochal events, and although he
declined the invitation of the Continental Congress to emigrate to America and assist in the financial administration of
the Revolution, he concluded his letter to the Congress with
the prophetic words that he looked "to the United States as
now the hope, and likely soon to become the refuge of
mankind." The liberal poet William Blake shared Price's
admiration for America in verses like these:

> Tho' born on the cheating banks of Thames,
> Tho' his waters bathed my infant limbs,
> The Ohio shall wash his stains from me:
> I was born a slave, but I go to be free.[9]

Views like those of Price and Blake were echoed in the
Opposition press. Centered in London and dominating the

8. (London) *Morning Chronicle*, November 20, 25, 1777.

9. John Sampson, ed., *The Poetical Works of William Blake* (Oxford, 1905),
p. 165.

newspaper circulation of the country, the Opposition press presented America's side and castigated the North Ministry throughout the war.[10]

Nor was discontent in England confined to intellectuals and polemical penmen. The extraordinary difficulty experienced by the North Ministry in recruiting for the armed forces evidenced the opposition or indifference of the masses to the war in America. War industries were beset with suspicions of sabotage, slowdowns, and even strikes. The eight days of June, 1780, that wild uprising in which the masses gave vent to their anti-Catholic prejudices, had ignoble ends, to be sure, but it provided a dramatic demonstration of mass discontent—social, economic, religious, and political, disorganized and fragmented, and flowing into illicit channels when it found no outlet elsewhere.[11] A more sober grass-roots movement of parliamentary reform, the quickening of whose activities came in response to the example from the Americans overseas, was led in the countryside by the Reverend Christopher Wyvill, ostensibly supported by the prestigious Marquess of Rockingham, and in London by that new darling of the mob, Charles James Fox. They spoke about fiscal reform, annual Parliaments, equalizing representation, even universal suffrage, but little was accomplished before the ministry of the younger Pitt took over and squelched the presumption of the radicals.[12]

One striking illustration exemplifying the massive impact

10. Solomon Lutnick, *The American Revolution and the British Press, 1775–1783* (Columbia, Mo., 1967).

11. See Richard B. Morris, *The Peacemakers* (New York, 1965), pp. 67–87.

12. See C. Wyvill, *Political Papers, chiefly respecting the attempt of the County of York and the Considerable Districts . . . to effect a Reformation of the Parliament of Great Britain* (6 vols., London, 1794–1808). See also Caroline Robbins, *The Eighteenth-Century Commonwealthman* (Cambridge, 1959), pp. 370–373; I. R. Christie, *Wilkes, Wyvill, and Reform* (London, 1962), pp. 68–72; Eugene C. Black, *The Association* (Cambridge, Mass., 1963).

of the American Revolution on British liberal thinking is the extraordinary exchange of letters between the reform-minded Earl of Shelburne, while prime minister of England, and Benjamin Franklin, a peace commissioner for a cluster of rebel states with whom the prime minister's country was at war. Shelburne asked Benjamin Vaughan, an intermediary with the Americans, to find out from Franklin what he thought about extending the suffrage in England. Though the peace preliminaries had not yet been signed, Franklin had no compunctions about passing on the advice that Parliament should be elected by all the people, and that the only way the lower classes would rise in England would be by elevating their education and political responsibility.[13]

Even had he so desired, Shelburne could not have implemented Franklin's advice. Nor could the radicalism of the late 80's and 90's, both American and French in its inspiration. Radicals like Major John Cartwright tirelessly reiterated the virtues of the American example of popular suffrage, adequate representation, and a written constitution, and pointed to the peace and felicity enjoyed under the new American government.[14] And if the political writers were unchecked in their admiration, the poets—Blake, Burns, Wordsworth, Southey, and Coleridge—were downright rhapsodic.

Distasteful though the American example may have been to the British government, it was the uncomfortably close lesson in regicide acted out across the Channel that sent chills up and down the spines of the rulers in England, impelling the government to call a halt to radical activity by instituting the treason trials of 1794–96 and enacting a batch

13. Benjamin Vaughan to Shelburne, Nov. 24, 1782. Emmons Transcripts, William L. Clements Library, University of Michigan.

14. See, for example, Cartwright's *An Appeal on the Subject of the English Constitution* (1796) and *The Constitutional Defence of England* (1796).

of repressive laws. As a result, it took two reform bills and a Chartist movement sandwiched in between to achieve in Britain something of the democratic upthrust that the American Revolution touched off in England's former colonies.

If the response in the mother country was delayed, other parts of the empire were more immediately affected by the coming and course of the American Revolution. Save perhaps for Bermuda and the Bahamas, which were riddled with subversion, Ireland, of all Britain's possessions, proved the most responsive to the revolutionary impulses that touched her shores from across the Atlantic. Irish and American patriots were quick to perceive how closely their respective situations paralleled each other and were alert to demonstrate how each suffered alike from discriminatory trade legislation and a denial of a role in decision making within the empire. Ireland's wrongs at England's hands should serve as a lesson to Americans, John Dickinson had warned. In his famous *Letters of a Pennsylvania Farmer*, issued in 1768, Dickinson devoted his tenth letter to Irish wrongs and bade his countrymen to "grow wise by the misfortunes of others." Contacts between American and Irish leaders were inevitable. In a visit to Ireland in 1771 Benjamin Franklin fortified the resolve of Irish patriots like the aged Charles Lucas,[15] and was himself encouraged to hope that Ireland and America might join forces to secure "more equitable treatment."[16] When the war came the American Congress, counting on Irish sympathy and support, drew up, together with its addresses to the people of England and of Canada, an address to the people of Ireland.

15. See J. Bennett Nolan, *Benjamin Franklin in Scotland and Ireland, 1759 and 1771* (Philadelphia, 1938), p. 148.

16. Franklin to Thomas Cushing, January 13, 1772, in John Bigelow, ed., *Works of Benjamin Franklin* (New York, 1887), IV, 445.

The Irish response offered every hope of active intervention by Irish patriots to support the American cause. By June of 1776 Horace Walpole could comment that "all Ireland is *America mad.*"[17] From the pro-American Irish press to the Dublin Liberty Boys public opinion seemed overwhelmingly sympathetic to the Americans, while Belfast and Cork petitioned the King for peace with America.[18] Sir Edward Newenham erected on the grounds of his Georgian mansion near Dublin a Gothic tower which he dedicated to George Washington. Part of the inscription on the tower ran: "Oh, ill-fated Britain! The folly of Lexington and Concord will rend asunder, and forever disjoin America from the empire."[19]

"Before you decide on the practicability of being slaves forever, look to America," Henry Grattan exhorted his compatriots. From his estate in Kerry, Shelburne reported that the regular toast of the Protestant Irish was "Success to the Americans," while Horace Walpole commented on a Dublin nonimportation agreement adopted in April, 1779, "It is now too publicly known to be disguised any longer, that Ireland has much the air of Americanizing."[20] Public enthusiasm notwithstanding, the Patriot party in Ireland constituted a minority of the managed Irish Parliament. Over the eloquent protests of the Opposition, that Parliament voted to

17. Walpole to the Countess of Upper Ossory, June 25, 1776, in Mrs. Paget Toynbee, ed., *The Letters of Horace Walpole* (16 vols., Oxford, 1903–05), IX, 380.

18. See Michael Kraus, "America and the Irish Revolutionary Movement in the Eighteenth Century," in R. B. Morris, ed., *The Era of the American Revolution* (New York, 1939), pp. 332–348.

19. Richard Lewis, *The Dublin Guide* (Dublin, 1787), p. 59, cited by Maurice R. O'Connell, *Irish Politics and Social Conflict in the Age of the American Revolution* (Philadelphia, 1965), pp. 25–35.

20. Lord Edmond Fitzmaurice, *Life of William, Earl of Shelburne* (3 vols., London, 1876), II, 401; Walpole, *Letters*, X, 408.

permit the dispatch to the American war of four thousand troops.

For a brief moment Ireland figured in the strategic planning of the War of the American Revolution. Once France, and then Spain, had joined forces against England, an invasion of both England and Ireland was seriously contemplated by the Allies. They counted on the kind of discontent that manifested itself from Ulster to the south of Ireland, on secret emissaries whose activities were noted by Lord Harcourt, the viceroy of Ireland, and, very heavily, on the propaganda efforts of Americans like Benjamin Franklin, who, in 1778, issued *An Address to the Good People of Ireland on Behalf of America*. In that broadside Franklin expressed the hope "that the liberation of your country has been effected in America" and held out the promise that, should England not lift the restraints on the Irish economy, "means will be found to establish your freedom in this respect, in the fullest and amplest manner."[21]

It was not the justice of the Irish cause but rather the threat of invasion posed by England's enemies that forced her to make concessions to reduce insurrectionary tension. In the spring of 1779 Benjamin Franklin dispatched Dr. Edward Bancroft to Ireland to report on the prospects for an invasion that was being projected by the Bourbon houses. Bancroft, who unknown to Franklin proved to be a double agent, toured northern Ireland, and what he saw he professed not to like. On his return he met Lafayette at Le Havre and told him "the fruit is not ripe," and that the military associations springing up in Ireland could be expected to resist the invaders rather than welcome them.[22]

21. Benjamin Franklin, *An Address to the Good People of Ireland, on Behalf of America*, October 4, 1778, ed. by Paul Leicester Ford (Brooklyn, N.Y., 1891).

22. See Richard B. Morris, *The Peacemakers* (New York, 1965), pp. 35–36.

Accordingly, the French and Spaniards agreed upon English Channel points as objectives for their ill-fated armada instead of Irish. But there was much truth in Bancroft's report, however suspect the source. The British government was forced to distribute arms to the forty thousand Irish Volunteers, and Parliament in the winter of 1779–80 enacted a series of bills giving liberal trade concessions to the Irish.

The patriots wanted more—a completely autonomous Parliament. "Look to America," exclaimed Grattan in the Irish House of Commons. Would Ireland be content with an English Parliament enacting laws for her, when Philadelphia, sending forth its ambassadors to the courts of Europe, "manifests to the world her independency and power?" When the North Ministry was finally forced to resign, the British Parliament in January, 1783, granted to the Irish Parliament a coordinate status under the Crown.

And so the Irish Revolution, touched off by the American, had run its course. "I trust," said Burke, "the last Revolution in Ireland." An Anglican minority had won political liberty —truly a small concession by the British Government—and it was not until the French Revolution that Irish Catholics were permitted to vote for members of the Parliament that ruled their country. Later insurrections, encouraged and bolstered by Ireland's emigrant sons in America, proved Burke to be a poor prophet indeed. For long, America and its Revolution stood as a model and reminder to Irish patriots of their own unfinished struggle.[23]

An exchange of communications between the Yankee Club of Stewartstown, county Tyrone, Ulster, and George

23. See R. Coupland, *The American Revolution and the British Empire* (New York, 1965), pp. 85–140, *passim;* R. B. McDowell, *Irish Public Opinion, 1750–1800* (London, 1943), pp. 49–50. For the support given the Fenian movement by Irish-Americans, see Florence E. Gibson, *The Attitude of the New York Irish Toward State and National Affairs* (New York, 1951), pp. 174–180, 182, 186–188.

Washington, as the American Revolution drew to a close, epitomized the interrelationship of the two movements and forecast the continuing impact of America on the prospects of Ireland. The county Tyrone patriots, in a letter addressed to Washington, expressed their rejoicing "to hear that the spirit of America had risen superior to the proud menaces of both regal and ministerial oppression." The committee was heartened by the example of "an infant country" successfully contending "with an antient, powerful and victorious nation." The address concluded by remarking that Washington's exertions had "not only vindicated the freedom of your country, but have also shed their benign influence over the distressed kingdom of Ireland," and expressed their gratitude to the General to whom they acknowledged themselves "indebted for our late happy deliverance from as baneful a system of policy as ever disgraced the rights of mankind." In a courteous reply, Washington expressed the hope that "if, in the course of our successful contest, any good consequences have resulted to the oppressed kingdom of Ireland, it will afford a new source of felicitation to all who respect the interests of humanity."[24] Stripped of its rhetoric, Washington's response reflected the expectation of America's own revolutionaries that their efforts would result in change and improvement everywhere.

Although nowhere else did it have so immediate an impact perhaps as in Ireland, throughout Europe the American Revolution evoked a sympathetic response. Its decisions on the relations of church and state coincided with the notions of religious liberty and toleration expounded by Enlightenment spokesmen, and its example in this respect was hailed

24. Address of Yankee Club of Stewartstown, June 7, 1783, reprinted in Colonial Society of Massachusetts, *Transactions*, XIV (1911–13), 198–199; from *Massachusetts Centinel*, May 22, 1784, pp. 1–2; Washington to Yankee Club, January 20, 1784, Jared Sparks, ed., *Writings of George Washington* (New York, 1847), IX, 13, 14.

by Richard Price and other English radicals. While lacking national identity, European Jewry took heart from the great events in America. Following news of the Preliminary Peace between the American States and Great Britain, a German Jew, presumably on behalf of a considerable number of coreligionists, proposed in a letter to the President of the Continental Congress that permission be granted for a substantial immigration of German Jews to the United States. The letter lays stress on the civil rights already accorded religious minorities in America in contrast to the discrimination prevailing in the Germanies and reveals how the American experience in religious liberty had aroused peoples of distant lands to take measures for their own betterment.[25]

The American Revolution did not by itself transform the status of the Jews in America, since from the outset Jews participated in the Revolutionary movement without discrimination, as some did as well on the Loyalist side of the struggle. However, bills of rights in Revolutionary state constitutions, beginning with Virginia's in 1776, guaranteed religious liberty, and the movement for the separation of church and state gained enormous momentum. In fact, the issue of religious liberty was a chief topic of debate in the Massachusetts Constitutional Convention of 1780, while the battle for disestablishment was waged in Virginia throughout the years of the Revolution. If Jews and other religious minorities were beneficiaries of these reforms in America, it was the federal Constitution which was to have so enormous an impact on the position of the Jews in America and, by example, on the Jews of Europe as well. Here were found the principles of separation of church and state, liberty of

25. The letter, published originally in the *Deutsches Museum* (June, 1783), pp. 558–566, was separately reissued four years later under the title *Schreiben eines deutschen Juden an den nordamerikanischen Präsidenten* (Frankfurt and Leipzig, 1787), with a prefatory letter allegedly written by Moses Mendelssohn.

conscience, the appointment to any federal office without religious tests, and other nondiscriminatory freedoms included in the Bill of Rights. It is to be noted that the first ten Amendments were proposed on September 25, 1791, just two days before the French National Assembly voted for the emancipation of the Jews. But Jefferson's bill for religious freedom, which also removed disabilities for religious opinion, had, through Madison's efforts, been adopted by the Virginia legislature five years earlier. This epoch-making measure was translated into French and Italian, and was considered abroad as a model for advanced legislation on the subject. Jefferson regarded the law as one of his three greatest achievements. In celebration of the ratification of the Constitution Jews joined fellow Americans. In Philadelphia their sensibilities were observed by providing for them a special table dispensing food that conformed to Jewish dietary laws.[26] Washington quite properly could applaud the "enlarged and liberal policy" of the new nation, in which "all possess alike liberty of conscience and immunities of citizenship." Significantly, the new President extolled the example of his nation "which gives to bigotry no sanction, to persecution no assistance," as "a policy worthy of imitation."[27]

This toleration toward Jews and Baptists, this acceptance of public worship by Roman Catholic soldiers of the King of France, reflecting in no small part Enlightenment currents, served as a spur to the movement in Europe for the emancipation of the Jews, so long victims of discriminatory laws—

26. Joseph L. Blau and Salo W. Baron, *The Jews of the United States, 1790–1840: A Documentary History* (New York and London, 1963), pp. xx, xxiii.

27. George Washington to Hebrew Congregation in Newport, Rhode Island, n.d., in Lewis Abraham, "Correspondence Between Washington and Jewish Citizens," American Jewish Historical Society, *Proceedings*, III (1895), 91–92.

an emancipation finally achieved by the French Revolution
and the Code Napoléon. A foremost spokesman for Jewish
emancipation was that grand product of the *Aufklärung,*
Moses Mendelssohn. So stirred was Mendelssohn by the
secular spirit evoked by America's War of Independence
that he wrote a new foreword to an older work, using the
Revolution as a pretext to set forth his ideas on the separation of church and state.[28]

If the American Revolution hastened the incorporation of
European Jewry into the respective national communities of
which they formed a part, it inspired national self-determination among the smaller states of Europe and accelerated the trend toward self-government. John Adams attested
to the reputation of that epochal event in both Holland and
Belgium, as well as on the larger European stage. "The
longer the war lasts," he wrote from Amsterdam in the fall of
1781, "the more the spirit of American government will
spread in Europe, because the attention of the world will be
fixed there as long as the war lasts."[29] Adams himself, as has
already been remarked, had brilliantly propagandized
among the Dutch the constitutional system adopted by the
Revolutionary American states.

Stirred by American Revolutionary ideologues and backed
financially by the French government, the Dutch patriots

28. Eric Werner, *Mendelssohn* (Glencoe, Ill., 1963), pp. 3, 4. Contemporaries recognized Mendelssohn's leading role in Jewish emancipation. See,
e.g., Comte de Mirabeau, *Sur Moses Mendelssohn, sur la Réforme Politique
des Juifs* (London, 1787); Abbé Henri Gregoire, *Essai sur la régénération
physique, morale et politique des Juifs* (Metz, 1789). For the relevance of
the American Revolution to the struggle for Jewish emancipation, see also
Christian Wilhelm Dohm, *De la Réforme politique des Juifs* (Dessau, 1782),
pp. 32–33, 119. For a recent critical, if controversial, appraisal of the attitude of Enlightenment figures like Voltaire toward the Jews, see Arthur
Hertzberg, *The French Enlightenment and the Jews* (New York and London,
1968).

29. John Adams to President of Congress, October 25, 1781. Jared Sparks,
Diplomatic Correspondence of the American Revolution, VI, 185.

revolted against the house of Orange in 1787. But the Orangists, supported extravagantly by the British and with a liberal use of Prussian troops, crushed the revolt easily. The result proved to be a victory of the aristocracy against a democratic bourgeois movement, a revolution put down by the force of a European counterrevolution and before the French Revolution had gotten under way.

Belgians had long followed with keen interest the reports of the rise of the new nation across the Atlantic[30] and were conversant with the texts of the state and federal constitutions, as well as with John Adams' *Defence of the American Constitutions,* published while he was in London in 1787–88.[31] Pro-American enthusiasts supported the republican cause in the provinces of Brabant and Flanders. In the former a member of the Sovereign Council, in an address delivered before the General Assembly in May, 1787, observed that liberty had been crushed in Poland; that it was struggling in Holland; that it was maintaining its position in England; and that it had triumphed in America. "What would be its lot in the Austrian Low Countries?" he asked. The author of a reformist tract, taking note of the efforts of Austria to make a trade treaty with America, pointed out that a prince who sought to form an alliance with America sanctioned, by that very act, "the revolution that had made them free." Such warnings to the Emperor contained at the least a veiled invitation to revolution. The poets proved less inhibited. For example, one quatrain composed in 1787 exhorted its readers:

> Je vous invite sans miséricorde,
> Pauvres Belgiques,

30. For John Adams' visit to Brussels in 1782, see L. H. Butterfield, *Diary and Autobiography of John Adams* (Cambridge, Mass., 1961), III, 32.

31. Thomas K. Gorman, *America and Belgium* (London, 1925), pp. iii, 15–54, *passim.*

> L'empereur tyrannique
> Suivons l'Amérique.[32]

Such effusions bestirred the right-wing French journalist Linguet, conducting his *Annales politiques civiles* from the comparative security of Brussels, to point out how dangerous an example the liberty of America was to Europe, how much like a virulent pest in its contagious and destructive propensities.[33] Liège-born Jean-Pierre Ransonnet visited the United States at the close of the Revolution, and upon his return advocated that the patriots of Liège and the Belgian provinces make common cause to set up a federation modeled on that of America.

The Belgian Revolution which broke out in 1789 found each province separately declaring its independence, with Flanders appropriating words from the American Declaration of Independence. When the conservative forces assembled in the so-called Estates General they adopted an Act of Union modeled upon the American Articles of Confederation, whose text was followed closely. The more radical party sought a modification of the electoral system and a reorganization of representation within the separate provinces in accordance with the American state constitutions. In short, each side took examples from the American Revolution to suit its case.

Belgian independence, a quick victim of foreign intervention, expired on December 2, 1790. That was the last of the republic, but the next time Belgium staged a revolt, in 1830, a more durable result was achieved. The leaders, disenchanted with the example provided by their revolutionary and counterrevolutionary neighbor France, preferred to

32. N. Schlitter, *Die Regierung Josefs II in des Österreichischen Niederlanden* (Vienna, 1900), I, 223.

33. *Annales politiques civiles et littéraires du XVIII siècle*, XIV, No. 111, 401.

make a "legal revolution" like the American to a more violent and less permanent one such as the French had attempted. While the leaders looked to the American federal Constitution and took counsel with the pro-American Lafayette, they adopted some but by no means all of its features. They introduced what was for Europe the radical innovation of separating church and state and adopted a bill of rights comparable in its sweep to those incorporated in the American state and federal constitutions. On the other hand, they chose a constitutional monarchy instead of a republic, but placed the sovereign under popular safeguards and made Parliament the organ of the popular will. Many years later the priest Désiré de Haerne, who had been active in shaping the Belgian Constitution, declared, with pardonable exaggeration:

> We are the only nation that has remained faithful in spirit to traditional rights and has followed America from the foundation of her political establishment and her liberal institutions. Yes, we looked upon England, on the one hand, as worthy of imitation in the march of progress in the path of true and practical liberty; but, at the same time, we were conscious that there were certain customs in the institutions of that country we would not adopt, and we cast our eyes beyond the Atlantic, where we found a great people worthy of entire imitation, and it is the institutions of that people we have chiefly inscribed upon our organic charter. We have followed their example in all that regards public liberty, the distribution of power, the election of representatives and decentralization of rule.[34]

This was not quite accurate, because while the independence of the judiciary was guaranteed, the executive was made largely dependent on the legislature by the parlia-

34. Quoted in Halvdan Koht, *The American Spirit in Europe* (Philadelphia, 1941), p. 24.

mentary system that was adopted. In support of a two-chambered legislature, with indirect elections, the drafters found their model in the American Senate as defined in the United States Constitution. The parliamentary system the Belgians adopted was to have a profound impact on subsequent constitutional developments on the European continent.[35]

It has been almost a cliché of the history textbooks to attribute the spread of revolutionary ideas in Europe to the French Revolution and the Napoleonic Wars. As we have already noted, revolutionary unrest in countries like Ireland, Holland, and Belgium antedated the coming of the French Revolution, while in still others what happened in France was rejected as a model for their constitutional systems. For a time, however, until like Beethoven they were to be cruelly disillusioned, European liberals hailed Napoleon as the authentic child of the Revolution—the embodiment of its spirit and the savior of its principles. If Bonaparte's arch-foe Metternich paid him the dubious compliment of denominating Napoleon "the Revolution incarnate," the Austrian in this instance proved both extravagant and undiscriminating. The accomplishments of Bonapartism cannot be ignored. As an administrator Napoleon showed extraordinary talent. With astonishing rapidity he reorganized the administration of his own country, unified its laws, and reduced its economic confusion. His Civil Code, with its pervasive influence, stands today as perhaps his most permanent contribution, but during his own time Napoleon's revolutionary nationalism seemed to pose the most dangerous threat to the status quo. At the peak of his success Bonaparte ruled an empire greater than the European holdings of the

35. See Henri Pirenne, *Histoire de Belgique* (Brussels, 1926), VI, 443; Franz von Kalken, *Histoire de la Belgique* (Brussels, 1954), pp. 541, 544; Jan-Albert Goris, ed., *Belgium* (Berkeley, 1946), pp. 32–33, 84.

Caesars or Charlemagne, but when he faded from the scene, England stood firmly at the crossroads of the seas, Russia had emerged as an important power in the West for the first time in history, and the way was prepared for a federation of German states under the domination of Prussia. Indeed, not democracy but nationalism proved to be the heritage that the citizen soldiers of revolutionary France left the world. In West Berlin's Kreuzberg there still stands a memorial to the Wars of Liberation. The monument bears such battle-scarred names as Leipzig. The liberation that is commemorated is, of course, the overthrow of the Napoleonic Empire, while at the opposite end of the city stands Plötzensee, stark memorial to those who died in the fight against a far more brutal tyranny.

It has sometimes been forgotten that the chief casualty of Napoleon's bold design was republicanism. Every museum and every memorial that perpetuates his deeds reveal that Napoleon's instincts were regal not republican. America, by rhetoric buttressed by battlefield victory, and France, at the national chopping block, had each ended kingly government. Napoleon promptly restored it in Europe, proclaiming himself emperor and setting up his relatives on the thrones of adjacent conquered lands, included newly-founded revolutionary republics. At the same time he made a shambles of the principle of popular sovereignty by turning the legislative bodies of France into ornaments, while he ran the nation by edict and a bureaucracy subservient to his will. In short, the antirepublican and anticonstitutional ends of Bonapartism proved counterrevolutionary both in purpose and in execution.[36]

Despite waves of reaction, revolutionary and reform

36. A more appreciative account of the connection of Napoleon with the French Revolution is found in the late Georges Lefebvre's two-vol. biography, *Napoleon*, trans. by F. Stockhold and J. E. Anderson (New York, 1968–69).

movements that had been kindled by both the American and the French Revolutions kept bubbling to the surface. Some were clearly in the French tradition; in others the leaders paid obeisance to the American rather than the French Revolutionary model. The Scandinavian countries may be cited as examples of the latter. In Sweden the United States' Constitution was almost immediately published in translation. Infected by American ideas and inspired by America's Washington whom Swedes placed in their pantheon of folk heroes, along with Cincinnatus and William Tell, members of the nobility talked darkly of a coup against the absolute monarch. When finally, in 1809, the revolution did come about, some of the leaders sought to establish a congress after the American pattern, but class interests proved stronger than democratic values and the old Riksdag of four estates was reconstituted.

In Norway the American influences also proved predominant. When that nation revolted in 1814 against its union with Denmark, Judge C. M. Falsen, called "the Father of the Norwegian Constitution," was inspired to name his son, who was born that year, George Benjamin for Washington and Franklin. At the constituent assembly convened at Eidsvold in April, 1814, one of the delegates brought along a copy of the French translation of the American state constitutions whose publication Franklin had arranged back in 1783. This very copy is still preserved at Eidsvold's Independence Hall. Another American work in demand was John Adams' *A Defence of the Constitutions of Government of the United States of America*.[37] Clearly visible in the Norwegian Constitution of 1814 are the borrowings from the American

---

37. For the influences especially of the Massachusetts Constitution on various proposed drafts, see Franklin D. Scott, *The United States and Scandinavia* (Cambridge, Mass., 1950), pp. 65, 66. See also Koht, *American Spirit in Europe*, p. 21.

models—for example, in the legislative power of the Stor-
thing, in the provisions for compensation to members and for
their security from arrest, and in the rules for impeachment
of members of the royal cabinet. That a liberal constitutional system on the American model has suited Norway can
be inferred from the fact that the Constitution of 1814 has
survived the dissolution of the union with Sweden in 1904,
and, save for a few modifications, survives today.

In a less direct but probably more significant way the
American Revolution fostered the liberalization of the governmental structures not only of Scandinavia but of other
European lands as well. Massive emigration to America
pried reforms from reluctant Scandinavian governments,
notably in the area of religious liberty, and accelerated the
process of social and economic change. Nor were radical
publicists remiss in praising America's civil liberties and her
other advantages which in combination proved to be irresistible to prospective emigrants.[38] Today a rather unique
tribute to both the libertarian image of America in Scandinavia and the common heritage of Scandinavians on two
continents takes the form of the annual celebration by Denmark of July 4, America's Independence Day, as a national
holiday. Since 1912 the heather-covered hills at Rebild have
become the focal point where Danes and Americans of
Danish origin from across the Atlantic celebrate the common themes of freedom and democracy to which the two
countries have been traditionally dedicated.[39]

Not only did the American Revolution serve as one of the

38. See Brynjolf J. Hovde, "Notes on the Effects of Emigration upon
Scandinavia," *Journal of Modern History*, VI (1930), 253–279; Adolph B.
Benson, "Cultural Relations between Sweden and America to 1830,"
Germanic Review, XIII (1938), 83–101.

39. See Peter Riismøller, *Rebild: The Fourth of July Celebrations in Denmark* (Copenhagen, 1952).

two classic models for the European revolutionary movements of the nineteenth century, but many Americans felt a
true affinity for the revolutionary yearnings of Europeans.
On at least two occasions the enthusiasm of Americans for
Europe's revolutions tested the official American position
toward other people's insurrections. Was the American
Revolution a self-contained and self-serving proposition or
did the United States have an obligation to spread the
contagion of liberty? So far as Europe was concerned,
America's first test came with the Greek struggle for independence against the Ottoman Turks. The outbreak of the
movement in 1821 coincided with the Latin-American revolutionary uprisings, and partisans of both causes wanted
America to intervene on behalf of the revolutionaries.

When, in 1821, the revolutionary Greek assembly at
Messina addressed an appeal to the American people, it
shrewdly pointed out that the liberty of Americans was "not
propped on the slavery of other nations," that it was the
Americans who had first proclaimed "those rights to which
all are by nature equally entitled," and that it was the
American example which had spurred Europe to abolish the
slave trade. "No," the Messinian Senate exhorted. "The fellow citizens of Penn, of Washington, and of Franklin will not
refuse their aid to descendants of Phocion and Thracybu-
lous, or Aratus and Philopoemon." Following hard on the
Greek Declaration of Independence and a provisional constitution, was the adoption in May, 1827, of the memorable
Constitution of Troezen, the charter of Hellenic liberties,
with its assertion of the doctrine of government resting on
the consent of the people, and of the principles of equality
before the law, freedom of speech, and safeguards against
arbitrary taxation and imprisonment without due process.
Some of these ideas reflected the counsel of Thomas Jeffer-

son who, in 1823, at the solicitation of the Greek patriot Adamantios Coray, advised that the state constitutions rather than that of the federal government might provide the more appropriate models.[40]

The spirited appeal of the Greek assembly at Messina evoked an enthusiastic popular response in America. Appropriately the citizens of Michigan set up the town of Ypsilanti near Detroit in honor of the Greek Demetrios Ypsilanti who had fought with the Continental army at Monmouth, and whose descendant commanded the revolutionary forces of Hellas. The American public subscribed generously to Greek war relief, and most intellectuals were moved to speak out for Greek liberty. Foremost among the latter was Edward Everett, then professor of Greek at Harvard. Among the humanitarians, Dr. Samuel Gridley Howe's heroic activity on behalf of the Greek cause constitutes an epic by itself.[41]

Despite popular enthusiasm, the United States Government scrupulously avoided intervention. The President's original draft of the Monroe Doctrine included references to the repressive policies of Spain as well as an expression of sympathy for the Greek rebels, but these were toned down at John Quincy Adams' behest. Adams insisted on the necessity of making the Doctrine "an American cause" and of adhering "inflexibly to that." Still, anyone listening to Monroe's message would know that the President was not neutral at heart. He alluded to the "heroic struggle of the Greeks" and expressed the fervent wish "that they would succeed in their contest and resume their equal station among the nations of the earth." That was as far as Monroe felt it prudent to go.

---

40. Jefferson to A. Coray, Oct. 31, 1823, in D. M. Robinson, *America and Greece* (New York, 1948), pp. 41–46; Harris J. Booras, *Hellenic Independence and America's Contribution to the Cause* (Rutland, Vt., 1934), pp. 60, 159.

41. *Ibid.*, pp. 157, 205–206. For the impact of the French Revolution in East Central Europe, see Fran Zwitter, *Les Problèmes Nationaux dans La Monarchie des Habsbourg* (Belgrade, 1960), pp. 36, 37, 51.

Statesmen like John Quincy Adams, who opposed intervention, insisted that America could save the world only by remaining free to save herself. President Andrew Jackson's Secretary of State, John Forsyth, epitomized America's foreign policy as a "national reserve," a deliberate abstention from the political relationships entered into by most states.

No responsible American considered intervening in the first Russian Revolution, the Decembrist movement, which broke out in 1825. That movement which gave birth to Russia's revolutionary tradition, culminating in its 1917 Revolution, came in response to currents of liberal reformism which found their roots in the American and French Revolutions.[42]

Although the Paris ideologues might fawn upon her and ply her with lavish and cloying compliments, the head of the Russian state was no friend of revolutions. Catherine II had backed up her arguments with cannon and bayonets to convince the reform-minded Polish diet of the error of its ways. Three years before the Declaration of Independence she had crushed the Pugachev rebellion and decapitated its principal ringleaders. Swayed by neither sentiment nor cajolery, Catherine placed Russia's national interest first in the War of the American Revolution. Although at the very beginning of the war she had rejected Britain's request for Russian troops to fight in America, she was disinclined to see England prostrate and the house of Bourbon in a position to lay down the law for Europe. However, if Catherine could be quoted as both favoring and opposing American independence depending upon her hearer, she scrupulously avoided any act which could be construed as even leaning toward recognition of the United States.[43]

42. For Lenin's appraisal of the importance of the Decembrist movement, see "In Memory of Herzen," in V. I. Lenin, *Collected Works,* ed. by Clemens Dutt (Moscow, 1963), XVIII, 25.

43. For Catherine's views and Russia's role as a co-mediator in the American Revolution, see Morris, *The Peacemakers,* pp. 159–190.

Apart from court circles, however, there was a considerable interest in Russia in the American Revolution, and extensive coverage in the Russian press. Recent light shed by N. N. Bolkhovitinov on Russian-American relations in the period from the American Revolution through the Napoleonic Wars[44] has documented the profound impact of that event upon Russian intellectuals. It may at first glance seem astonishing that the American Revolution received more coverage in the Russian press than did the French Revolution, but it must be borne in mind that the latter was considered by the Russian government to pose a more direct threat to the status quo and therefore demanded tighter press censorship. While the two newspapers existing in Catherine's Russia depended upon the same English sources for their news about the American Revolution, the *Moskovskie Vedomosti* edited by Nikolai I. Novikov contained news more favorable to the American cause than did its more rigidly controlled St. Petersburg counterpart. Not only were military events extensively treated in the Moscow paper, but much attention was paid to informing its readers of the opposition to the war in England and the rising peace movement. That the *Moskovskie Vedomosti* ventured to slant its news coverage toward freedom is suggested by an allegorical fable, "The Tomtit in the Field," which it published on September 10, 1782, on the eve of the conclusion of a preliminary peace between Britain and the United States. It told of a tomtit that had been captured by a lady of the nobility and encaged, but one fine day the tomtit broke out and flew away. The lady ordered her servants to convince the bird to return, promising that she would then release it. But the bird answered that it already possessed what was now being promised. "It is you who must suffer in her power," the bird

44. N. N. Bolkhovitinov, *Stanovlenie russko-amerikanskikh otnoshenii, 1775–1815* (Moscow, 1966).

told the servants, "but I am enjoying independence." To this fable which rings so true, the editor added, "each may draw a picture of reality, and although I shall not name the lady, shamed be he who thinks evil of her." To be doubly sure that his readers were familiar with *"Honi soit qui mal y pense,"* Novikov elaborated on the last phrase: "It is known that that is the motto on the English coat of arms."

Novikov devoted much attention to the principal Founding Fathers, to John Adams, to Franklin, and, above all, to Washington. Not only did Novikov continue to show by newspaper coverage a lively interest in the fate of the new republic after the war, but in his magazine *Prebavleniia k Moskovskim Vedomostian,* he published an article by a Professor Geberlin on "The Influence of the Independence of the United States upon the Political Situation in Europe," in the course of which the writer hailed the Declaration of Independence as "among the most important occurrences of our century."[45]

The idea of America and its new civilization had long been a theme among Russian writers, such as M. V. Lomonosov and the poet A. P. Sumarakov. It was the American Revolution, however, which made America a more compelling theme in Russia. In 1783, the year that marked the close of the war, there appeared in St. Petersburg the first book by a Russian author devoted to the new United States, a pocket reference work by D. M. Ladigin, while Novikov had to furnish his readers with abundant information on America in the supplement to his Moscow paper.

Outstanding among the admirers of the reforms instituted in America in the Revolutionary Era was A. N. Radishchev, whose stirring *Journey from St. Petersburg to Moscow* was

---

45. M. N. Shprygova, "The American War of Independence as Treated by N. I. Novikov's *Moscow Gazette,*" *Soviet Studies in History,* I (1962), 51–62.

the first notable example of a literature of protest in Russia. Inspired by a reading of Rayneval's *Révolution de l'Amérique*, Radishchev wrote an ode, entitled "Liberty," which apostrophizes Washington, and informs the people of America that their "example has set a goal for us—We all wish for the same."[46] Radishchev, in reporting the celebrated journey that he made in the year 1775, discusses approvingly the civil libertarian provisions of the American state constitutions, which he favorably compared with the censorship imposed in France during its revolution. He urged Russian judges to visit Pennsylvania and study the Quaker penal system, under which both capital and corporal punishment were abolished and emphasis was placed on reformation of criminals rather than punishment.[47] Catherine, naturally, did not appreciate Radishchev's radical ideas and had him exiled to Siberia as an example to other literary subversives.

Radishchev's dissatisfaction with the status quo sparked the reformist impulses behind the Decembrist movement, with its twin objectives of abolishing serfdom and establishing a representative government to limit autocratic power. More extreme malcontents aimed for a republic.[48] Significantly, both the "radical" Decembrists who advocated a republic and their more conservative associates who favored a constitutional monarchy were greatly influenced by the American constitutional system. The radical leader, Pavel Ivanovich Pestel, was enthusiastic in his regard for the American republic, while his more conservative counterpart,

46. A. K. Borozdin, *et al.*, *Complete Works of A. N. Radishchev* (Akenfieva, 1907), I, 318–330.

47. Aleksandr Nikolaevich Radishchev, *A Journey from St. Petersburg to Moscow*, trans. by Leo Wiener (Boston, 1958), pp. 184–186; Jesse V. Clardy, *The Philosophical Ideas of Alexander Radishchev* (New York, 1964), p. 103.

48. See Anatole G. Mazour, *The First Russian Revolution: 1825* (Berkeley, 1937).

Nikita Muraviev, based his constitutional program primarily on the United States constitutional system. Another Decembrist, Prince Sergei Volkonsky, contemplated a visit to the United States as early as 1814 because, as he later explained, "the North American States filled the minds of Russian youth at that time," inspiring them with "their independent mode of life and their democratic political order."[49] Although this palace revolution was crushed, its ruthless suppression aroused the liberal socialist Alexander Herzen and other reformers, who enlarged upon the Decembrist program and broadened its appeal.[50]

A cosmopolitan Russian nobleman, Herzen was thoroughly familiar with Alexis de Tocqueville's *Democracy in America* and with a number of American writers, including James Fenimore Cooper, Washington Irving, and Harriet Beecher Stowe. In a sketch of a drama, *William Penn,* written in 1838, Herzen idealized Pennsylvania as a Christian Socialist colony, and paid tribute to Washington and Franklin. After 1848 America remained a source of hope to Herzen, depressed by the failure of the mid-century revolutions. He saw America as a fluid society without hunger, and advised all who could slough off the "Old Adam of Europe" and be reborn "a new Jonathan," to take "the first steamer to America and then to migrate to some place in Wisconsin or Kansas," away from "decaying Europe." Herzen saw America as "destined to a great future," and paraphrasing Goethe, thought of "America: strong, rude, powerful, energetic, without the ruins of a past which would encumber the route of the present." Truly, America could "take care of herself,"

49. David Hecht, ed., *Russian Radicals Look to America, 1825–1894* (Cambridge, Mass., 1947), pp. 17–18.

50. For the importance of the year 1825 in Russian historiography, see Anatole G. Mazour, *Modern Russian Historiography* (2nd ed., New York, 1958), pp. 175, 176.

and therefore should be left to the Americans. Believing that centralization was "incompatible with freedom," Herzen fully appreciated the potentialities of American federalism. Writing to the French historian Michelet in 1868, Herzen stigmatized the Russian Empire as a "monstrosity" and expressed the "wish and hope" to see it transformed into "a federation on the American order." Herzen's fierce opposition to slavery in America and to the Confederacy came naturally to one who was a passionate partisan of the abolition of serfdom in Russia; and in the post–Civil War years he remained an untarnished optimist about the future of America and a warm advocate of Russo-American friendship.[51]

Quite distinct from Herzen in the goals he set for the reformation of society but equally impressed by the American constitutional example was that fountainhead of Russian anarchism, Michael Bakunin. Exiled for his radical activities, Bakunin visited America briefly in 1861, with stops at San Francisco, New York, and Boston, whence, after hobnobbing with the leading Brahmins, he departed for London to commence anew his revolutionary activities. Written seven years after his American visit, Bakunin's essay entitled *Federalism, Socialism, and Anti-Theologism* eulogized the United States for being the one place where the workers never starved and were "better paid" than their European brothers. To Bakunin the colonists' experience in self-government laid the foundations for a "new world of liberty," one "free from the obsessions of the past," and he characterized the American Revolution as "the cause of liberty against despotism." Laying great stress both on the "traditional spirit of liberty" imported by the colonists from England and on the existence in America of vast tracts of free land, Bakunin anticipated by a quarter of a century the "safety-

51. Alexander Herzen, *Memoirs* (English trans., London, 1924–27), I, 299–302; II, 198; III, 105, 135–136, 185–186.

valve" theory appropriated by Frederick Jackson Turner. Repeatedly, he characterized America as "the classic land of political liberty" blessed with "the most democratic institutions," and to the end he remained an enthusiast both for the republican system as exemplified in America and for federalism, which he believed to be worthy of emulation by European socialists.

Bakunin saw the less attractive side of the coin in America, too. He cautioned that a proletarian class was emerging in American cities, thus posing in America the social question that had been raised so much earlier in Europe. On occasion he expressed the view that universal suffrage and representative government benefited only the bourgeoisie, and toward the end of his life he predicted that for "popular self-government" to become a reality "another revolution" far more profound would be necessary.[52]

If, as Lenin saw it, Herzen started the revolutionary agitation in Russia, it was the "revolutionary commoners," beginning with Nicholas Chernyshevski and ending with "the heroes of the 'People's Will,'" who carried that agitation to completion. Chernyshevski possessed an extraordinary familiarity with American institutions. He saw America as a model for a progressive Western Europe, one which stood as a living refutation of the principles of conservatism. Paying tribute to America's "glorious past," he was enthusiastic in his admiration for American energy and social mobility, the absence of a top-heavy bureaucracy in America, and the success of its experiment in federalism, withal stoutly contesting Tocqueville's opinion that democratic governments

52. Michael Bakunin, *Oeuvres*, ed. by James Guillaume (Paris, 1895–1913), I, 12, 13, 22, 170–174; III, 166; IV, 183, 289, 499; Oscar Handlin, "A Russian Anarchist Visits Boston," *New England Quarterly*, XV (1942), 107; Hecht, *Russian Radicals Look to America*, pp. 49–77; Hans Rogger, "Russia and the Civil War," in Harold Hyman, ed., *Heard Round the World* (New York, 1969), pp. 249–250.

possessed a special affinity for centralization. From the readily available freehold land system of the United States,
Chernyshevski drew the conclusion that "state lands" had to
"predominate in a country over those distributed in private
property" and that in any scheme for the emancipation of
the serfs the peasant commune must be preserved.[53]

Imbued as the Russian radicals were with a sometimes
uncritical enthusiasm for the American Revolutionary example, it was to be expected that the commemoration of the
centenary of Pugachev's revolt, which was celebrated in
1873, would provide the occasion for comparisons between
that ill-fated uprising and the successful revolution in America. The radical propagandist Peter Lavrov, spokesman for
the Russian Populist movement, stressed the parallel between the two events, and professed to find a revolutionary
link between "the Washingtons and the Hamiltons" and the
"Dantons and Robespierres." Seeing in the American Revolution the fulfillment of the ideals pronounced in the Declaration of Independence, Lavrov praised Washington for
spurning the opportunity at war's end of setting up a
dictatorship by a military coup. Finding the Confederation
interlude to be a truly "critical" period in the sense that John
Fiske used it, Lavrov regarded the new constitution that
emerged as productive of "tremendous political power" and
accelerating economic development. Nevertheless, as a radical, Lavrov felt that the achievements of the heroic age of
the American republic were now "exhausted," and that the
rising "social question" had "buried the political creations of
the revolutionary period."[54]

Even Lenin, whose brand of Marxism betrayed little enthusiasm for America's bourgeois liberties, took the occasion
of "A Letter to American Workers" to eulogize America's
revolutionary tradition, to refer to the American Revolution

53. Hecht, *Russian Radicals*, pp. 88–137.
54. Hecht, *Russian Radicals*, pp. 142–195, *passim*.

as a "really liberating" anticolonial war, and at the same time to scold "the American people," who, after giving "the world an example of a revolutionary war against feudal subjection," now appeared "as a new, capitalist wage slave of a handful of billionaires," strangling the Philippines under the pretext of "liberating them," and "strangling the Russian Socialist Republic in 1918 under the pretext of 'protecting' it from the Germans."[55] Rather consistently, then, Russian radicals from Catherine II's day to our own have paid tribute to the American Revolution and to the principle of popular sovereignty for which it was fought, although that doctrine has been interpreted quite differently in the Marxist-Leninist credo from that of Jefferson. Thus, what they profess to find fault with in American society since the Civil War has been the destruction or debasement, as they see it, of its revolutionary tradition.

Naturally one would expect the protagonists of the March '17 Revolution to adopt a different line toward American libertarian and constitutional doctrines than the leaders of the subsequent October Revolution. The former was hailed in America, prompted parallels to the American Revolution, and was followed by speedy *de jure* recognition of the Russian provisional government. Understandably, in light of the Russian liberal-radical tradition that we have considered, that government contained figures like Foreign Minister Paul N. Miliukov, the historian, who never concealed his admiration for America.

By October a chill had descended upon Russia and the honeymoon with America was over. But even the Bolsheviks, critical as they were of American institutions, found it expedient to deviate from orthodox Marxism and pay grudging tribute to the American systems of constitutionalism and federalism in their 1918 constitution. To be sure, Soviet

55. V. I. Lenin, *A Letter to American Workers* (New York, 1934), pp. 9–10.

constitutionalism and federalism, like Soviet civil liberties, are paper doctrines that can be conveniently trotted out at strategic moments in the East-West confrontation, but it is nonetheless significant that even so implacable a foe of bourgeois democracy does not dare repudiate some of its most innovative doctrines.[56]

The Revolutions of 1848, which swept Europe from the Channel ports to the frontiers of Russia, marked the end of a thirty-three-year period when a counterrevolutionary philosophy had held the Continent in its iron grip. Though touched off by economic discontent and by a few confrontations between the proletariat and the military, 1848 was primarily a revolution of the intellectuals. Of the various systems that were concocted in the fertile brains of French reformers, none had special relevance to the American Revolutionary tradition. Most could be traced to Robespierre or Babeuf. In France, the reformist projects carried authoritarian rather than constitutional overtones, and the impulses that stirred them were messianic and utopian.[57] After the savage class war of the "June days" a liberal Constitution was adopted, establishing universal suffrage, a single-chambered legislature, and, on the model of the United States, a President of the Republic, with executive powers, elected for a term of four years but ineligible for re-election. That Prince Louis Napoleon Bonaparte, who was elected to that office, would soon overthrow the republic, was not foreseen at the moment. Indeed, Americans, in their enthusiasm for the revolutionary movements of '48, were not prepared to discriminate between revolutionaries. Richard Rush, the American minister at Paris, was the first to recognize the Second French

56. See Franz Neumann, "Federalism and Freedom: A Critique," in Arthur W. MacMahon, Federalism—Mature and Emergent (Garden City, N.Y., 1955), pp. 44–57.

57. See Georges Duveau, 1848: The Making of a Revolution, trans. by Anne Carter (New York, 1967), pp. 209–229.

Republic. Rush's maneuver won the cordial endorsement of President Polk and the Senate.

The men of '48 sought popular sovereignty in both the American and French Revolutionary senses. They settled for constitutionalism. The ambivalence of the movement was best exemplified by the men at Frankfurt, who sought freedom for Germans, but condemned the revolutionary activities of the oppressed non-German nationalities,[58] an attitude not unlike that of the Hungarian revolutionaries toward their non-Magyar minorities. It is difficult for us today to reconcile the stereotype of Germany under Hitler with any other Germany, in which principles derived from the American Revolutionary tradition and constitutional experience could have exerted a significant force. The Iron Chancellor, the mountebank Kaiser, or the paranoid Führer do not seem to have been cast in the same mold as America's Founding Fathers. Nevertheless, it must be remembered that over an extended period of time liberal intellectuals in Germany sought to reconstruct the German states after a more progressive, if not revolutionary, pattern.

The German mercenaries, who comprised some 50 percent of George III's armed forces in America during the Revolution, had a chance to see at close range how revolutionary states were being fashioned, and many of them preferred what they saw to what they had experienced at home. Not only did German deserters, many coming from the Convention Army which capitulated at Saratoga, melt into the American scene, but still others received permission at the end of the war to remain in America.[59] The German press devoted much attention to the war in America. The com-

58. This thesis is brilliantly expounded in L. B. Namier, "1848: The Revolution of the Intellectuals," British Academy, *Proceedings,* XXX (1946).

59. E. J. Lowell, *The Hessians in the Revolutionary War* (New York, 1884); Bernhard A. Uhlendorf, ed. and trans., *The Siege of Charleston* (Ann Arbor, Mich., 1938), p. 3.

ment of one German enthusiast that "a secret bond . . . links the cause of the Colonies with the welfare and uplifting of the human race" could be duplicated many times.[60] Granted that the aspects of the American Revolution that contemporary Germans most clearly perceived were those which seemed congenial to Enlightenment thinking—notions of liberty and equality—whereas they failed at the time to grasp the significance of republicanism, popular sovereignty, and federalism. In the longer run these latter aspects had their impact on German political thinking.

Contributing so much to that enlarged understanding was the German historian Christopher Daniel Ebeling. During the years 1777–78 Ebeling published in Hamburg four numbers of *Amerikanische Bibliothek*, the first German periodical devoted to America, and followed with his *Amerikanische Magazin*, which acquainted Germans with American constitutional documents, books, and miscellaneous news of life overseas. The culmination of his American interest was the publication in seven bulky volumes issued between 1793 and 1816 of his *Erdbeschreibung und Geschichte von Amerika*, providing reactionary Europe with what he in his own words considered to be a "faithful picture of a truly free republic."[61]

The American example found reflection on a more official level, as well. Despite its lack of enthusiasm about revolutions and Frederick the Great's own pessimism about the success of the American experiment,[62] the Prussian Gov-

60. See Alfred Kroger, *Geburt der USA, German Newspaper Accounts of the American Revolution* (Madison, Wis., 1962), pp. 304–306.

61. Ebeling to William Bentley, June 29, 1805, "Letters of C. D. Ebeling," American Antiquarian Society, *Proceedings* (October, 1925), p. 371.

62. See Frederick II to Thulemeier, May 26, 1783, Marvin L. Brown, *American Independence Through Prussian Eyes* (Durham, N.C., 1959), p. 201. *Per contra*, creative writers. *Americana Germanica*, III (1899–1900), 336–385.

ernment was happy to conclude a treaty of commerce and amity with the United States in 1786, incorporating therein the advanced American position, long advocated by Franklin, stipulating the protection of innocent persons and private property in wartime. Prussia took the initiative in 1818 in the organization of a customs union or *Zollverein*, which by 1836 included most of Germany within its free-trade area. Nor is it by accident that one of its chief advocates was the political economist Friedrich List, who had gained a firsthand acquaintance in America with the working of the Hamiltonian system and who, as United States consul in Leipzig, helped further commercial relations between America and the German states. The parallel between the American federal union and the *Zollverein* as a customs union is one that German statesmen could not ignore.[63]

The men of the Frankfurt Assembly meeting in the Paulskirche were, despite their own strong nationalist impulses, by no means impervious to the American example in constitutionalism. By the time of the Revolutions of 1848, American ideas had been widely disseminated in Germany. In his *Reminiscences* Carl Schurz tells how as a boy brought up in a German village he had first heard about America, how his father and his uncle had talked ceaselessly about "that young republic where the people were free, without kings, without counts, without military service, and, as was believed in Liblar, without taxes." In that village everything about America that could be procured was eagerly read. Schurz's father held up Washington to him as an example of the true patriot, who "had voluntarily divested himself of his power and returned to the plow as a simple farmer."[64] Aside from the villager's romantic log-cabin image of America,

63. See Henry M. Adams, *Prussian-American Relations, 1775–1871* (Cleveland, 1960), pp. 22, 24, 53, 54.

64. Carl Schurz, *Reminiscences* (New York, 1907–08), I, 29.

much accurate documentation on the United States was available in Germany thanks in no small part to the efforts of that brilliant pamphleteer and traveler, Count von der Goltz, and to the constitutional treatises of Robert von Mohl. Rotteck and Weeker's *Staatslexicon* devoted almost as many pages to Benjamin Franklin as to Joseph II and Napoleon put together. Now, again, in 1848, copies of the Declaration of Independence and the Constitution were sent to Germany and widely circulated.[65]

The men of the Frankfurt Assembly seemed fascinated by the American constitutional example and talked about it incessantly. They borrowed from the American Constitution both in broad matters of principle and in the specific details of drafting. The monarch was consciously fashioned upon the American Chief Executive and the Reichsgericht modeled upon the United States Supreme Court.[66] In conferring upon the new German union exclusive authority over foreign relations and in providing for direct elections to the Reichstag, the Frankfurt Constitution drew directly from the American. Reversing the intention of the American Bill of Rights, the German framers had the new German union guarantee the fundamental rights of its citizens against incursions by the member states. The drafters actually thought they were imitating the American Bill of Rights, which protected the people from inroads against their civil liberties on the part of the federal government, not the

---

65. Henry M. Adams, *Prussian-American Relations*, p. 59. See also Erich Angermann, "Der Vereinigten Staaten von Amerika von Friedrich von Gent (1814) bis zum Frieden von Versailles," *Historia Mundi*, X, 253–331.

66. See Anton Scholl, *Der Einfluss der nordamerikanischen-Unionsverfassung auch die Verfassung des Deutsches Reichs von 28 Maerz 1849* (Borna-Leipzig, 1913), p. 47; Carl J. Friedrich, *The Impact of American Constitutionalism Abroad* (Boston, 1967), pp. 44, 81 *et seq.*; Eckart G. Franz, *Das Amerikabild der deutschen Revolution von 1848–49* (Heidelberg, 1958).

states. If they did not emulate the Bill of Rights in structure, they did in spirit. On the other hand, the American elements of the Frankfurt Constitution, those embodying the federal principle, kept Austria out of the union on the ground that no state could be permitted to be partly in, as regards domestic affairs, and partly out, as regards control over foreign policy.[67]

The failure of the men at Frankfurt proved a fatal setback for democracy in Germany. George Bancroft, the American minister to Berlin who was predisposed to see the best side of Prussian life, eulogized the Constitution adopted by the North German Diet in 1867, and largely written by Bismarck, as expressing "many sentiments characteristic of the American people." But his judgment was flawed by optimism.[68] True, there was a two-house legislature, with the lower house elected by universal manhood suffrage. While the Prussian solution may have appeared to move in a democratic and even a federal direction,[69] in effect it promoted greater centralization and violated the federal principle presumably borrowed from the United States. After 1871 it should have been clear to any knowledgeable observer that the façade of federalism ill-concealed the reality of Prussia's absorption of Germany and that an empire had been created on principles largely divergent from American constitutional experience. The subsequent history of the Second Reich made that point transparently clear, even though Bancroft failed to see it. It was not until the post-

67. Robert C. Binkley, "The Holy Roman Empire Versus the United States," in Conyers Read, ed., *The Constitution Reconsidered* (rev. ed., New York, 1968), pp. 271–284. For the influence of American federalism on the Swiss Constitution, see William E. Rappard, *La Constitution fédérale de la Suisse* (Boudry, 1948), p. 134.

68. Adams, *Prussian-American Relations,* pp. 94–95.

69. J. A. Hawgood, *Modern Constitutions since 1787* (London, 1939), pp. 239–244.

World War I interlude that the Germans seriously turned to the American Constitution once more for their examples, as they had done long before at Frankfurt.

Of all the revolutionary movements of 1848 it was the uprising in Hungary against the house of Hapsburg that touched off the greatest emotional response in the United States. For a brief moment it seemed as though the United States might even intervene to insure Hungary's independence. In a screech-eagle message Secretary of State Webster dismissed the protest of the Austrian government against the apparent readiness of the United States to recognize the Hungarians. In comparison with the extent of the United States, this diplomat pointed out with characteristic American bombast, the possessions of Austria were "but a patch on the earth's surface." "Verily, we are the people to lecture Austria!" was the sardonic comment of New York's abolitionist leader, William Jay, who took the occasion to underscore the moral hypocrisy of America's support for the institution of slavery.[70]

When the Hungarian uprising collapsed and Hungary's magnetic hero, Louis Kossuth, came to America to secure aid for his cause, he was wined, dined, and lionized everywhere. Daniel Webster addressed a congressional banquet in his honor, acknowledging the justice of the Hungarian cause and expressing a wish to see the Hungarians win their independence. The Hungarian patriot, who referred to the Declaration of Independence as "that noblest, happiest page of mankind's history," and reiterated eulogies to the Founding Fathers, sought to bring home to Americans the relevance of their revolutionary heritage to Europe's contemporary revolutionary stirrings. If, as Kossuth declared,

70. "Letter to William Wilson on Mr. Clay's Compromise," New York, February 11, 1850, in William Jay, *Miscellaneous Writings on Slavery* (Boston, 1853), p. 568 n.

America's destiny was "to become the cornerstone of Liberty on earth,"[71] the American government did not feel it incumbent on a cornerstone to pledge intervention in Hungary's cause. In these efforts he was no more successful than were latter-day Hungarian liberals, who sought such a commitment from President Eisenhower to intervene in their more recent and equally tragic revolution.

While Kossuth left this country a sadly frustrated patriot, he had in six hundred speeches stirred the imagination of Americans, heartened by the vision of a republican Europe with governments based, of course, on the model of the United States. Within the Democratic party the '48 Revolution led to a split over foreign policy. One segment of the Democratic party supported the "Young America" movement, which, combining the themes of capitalistic progress, romantic nationalism, and democratic universalism, befriended republican stirrings abroad. The leader of the "Young America" movement was George Sanders, who had been personally involved in dealings with European revolutionaries. Appointed United States consul to London, Sanders' London residence provided a rendezvous for Europe's most famous revolutionary exiles. Surely Kossuth, Mazzini, Garibaldi, and Herzen, all sitting around Sanders' dinner table at one time, must have created a combustible atmosphere. Sanders' appointment was taken as an affront by the Austrian foreign office, and he was refused confirmation by the Senate. From The Hague, August Belmont, the American minister to the Netherlands, expressed his complete sympathy with Sanders' support for European republicanism. "The day is not far distant," Belmont stated, "when self-preservation will dictate to the United States the necessity of throwing her moral and physical force into the scale of

71. See *Select Speeches of Kossuth*, condensed and abridged by F. W. Newman (London, 1853), pp. 144, 145, 281, 310 *et seq.*

European republicanism." Belmont's remarks were indeed prophetic, but the day was far more distant than he had imagined. Except for promoting America's self-image, the "Young America" movement had no practical results in its day.[72]

The roots of the movement for Italian independence and unity, accelerated by the '48 revolutions, can be traced at least as far back as the poet Vittorio Alfieri, the great prophet of the *risorgimento*. The American Revolution aroused Alfieri's ardent enthusiasm. In a treatise, *Della tirannia*, written at Siena in 1777, he cited "la nuova America" in support of the view that liberty is greater in Protestant lands than in others, and in his treatise, *Del principe e delle lettere*, begun in 1778 but not completed until 1786, he eulogized both the Roman republic and the new republic which had arisen across the sea, ranking Washington with Brutus, William Tell, and William of Orange. At the very end of 1781 Alfieri published the first four odes of *L'America libera*, with its account of the origins of the American Revolution and its eulogies of Franklin, Washington, and the youthful Lafayette and, in the next year, he dedicated his revolutionary drama *Brute* to Washington.[73]

Others shared Alfieri's admiration for the American example, from Daniel Dolfin, Venetian ambassador to Paris, who recognized the event as the "most important revolution of the century," to the Milanese Count Luigi Castiglione, whose glowing appraisal of the American Revolution found in his book, *Travels in the United States of North America*, was the result of firsthand observations on a visit to the United States at the close of the war. The virtues of Benja-

72. See Merle E. Curti, "Young America," *American Historical Review*, XXXII (1926), 36, 37–55.
73. Charles R. D. Miller, "Alfieri and America," *Philological Quarterly*, XI (1932), 164–166.

min Franklin, a special hero of the Italian illuminati, were celebrated in translated editions of his political and philosophical works by the indefatigable Pietro Antoniutti; reformers like Gaetano Filangeri consulted Franklin about his program for penal reform, and the state constitutions made available in Italy through Franklin's efforts excited much favorable comment. It is perhaps significant that the Pennsylvania Constitution, the one closely identified with Franklin, was the one Italianized by Bernardo Maria Calura and Antonio Marcontoni for the use of the Venetian republican restoration just before Napoleon snuffed out the life of that ephemeral democracy.[74] This was perhaps exceptional, for many of the Italian city-states based their constitutions of the 1790's on the French Revolutionary models, examples whose relevance was made obvious by the presence of the French army.

The enthusiasm of Italian intellectuals for the American example is further underscored by the significant fact that the earliest historians of the American Revolution were Italians, and that the interest of Italian historians in that successful revolution was only intensified by their own disillusionment with the results of the French Revolution. Of these only Carlo Botta produced a work on a grand scale. The Piedmontese physician, whose multivolume *History of the War of Independence of the United States of America* was originally published in Italian, laid great stress on the worldwide character of the American Revolution, recognized the connection between Irish discontent and the American struggle, and contributed to building the myth of the Founding Fathers as classic monuments rather than men.

The revolutionary movements of the 1790's collapsed in reaction, stirred briefly in 1848, but caught fire with the

74. Antonio Pace, *Benjamin Franklin and Italy* (Philadelphia, 1958), pp. 113, 128–134, 142–143, 156, 157, 169–170.

march of Garibaldi and his Thousand in 1859. Garibaldi may have been likened by his compatriots to Washington, but he seems to have been imbued with an enthusiasm for republics far more from his association with Giuseppe Mazzini, whose republicanism stemmed more directly from the French Revolutionary tradition, than from his stay in exile on Staten Island. Nonetheless, on a number of occasions Garibaldi expressed his admiration of Franklin, contrasting his true nobility and humble garb with the empty pretensions of the upper class.[75] To launch the famous attack on the Kingdom of the Two Sicilies Garibaldi was carried across the strait of Messina to Calabria in a wooden sidewheeler named *Franklin,* while one of his leading co-conspirators in the spadework preparatory to the march of the Thousand was one Nicola Mignogna, who had veiled his identity under the alias of "Franklin."[76] Cavour, on the other hand, was in his youth a passionate admirer of America and Americans. Although his enthusiasm was somewhat tempered by the sober lesson of the American Civil War, it is indubitable, and Cavour himself admitted as much on his deathbed, that the American constitutional tradition constituted an important ingredient in his liberal system.[77]

The American Civil War, testing the durable nature of a great republican experiment in federalism and dramatizing the issue of slavery versus freedom, bestirred liberals and radicals throughout Europe to re-examine the meaning of the American tradition. Nowhere was the issue dramatized

75. *Memorie, nella redazione definitiva del 1872* (Bologna, 1932), pp. 45–46.

76. Pace, *Franklin in Italy,* pp. 182, 183.

77. W. de la Rive, *Le Comte de Cavour, Récits et Souvenirs* (Paris, 1862), pp. 439, 440; W. R. Thayer, *The Life and Times of Cavour* (Boston, 1911), I, 519, 520. For Mazzini's enthusiastic reaction to the Union triumph in the Civil War, see J. Donaldson and E. J. Pratt, *Europe and the American Civil War* (Boston, 1931), p. 266.

as eloquently as in England, where liberals like Bright and Cobden recognized the intimate relation between the success of the Union cause and the future of liberal England. To Bright the Civil War was God's instrument for the destruction of slavery, and he implored his American friends to bring pressure on their government for emancipation. He took every occasion to counter pro-Confederate propaganda and sentiment in England by reminding his listeners what Americans had to teach the world about democratic suffrage, public education, the secret ballot, and humanitarian reforms.[78] If all Britain did not share Bright's enthusiasm, the Unionist North was delighted with his support. As he confessed to Harriet Beecher Stowe, he was an American at heart.[79] Bright voiced his passion for the American republic in a letter to an American historian, wherein he stated: "I have been a friend of your country from a belief that on your continent and with your institutions our race seems to have a chance of a better time, and I live in the expectation that from you much will be learned that will advance the cause of freedom: not in Europe only, but throughout the world."[80]

European Socialists as well as liberals were heartened by the Union's antislavery stance. Karl Marx hailed the Emancipation Proclamation as "the most important document of American history since the founding of the Union, a docu-

78. See Frank Moore, ed., *Speeches of John Bright, M.P., On the American Question* (Boston, 1865).

79. Bright to Harriet Beecher Stowe, March 9, 1863, Chicago Historical Society.

80. Bright to J. K. Hosmer, May 4, 1864, cited by Herman Ausubel, *John Bright, Victorian Reformer* (New York, 1966), p. 139. Scholars are divided over the impact of the U.S. on the Parliamentary Reform Bill of 1867. For an affirmative view, see G. D. Lillibridge, *Beacon of Freedom* (New York, 1955), p. 122; Henry Pelling, *America and the British Left* (London, 1956), pp. 7–29; H. C. Allen, "Civil War, Reconstruction, and Great Britain," in Hyman, ed., *Impact*, pp. 40–83, *passim*. Contrariwise, see Gertrude Himmelfarb, *Victorian Minds* (New York, 1968), pp. 333, 348.

ment that breaks away from the old American Constitution."
Although Lincoln "was not born of a people's revolution,"
Marx grudgingly conceded, although he was but "an ordi-
nary man of good will," yet the "victory scored by the New
World," which the Proclamation epitomized, showed how
"ordinary people of good will can carry out tasks which the
Old World would have to have a hero to accomplish!"[81]

The time did arrive, in another century, when, unlike
1848, America contributed on a massive scale to the liberation and reconstruction of Europe, and, in a reversal of
long-standing policy, directly promoted revolutions abroad.
However hollow terms like "liberty" and "consent of the governed" may sound in today's world of confrontation politics,
American statesmen recognized the revolutionary potential
of ideological weapons drawn from America's own political
traditions, and the American people supported both world
wars out of a profound conviction that the traditional democratic values had relevance for the rest of the world.
Revisionists, old or new, may choose to attribute American
intervention in both wars to self-interest, to fear of totalitarian aggression, to balance-of-power politics, or imperialist
aggrandizement. Not so the American people at the time,
however. They were aroused by Woodrow Wilson's eloquent
reaffirmation of the Declaration of Independence, the universality of whose principles he now proposed to test, and
equally committed to Franklin Delano Roosevelt's "Four
Freedoms" and Atlantic Charter as a blueprint for humanity.

In his historic war message of 1917 Wilson described "the
things which we have always carried nearest in our hearts."
These he pronounced as the ends for which Americans
would now fight—"for democracy, for the right of those who
submit to authority to have a voice in their own government,

81. *Die Presse*, Oct. 12, 1862, reprinted in Karl Marx–Friedrich Engels,
Werke (Berlin, 1961), XV, 553.

for the rights and liberties of small nations, for a universal domination of right by such a concert of free peoples as shall bring peace and safety to all nations and make the world at last free." These objectives Wilson spelled out in his Fourteen Points, a set of peace aims which imbued the American cause with an idealistic and proselytizing dimension. Wilson has been paired with Lenin in aiming at achieving through diplomacy and propaganda a revolution in Germany. The Bolshevik appeal agitated the German left wing while Wilson's heartened the non-Socialist elements in the growing Reichstag majority.[82] Wilson's primary audience, then, was not America but Europe. Frustrated in his efforts to secure a consensus in the United States on peace aims, he was remarkably successful in achieving an overthrow in Germany of the twin evils of the Hohenzollern autocracy and the military imperialists. As H. G. Wells saw it, America, with Wilson as her spokesman, was "under no delusion; she is fighting consciously for a German Revolution as the essential War Aim."[83] Realizing that a great diplomatic duel was shaping up between Wilson and Lenin for control of Europe's revolution, Romain Rolland confessed privately that Wilson, "heir of Washington and Abraham Lincoln," was aiming "at realizing throughout the world the ideal of the bourgeois republic of the Franco-American type."[84]

That duel was most dramatically focused on Central and Eastern Europe. For a time it appeared that Wilson would triumph over Lenin in Germany, and the emergence of a totalitarian Right was not foreseen. The much maligned Weimar Constitution drew heavily upon the American. Most notable among its draftsmen, the eminent sociologist Max

82. See Arno J. Mayer, *Political Origins of the New Diplomacy* (New Haven, 1959), p. 354.

83. H. G. Wells, *In the Fourth Year* (London, 1918), p. 71.

84. Romain Rolland, *Les Précurseurs* (Paris, 1920), pp. 217–218.

Weber, had become imbued with republicanism and had the audacity to take the fight for constitutional reform to the public even while the war was still being waged. In his pamphlet *Parliament and Executive in a Reformed Germany*, Weber looked to the democratic experiment to control the executive. Once the monarchy had broken down and the war had been lost, Weber proposed in a series of articles in the *Frankfurter Zeitung* in November, 1918, that there be a popularly elected president, and at the same time a politically responsible parliament—thus combining the American and French systems, notions finally embodied in the Weimar Constitution. However, the introduction of proportional representation prevented the evolution of an effective two-party system and rendered the Reichstag ineffective.[85] A similar compromise between the American and the parliamentary systems may be noted in the basic law of May 23, 1949, which serves as the constitution of the Federal Republic until a peace treaty permits the establishment of a unified government for Germany. The indirect election of the President is perhaps comparable to the electoral college in the United States, while the federal council possesses some of the features of the Senate. But the absolute veto which the federal council possesses over legislation affecting the provinces suggests that the centralizing trends increasingly manifest in the United States have been rejected in favor of a looser federalism, almost akin to that in America under the Articles of Confederation.[86] While the German drafters took over the device of judicial review, they failed to incorporate the unifying supreme court so distinctive to

85. See articles by F. Meinecke and W. Jellinek, in *Handbuch des deutschen Staatsrechts*, ed. by G. Anschütz and R. Thoma (Tübingen, 1930–32); Max Weber, *Politische Schriften* (Munich, 1921); Hajo Holborn, "Verfassung und Verwaltung der deutschen Republik: ein Verfassungsentwürf Friedrich Meinecke aus dem Jahre 1918," *Historische Zeitschrift*, CXLVII (1932), 115 *et seq.*

86. See Friedrich, *Impact*, pp. 67, 68.

the American system. Much closer to that American model is the Austrian Constitutional Court, although its functions are more specialized than that of the United States high court.[87]

Profound as was the impact of Wilsonian doctrine on the liberation of Eastern Europe, its implementation achieved results which could hardly have been a source of unalloyed satisfaction to its author had he lived to appraise more recent currents. That Wilson was ideologically and dogmatically committed to the principle of "government by the consent of the governed" should have been clear to both the Allies and the Central Powers. He deemed these principles to be not only "American" but "the principles of mankind" as well, and had them spelled out in his "Peace Without Victory" Address to Congress of January 22, 1917, and in his "Fourteen Points." That the latter soon caught him up in a maze of difficulties hardly merits amplification at this late date. The "Fourteen Points" contained an unqualified commitment to Poland, but the effort to bolster a pro-Allied regime signally failed to achieve democracy in that newly revived but ancient nation. Contrariwise, Wilson had merely held out to the non-German and non-Hungarian nationalities within the Austro-Hungarian Empire the promise of autonomy rather than independence, as he fondly but mistakenly hoped to induce Austria-Hungary to drop out of the war. When that prospect proved unrealistic and when pro-Czech and Slovak sentiment mounted in America, Wilson turned full circle and recognized the independence of Czechoslovakia.

Now, if you read the recent Communist historians,[88] you will learn that Czechoslovakia's independence came as a

---

87. For the nineteenth-century origins of the court, see Gerald Stourzh, "Die österreichische Dezemberverfassung im 1867," *Österreich in Geschichte und Literatur*, I (1968), 12, 13.

88. See, for example, J. S. Hájek, *Wilsonovská legenda v dějinách Ceskoslovenské Republiky* (Prague, 1953).

product exclusively of an internal social revolution set in motion by the Bolshevik Revolution in Russia, and that Wilson was really an enemy of the Czech and Slovak people. As one writer puts it, not the star-spangled banner, "but the red star of the Great October Socialist Revolution" inspired the Czechs in their struggle against Austria-Hungary.[89] This is current fiction, and the line has been hewed to by Communist historians writing of other national independence movements as well. Yet so knowledgeable a student as Victor S. Mamatey has shown that, from 1917 on, both Czech Socialists and nationalists worked in close cooperation toward the same goal: Czechoslovak independence. Wilson proposed autonomy; the Bolsheviks, nothing. Granted that these peoples took the initiative to attain their liberation and unification. Granted, too, that Wilson had originally hoped to drive a wedge between Germany and her Austrian ally by avoiding the breakup of the Hapsburg Empire. What is important is that Wilson responded to the developing events, reversed his course, and became an advocate of the cause of the oppressed nationalities of Austria-Hungary. What part the Czech legions played in the conversion, what part Secretary of State Lansing and American public opinion, would be difficult to determine precisely, but, as Mamatey felicitously remarks, this was an instance where *vox populi* became *vox Dei*.[90] In Masaryk's own view, Wilson's reversal of his original autonomy stand proved the decisive factor in achieving Czechoslovak independence.[91]

By way of a footnote it might be added that Wilson's conversion to Czechoslovak independence was no more dra-

89. *Ibid.*, p. 109 *et seq.*

90. For Czech propaganda in America, see Otakar Odlozilik, in Joseph P. O'Grady, ed., *The Immigrants' Influence on Wilson's Peace Policies* (Lexington, Ky., 1967), pp. 204–223.

91. See Thomas G. Masaryk, *The Making of a State: Memoires and Observations* (London, 1927), pp. 269–272, 340–342.

matic than was his backing for a united Yugoslavia and his disdain for Italy's pretensions based on the Secret Treaties toward which the American president repeatedly exhibited extraordinary repugnance. Wilson's support of a compromise between the principle of nationality, to which he was so sympathetic, and strategic considerations must, in historical perspective, be considered the essence of realism.[92]

In terms of the recent past it is easy to forget that, of all the small nations of Central Europe whose self-determination and independence were spawned by the Wilsonian program, Czechoslovakia stood for a score of years as the most authentic child of the American Revolutionary tradition. It was the liberal philosopher-statesman Thomas G. Masaryk heading a Czech government-in-exile who, less than a month before the Armistice, issued the Czechoslovak Declaration of Independence, so alike in both phraseology and spirit to the document drawn up long before in Philadelphia.[93] Presiding in Philadelphia at a conference of the Mid-European Democratic Union, Masaryk sat in the chair once occupied by George Washington when he presided over the Constitutional Convention of 1787. While Masaryk signed the "Declaration of Common Aims of the Independent Mid-European Nations," a bell, a replica of the Liberty Bell of '76, rang out, and the Declaration was then read to a crowd gathered in front of Independence Hall. Once again, an emerging nation paid obeisance to the ritual of the oldest revolution of modern times.

Masaryk was a discriminating admirer of America's revolutionary and democratic traditions. In his pantheon of political heroes, Washington and Lincoln occupied honored niches. To Masaryk, the American republic, lacking dynasty,

92. See Dragan R. Zivojinović, "The Emergence of American Policy in the Adriatic: December 1917–April 1919," *East European Quarterly* (Boulder, Colo.), I (1967), 173–215.

93. See text in *Foreign Relations, 1918*, Suppl., I, 847 *et seq.*

aristocracy, and militarism, seemed a more suitable model for emulation than the French republic which inherited from the *ancien régime* both an aristocracy and a military caste. Out of a lifetime study of the American constitutional system, Masaryk found especially worthy of emulation the institution of the Presidency, which he saw as a check on the prevailing shortcomings of European parliamentarism, the power of the Supreme Court to rule on the constitutionality of laws, and the American federal system. Most of all, Masaryk recognized the leadership void that occurred in the transition from a monarchical aristocracy to a democracy. Hence, to him the first order of business in his new republic was "to educate its citizens in democracy."

Masaryk's political heir, Eduard Beneš, paid tribute on more than one occasion to the constructive achievements of the American Revolution, to the various American bills of rights, and to the role played by the revolutionary movements in America and France in spreading "an enlightenment and vitality," setting off thereby "a kind of second Renaissance and Reformation." Beneš, rejecting the socialist doctrine of the class struggle as contrary to the "essential principles" of the two great revolutions, as he also rejected the "antirationalist, antihumanist, antiequalitarian" fascist and national socialist doctrines, foresaw a struggle to transform "bourgeois democracy" into a "deeper and more perfect democracy" which he chose to call "humanitarian democracy." Addressing the Congress of the United States on May 13, 1943, the exiled President Beneš pledged the restoration of a democratic Czechoslovak nation committed to freedom and peace, and "considering itself again the godchild of the great and glorious Republic of the United States."[94]

94. Thomas G. Masaryk, *The Making of a State: Memoires and Observations* (London, 1927), pp. 212–215, 419–421; Eduard Benes, *Masaryk's Path and Legacy* (Prague, 1937), pp. 13, 14, 18; *Democracy: Today and*

When Beneš made his commitment to freedom, he counted on the support of the United States, upon F.D.R.'s backing for self-determination, as reaffirmed in the peace aims written into the United Nations Declaration of January 1, 1942, and adopted by all the allies against Nazi Germany. The American Revolutionary principle of government by the consent of the governed was articulated in the pledge to see no territorial changes "that do not accord with the freely expressed wishes of the peoples concerned," and with the proclamation of the right of all peoples to choose their own form of government. At the Yalta Conference the United States presented the project of a "Declaration on Liberated Europe," according to which the American, British, and Russian governments undertook jointly to assist "the people in any European liberated state or former Axis satellite . . . to form interim governmental authorities broadly representative of all the democratic elements in the population and pledged to the earliest possible establishment through free elections of governments responsive to the will of the people; and to facilitate where necessary the holding of such elections." If Joseph Stalin, who affixed his signature to the "Declaration," had any scruples about it, the record is silent. He might easily have reconciled the pledge with his Marxist conscience, which excludes the bourgeoisie from that mystical body known as "the people."

As an aftermath of the recent Soviet military invasion of Czechoslovakia and the institution of curbs on provocative democratic impulses, an interesting semantic debate took place between spokesmen for the Soviet government and the Czechoslovak Academy of Sciences. The Russians affirmed the rectitude of the invasion on the ground that the Red

---

Tomorrow (London, 1937), pp. 5–8, 14, 15, 98, 99, 106, 144, 145, 177; *Eduard Benes in His Own Words* (New York, 1944), pp. 131, 136; "Speeches of Jan Masaryk in America," *Czechoslovak Sources and Documents*, No. 1 (September, 1942), pp. 52.

Army was "defending the interests of all of world socialism, of the entire world revolutionary movement" since the assertion by the Czechs of self-determination constituted an "encroachment upon the vital interests" of the European socialist countries. The refutation by the Czech scholars serves to dramatize the wide cleavage, not alone between Western democracies and orthodox Communist countries, but also within the European socialist community itself over terms like "consent of the governed," "liberty," and that "separate and equal station" which the Declaration of Independence affirmed all people were entitled to "by the Laws of Nature and of Nature's God."[95] One can well understand why in Czechoslovakia, whose origins were so colored by Jeffersonian and Wilsonian doctrine, the values that most of the Free World cherishes are too profoundly rooted to be silenced even by a Nazi occupation, a Communist postwar coup, or a recent invasion of that nation by her Communist neighbors.

Writing in the *Neue Zurcher Zeitung* on October 27, 1918, the German-born Swiss essayist and playwright, Hermann Kesser, recognized the revolutionary approaches of both Wilson and Lenin as well as the differences in their objectives. "There can be no question that *sub specie aeternitatis*," he affirmed, "Wilson and Lenin will appear merely as men with different methods. It is certain that mankind must make up its mind either for Wilson or for Lenin." As a dramatist, Kesser chose to personalize his protagonists. Perhaps we do less violence to historical facts if we choose to ground them more broadly and say that mankind must make up its mind either for the July '76 Revolution in America or the October '17 Revolution in Russia. Mankind is still going through the very painful process of making up its mind.

95. See *The New York Times*, Sept. 27, Oct. 24, 1968. See also Robert Litell, ed., *The Czech Black Book* (New York, 1969), pp. 292–314.

IV

THE AMERICAN REVOLUTION
AND THE EMERGING NATIONS OF
THE WESTERN HEMISPHERE

In his well-known restrospective judgment the British Tory statesman George Canning remarked that the operation of the example of the American Revolution was "sooner or later inevitable."[1] Canning realized that so epochal an event could not have failed to have an enormous impact, if only by example, on the Western Hemisphere, where neighboring colonial peoples had long chafed under the rule of Spain and France. Possessor of a vast and treasured empire in America, Spain was immediately put on guard when the Thirteen Colonies declared their independence of England, and then thrown into a state of alertness, if not alarm, when it appeared that the American Patriots would triumph.

The Spanish stance was thoroughly logical, for, by the year 1782, the American Revolution posed a greater threat to the empire of Spain than to any other power in the world. England, confronted with a *fait accompli,* had to work out

1. Sir Charles Webster, *Britain and the Independence of Latin America, 1812–1830* (2 vols., London, 1938), I, 6.

some kind of face-saving formula to keep its honor while losing its colonies, as Spain, with forebodings, prepared for the troubles that most certainly lay in wait.

Already revolt had shaken Spain's Latin-American colonies. First, the Creoles, the educated Spanish-speaking colonists of Latin America, aroused by the inequitable operation of the colonial commercial system and more immediately by a revised taxation policy, moved from political maneuvers and protests to armed risings. As early as 1780 insurrections had broken out in Cuzco, Arequipa, La Paz, and Cochabamba.[2] While one segment of the colonial population was aroused over the issue of taxation, another and far larger element shook the very foundation of colonial rule with an extraordinary rebellion. In November, 1780, an Inca Indian leader, Tupuc Amaru, called on the natives, long the victims of cruel colonial exploitation, to rise. Within a few months he controlled much of what is now southern Peru, most of Bolivia, and some of Argentina. Spanish reinforcements summoned from Buenos Aires and Lima suppressed the revolt. Punishment was pitiless. Tupuc Amaru witnessed the execution of his wife, sons, and aides. Then his tongue was cut out and he was torn to pieces by horses attached to his arms and legs. The bleeding members of his body were fixed on poles and exhibited in the village which had supported him. Instead of ending the revolt the barbaric executions only fired the Indians to continue and expand the insurrection for many months. Before it was put down the victims on both sides numbered not less than eighty thousand.[3]

2. Sergio Villalobos R., "Opposition to Imperial Taxation," in Lewis Hanke, ed., *The Origins of the Latin American Revolution, 1808–1826* (New York, 1965), pp. 124–137.

3. George Kubler, "The Quechua in the Colonial World," *Handbook of South American Indians*, II (Washington, D.C., 1946), 331–410.

To the Spanish government this revolt was a harbinger of what might happen if the Creoles were to embrace the revolutionary ideology of the North Americans. For a moment the possibility loomed large, for in 1781, the Spanish authorities had to deal with a plot for independence hatched in Chile by a landowner, a French-born teacher, and an inventor. While this amateur "Conspiracy of the Anthonys" (the given names of all three conspirators) to make Chile a republic failed, the authorities took pains not to publicize it at the time.

Portuguese Brazil also had its revolutionary conspiracies. Among intellectuals influenced by the Enlightenment and inspired by the example of constitution-making in Philadelphia, there was deep discontent, notably in São Paulo and Minas Gerais. That discontent came to a boil in 1789 in the so-called Conspiracy of Tiradentes, led by a disaffected army officer. Tiradentes was hanged, and Brazil did not become independent until 1822.[4]

In Paris, Spain's ambassador, the Conde de Aranda, frustrated by his inability to procure from the stubborn and tenacious John Jay a waiver of America's claim to the trans-Appalachian territory and to the free navigation of the Mississippi, reputedly prepared a secret memorial to his King, Charles III, pointing out the dangers that the new American nation posed to the Spanish Empire. He is supposed to have proposed as a counterweight to American expansion and annexation that Spain turn over all her colonies except Puerto Rico and Cuba to royal princes, exerting regal powers in their respective domains, while the Spanish King assumed the title of Emperor. The Spanish realms would be united by offensive and defensive alliances and enjoy trade reciprocity. Although the genuineness of this

4. See P. A. Martin, "Federation in Brazil," *Hispanic American Historical Review*, XVIII (1938), 144.

memorial has been questioned by some scholars, it is incontestable that even earlier Aranda had gone on record warning that the United States, though a pygmy in infancy, would some day become the colossus of the West and a formidable menace to Spain's possessions. Still concerned about the effects of American independence on Spain's colonies, Aranda in 1786, three years after the memoir was allegedly written, proposed to establish one infante in Spanish America, not three. The Spaniards never moved quickly enough to embrace this idea, although for other reasons Portugal managed to transplant its monarchy to Brazil in 1808.[5]

In short, the only significant impact of the American Revolution at the time proved to be a negative one. The example of America's successful insurgency aroused the Spanish government to the danger of widespread insurrection and fortified Spain in her disinclination to permit American trade on the Mississippi or to establish contact with Spanish colonials. As Secretary for Foreign Affairs of the new American nation, John Jay found the going rough when he sought to work out with Don Diego Gardoqui, Spain's minister to the United States, a treaty opening up the Mississippi. That issue was only temporarily settled during the French Revolution and not permanently until the purchase of the Louisiana Territory from France in 1803.

What more immediately triggered the Latin American revolutionary movements were the French Revolution and the Napoleonic Wars.[6] When the French Revolution broke out in 1789, the island of Saint Domingue—now Haiti and

5. See R. B. Morris, *The Peacemakers* (New York, 1965), pp. 424, 425 and footnotes 69, 70.

6. For the view that Rousseau had a far greater impact than Franklin or Hamilton, see Charles K. Webster, *Britain and the Independence of Latin America, 1812–1830*, 2 vols. (London, 1938), I, 6–12.

the Dominican Republic—was the first to react. Indeed, the French Revolution set off the explosion on the island by outlawing slavery. In the riotous atmosphere that ensued on Haiti, a strange and tragic leader, Toussaint L'Ouverture, the slave grandson of an African king, led his armies of illiterate Negroes in a ten-year war over mountains and valleys, striking now at the French, then at the British and Spaniards who intervened. By 1801 he not only controlled Haiti, but the eastern end of the island—Spanish Santo Domingo. When he finally was talked into surrendering to the French General Leclerc, he was treated much as Tupuc Amaru had been. He was treacherously seized, chained, thrown on a ship, and consigned to a French prison, where he died in 1803. Toussaint had lost the battle, but Haiti won its independence a year later, the first area in all Latin America to cut its ties with the Old World.

The reaction of the United States to the Haitian uprising provided a stern test of the notion that the American Revolutionary tradition might be for export. During a debate in the Pennsylvania legislature in 1791 on sending aid to Santo Domingo planters, one legislator was reported to have declared that "it would be inconsistent on the part of a free nation to take measures against a people who had availed themselves of the only means they had to throw off the yoke of the most atrocious slavery; if one treats the insurrection of the Negroes as rebellion, what name can be given to that insurrection of Americans which secured their independence?"[7]

A few antislavery figures in the North might rejoice, but elsewhere the reports of appalling atrocities aroused enor-

7. Reported by Jean de Ternant to Comte de Montmorin, Philadelphia, September 30, 1791. Frederick J. Turner, ed., *Correspondence of the French Minister to the United States, 1791–1797* (American Historical Association, *Annual Report* [1903]), II, 53.

mous antipathy and raised fears, shared by Secretary of State Jefferson, that Santo Domingo might spark a slave conflagration in the South.[8] Typical of this ambivalence of American leaders toward other people's revolutions was Rufus King, America's minister to England. While cordial to befriending revolutionary movements on the Latin American mainland, King felt far less enthusiasm for Toussaint's social and racial insurrection. Not only did he take it upon himself to deny that the United States had fomented rebellions in the colonies of other powers, a denial which was technically true; King felt impelled to assure Britain's Foreign Secretary, Lord Grenville, that "there was no likelihood of our becoming zealous in the propagation of the new doctrines of liberty and the rights of man." At the same time he was almost pathologically fearful that France might use Santo Domingo as a base of operations against the mainland of North America, and hoped, above all, that somehow the restoration of French power might be prevented and racial and social passions on the island cooled.[9]

True, the United States had contributed to Toussaint's victory by joining with Great Britain in concluding a trade agreement with Toussaint, and its naval squadrons in conjunction with the British blockaded harbors and even bombarded forts controlled by Toussaint's opponent, a French-supported mulatto. President Jefferson, however, did not view Toussaint's black republic with equanimity, and for a time was reported to be considering action in concert with France and England to put down the insurrection. A move in that direction was made in 1806, when Congress banned

8. See Winthrop Jordan, *White Over Black* (Chapel Hill, N.C., 1968), pp. 375–386.

9. Rufus King's Notebook entries for January 10, 1799, December 26, 1801. Rufus King Papers, New York Historical Society.

trade with the island.[10] The United States put off recognizing Haiti until after the Civil War.

The uprisings of the real proletariat of Latin America—the native Indians and Negro slaves—did not forecast the shape of things to come. The classic Latin American revolutions were led by Creoles rebelling against rule by Peninsulares, as the governing class from the mother country was called. The initial exclusion of the Creoles from higher office had created among them a sense of frustration and contributed to their growing alienation from Spain and the Spaniards, evidenced by the tendency Alexander von Humboldt observed, of their considering themselves as Americans rather than Spaniards.[11] Earliest of these Creole rebels was the long-time conspirator, Venezuelan-born Francisco de Miranda. Miranda visited England in 1790, and found a sympathetic listener in Rufus King, the United States minister to the Court of St. James. Concerned that Spanish America might fall into French hands, King wrote Secretary of State Pickering urging that the United States cooperate with England in securing Latin American independence, "which, looking forward to the destinies of the New World, shall in the beginning by great and generous deeds lay deep and firm the foundations of lasting concord between its rising Empires." Should the United States fail to guide the revolution in South America, King maintained, France would do so, to the detriment of American liberties.[12] Alex-

10. Carl L. Lokke, "Jefferson and the Leclerc Expedition," *American Historical Review*, XXXIII (1927–28), 322–328.

11. Alexander von Humboldt, *Essai Politique sur la Royaume de la Nouvelle-Espagne* (5 vols., Paris, 1811), II, 3. See also Sergio Villalobos R., "The Creole Desire for Office," in Hanke, *op. cit.*, pp. 250–255.

12. King to Pickering, February 26, 1798, King Papers, New York Historical Society; King to Theodore Sedgwick, May 21, 1799, Sedgwick Papers, Massachusetts Historical Society. See also Robert Ernst, *Rufus King: American Federalist* (Chapel Hill, N.C., 1968), pp. 262–267.

ander Hamilton was equally sympathetic to encouraging a liberation movement in Latin America under Miranda's auspices while refusing to participate overtly in Miranda's project without his government's approval.[13] On the other hand, in Hamilton's planning, Louisiana and the Floridas were to be liberated by the Americans by way of annexation. How much farther Hamilton would have gone if his plans as inspector general of the American armies under Washington had not been thwarted by President Adams must be left to speculation. As he wrote Secretary of War McHenry in June of 1799, "Besides eventual security against invasion, we ought certainly to look to the possession of the Floridas and Louisiana, and we ought to squint at South America."[14] With men, ships, and funds from Federalist supporters in New York, Miranda undertook an ill-planned expedition to Venezuela in 1806, which proved abortive, and its alleged American backers were prosecuted by the Jefferson administration seeking to make political capital out of their adversaries' indiscretions. Miranda returned in triumph to Venezuela in 1810 to head an independent junta, only to be soon defeated by royalist troops and turned over to the Spanish authorities by revolutionary hotheads, including Simón Bolívar. The unstable Miranda died in a Cádiz prison in 1816.[15]

What gave the Creoles their great opportunity was the invasion of the Iberian Peninsula by Napoleon's armies. Unlike the American revolutionaries who defied their King, the Creoles ostensibly took their stand in support of the

13. Hamilton to Miranda, August 22, 1798. Hamilton Papers, Library of Congress.

14. Hamilton to Harrison Gray Otis, January 26, 1799 (copy); to McHenry, June 27, 1799. Special Collections, Columbia University Libraries.

15. William S. Robertson, *The Life of Miranda*, 2 vols. (Chapel Hill, N.C., 1929).

displaced Ferdinand VII and against the upstart Joseph whom Napoleon had placed on the throne. Thus, the revolutions beginning in the year 1810 sought to fill a vacuum in imperial control. What occurred was a series of municipal revolts in Caracas, Buenos Aires, Bogotá, Quito, and Santiago, led by the wealthy Creoles in opposition to the Peninsulares, although these groups were themselves torn into some half-dozen factions of which the pro-independence group was tiny at the start. The rebels aimed at self-government for Creoles, not necessarily for the overwhelming majority of Indians and Negroes.[16]

Inevitably, the clash of race and class could not be avoided, and it took place in Mexico. There the revolt started in the countryside, in the mining region, rather than in the cities, and only in one province did it resemble in any way the social revolution of France. In fact, the parish priest who led the revolt, Father Hidalgo y Costilla, was an avid reader of the French *philosophes,* especially Rousseau, and he instinctively took the side of the dispossessed underdogs, the Indian and the mestizo, or half-castes. Victorious in numerous bloody battles, Hidalgo issued a proclamation from Valladolid calling upon a congress composed of representatives from the cities and villages to "enact mild and beneficent laws." Finally, he too, like Toussaint, was captured by trickery and executed. When independence was finally secured in 1821 it came as the result of a revolt under Agustín de Iturbide, shabby leader of the rebel remnants.[17] Thus, in its early phase the Mexican Revolution bore only superficial resemblance to the American Revolution in that it was supported by a wealthy colonial elite. Otherwise, the

16. See R. A. Humphreys, *Tradition and Revolt in Latin America* (London, 1969), p. 10.

17. W. S. Robertson, *Iturbide of Mexico* (Durham, N.C., 1952), is the definitive biography.

parallel could be sustained only if the Whig Opposition party had gained control in England in 1770 or 1774, and the American Patriots had rebelled against a liberal, reformist regime, a supposition quite the contrary to the fact.

Latin America was destined, however, to have revolutionary leaders of stature. The pair, who might well be called the Founding Fathers of Latin America, were Simón Bolívar, Caracas-born of an affluent family, and José de San Martín, Argentine-born, but reared in Spain where he worked his way up through the military ranks, only to return to Argentina to fight Spaniards and to free Latin America. Ardent, articulate, Bolívar was something of an ideologue, while San Martín was a modest, reticent man of action. Both knew something about the American Revolution and the constitutional system that had come out of it; both approached the North American system with reservations. For San Martín, the model of American federalism seemed to have at best a shaky application to Latin America, and he preferred a constitutional monarchy to a republic.

Intellectually, Bolívar was the more radical of the two. Educated by a tutor who was an enthusiast for Rousseau's *Émile*, Bolívar later acknowledged his teacher's influence. "You have molded my heart for liberty, justice, greatness and beauty," was his generous tribute. Bolívar, a true child of the Enlightenment,[18] shared a number of political notions with at least some if not all of the American Founding Fathers. He believed in democracy in Hamilton's sense rather than in Jefferson's. His political system was primarily paternalistic, and he conceived a transitional period during which the Latin American people in time would be educated to participate in a complete democracy. He felt strongly that

18. Jefferson R. Spell, *Rousseau in the Spanish World Before 1833* (Austin, 1938); A. P. Whitaker, ed., *Latin America and the Enlightenment* (New York, 1942).

the United States Constitution would not be suited to Latin Americans. The North Americans, he pointed out, had enjoyed self-government as colonists whereas the people of Colombia, he insisted, needed time before fully participating in government. Until they had acquired "the abilities and political virtues" that distinguished their political brothers to the north, popular democracy would, he warned, "bring about vices that one learns under the rule of a nation like Spain, which has only distinguished itself in ferocity, ambition, vindictiveness, and greed."

As to the system of federalism, which Venezuela had copied from the North Americans, Bolívar was similarly pessimistic. "It is a marvel," he remarked in 1819, "that its prototype in North America endures so successfully and has not been overthrown at the first sign of adversity or danger." Indeed, it was a marvel, as Bolívar saw it, that "so weak and complicated a government as the federal system" worked effectively for the people of North America, whom he described as "a singular model of political virtue and moral rectitude," and he steadfastly praised the United States as a "nation cradled in liberty, reared on freedom, and maintained by liberty alone." But that system was all right for the North Americans, and unadaptable, he contended, for the people of Venezuela. He conceded that the Venezuelan legislators "yielded to the ill-considered pleadings of those men from the provinces who were captivated by the apparent brilliance of the happiness of the North American people, believing that the blessings they enjoy result exclusively from their form of government rather than from the character and customs of the citizens."

"Who could resist the powerful attraction of full and absolute enjoyment of sovereignty, independence, and freedom?" he wrote. "Who could resist the devotion inspired by an intelligent government that has not only blended public and private rights but has also based its supreme law respecting the desires of the individual upon common consent?" But the Venezuelans were not prepared to enjoy such a beneficent government "immediately upon casting off their chains," he argued. Such a government was more suitable to "a republic of saints." Following Montesquieu's *L'Esprit des Lois*, which recommends that laws should be suited to the people for whom they are made, Bolívar warned his constituents to take into account the physical and social conditions of their own country. "This is the code we must consult, not the code of Washington!"

On the other hand, in one area, a strengthened central executive, Bolívar expressed his preference for the United States Constitution to the weak executive system of the Venezuelan Constitution. As regards the legislative branch, Bolívar considered the two-chambered legislatures of America and England, rejected the Abbé Sieyès' insistence on only one, which he called "a classic error," but proposed to the Congress of Bolivia a three-chambered system.[19]

Bolívar's rejection of many of the ideas embodied in the American Constitution on very practical grounds should not lead us to assume that he was hostile to the North American experiment. Quite the contrary, he praised the American Revolution on numerous occasions, and regarded the American Patriots as worthy of emulation. In advice to a Peruvian delegate to the Congress of Panama, Bolívar wrote in 1825:

> . . . expel from your heart and from your thoughts all the heat of that torrid zone that consumes you and dwell in the waters of the Pacific and the Atlantic—you have them close by—so as to develop your ideas with a temperament as cool as Washington's while still abiding on the heights of

19. *Selected Writings of Bolívar*, compiled by Vincente Lecuna, trans. by Lewis Bertrand (New York, 1951), I, 103, 179–181; II, 597–598. See also Victor Belaunde, *Bolívar and the Political Thought of the Spanish American Revolution* (Baltimore, 1938).

Franklin, who with his hand wrested lightning from the sky.[20]

Bolívar sought to have himself identified with the great Washington, whom he called "the outstanding architect of human freedom," so that "zealous republicans" would remember that there was that "occasional exception" of the selfless patriot. True, Bolívar conceded, Washington was that exception, for men in Bolívar's position had "always been ambitious" and it was difficult to counter "the long history of a world that had always been oppressed by the powerful."[21] The Latin-American liberator took pains to publicize the laudatory opinion that Lafayette, Washington's favorite aide, held of him. "Have the General praised in glowing terms, and send plenty of copies to Buenos Aires," he instructed General Antonio José de Sucre when Lafayette wrote him that he was to secure a medallion of Washington as a gift from the American General's family.[22]

Despite the influence of European Enlightenment thought on the Spanish-American liberators and their rejection of a number of North American constitutional principles as unadaptable to the condition of their constituents, it is remarkable just how much the Latin American nations borrowed from the American Revolutionary experience. In the first place every state on revolting issued a Declaration of Independence. Argentina's, for example, is strikingly parallel to Jefferson's. Oddly enough, in one country, Brazil, the declaration was proclaimed by a single man, the Prince Dom Pedro, who, while indubitably voicing the will of the majority, drew up no document but made his declaration verbally.[23]

20. *Selected Writings*, II, 525.

21. *Selected Writings*, II, 5, 579.

22. *Ibid.*, II, 565.

23. See Bradford E. Burns, ed., *A Documentary History of Brazil* (New York, 1966), No. 29, and compare with Charles Gibson, *The Spanish Tradition in America* (New York, 1968), p. 239.

Every new nation save Brazil felt called upon to have her constituent assemblies adopt constitutions along a republican plan. These constitutions, as in Argentina, ranged from the first of 1819, which was too centralized and monarchical, to that of 1826, which assured autonomy to the provinces. The latter led to the tyranny of regional chieftains, and finally to the dictatorship of Manuel de Rosas, who entered office as a federalist but in fact exercised absolutist control over the provinces until defeated by rebels in battle in 1852 and forced into exile. Finally, in 1853, a Constitution based on a working draft prepared by that penetrating liberal thinker Juan Bautista Alberdi was closely patterned after the instrument adopted in Philadelphia in 1787.[24]

Federalism, that seminal contribution of the Founding Fathers, played a central role in the constitutional thinking of many Latin American statesmen.[25] In Argentina the drafters of the Constitution of 1853 sought to assure local government to the provinces while conferring large powers upon the president and the federal government, which was specifically empowered to intervene in any province where republican government was threatened by internal disorders or foreign invasion. Like the American, the Argentinian Constitution provided for a federal system of representative government based on a division of power between the central government and the provinces, and on the separation of powers of the executive, legislative, and judicial departments. Like the American, the Argentine Constitution provided for a president, a bicameral congress (Senate and Chamber of Deputies), and a hierarchy of federal courts headed by a Supreme Court, with the three powers interconnected by a system of checks and balances. In fact, the

24. See D. F. Sarmiento, *Life in the Argentine Republic in the Days of Tyrants,* translated by Mrs. Horace Mann (New York, 1961).

25. See Belaunde, *Bolivar and the Political Thought of the Spanish American Revolution,* p. 1.

resemblance to the American model was so close that for many years Argentine courts went so far as to interpret their country's Constitution in the light of the interpretations of the United States Constitution by its courts and leading commentators. "The system of government under which we are living was not our creation," the Argentine Supreme Court declared in an opinion rendered in 1887. "We found it in operation, tested by the experience of many years, and adopted it for our own system."[26]

In his *Bases*, Alberdi counseled some variations from the American model, which were dutifully adopted, including a six-year term for the president without immediate re-election and the coupling of a provision for state support of the Roman Catholic Church with a guarantee of freedom of conscience and public worship for other religious faiths. While the United States has shown great restraint in exercising its constitutional powers to intervene in a state to maintain republican institutions—after all, it can be argued that we have not had republican institutions in most of the Southern states for at least a hundred years—the Argentine federal government has intervened in the provinces many, many times. By 1943 some 142 interventions were recorded; hence their system, though nominally federal, has been converted into a highly centralized, unitary state in fact.[27] The case could be made that the increasing assumption by the American federal government of responsibility for the general welfare is having the same effect here.

Brazil also paid tribute to American federalism. Its merits were eloquently argued at the Constituent Congress of 1824, but the first concrete impact was the Ato Adicional of

26. L. S. Rowe, *The Federal System of the Argentine Republic* (Washington, 1921), p. 2. See also José Luis Romero, *A History of Argentine Political Thought*, trans. by Thomas F. McGann (Stanford, Calif., 1963), p. 152.

27. Romero, *A History of Argentine Political Thought*; Arthur P. Whitaker, *Argentina* (Englewood Cliffs, N.J., 1964), pp. 25–26, 33–34.

1834, which gave the provinces increasing authority. Inspired directly by the United States Constitution, Ruy Barbosa incorporated not only the presidential system but also the federalist principle into Brazil's 1891 Constitution, which remained in force for forty years.[28] Thereafter federalism took a zigzag spiral downward, suffering body blows under the regime of Dr. Getulio Vargas, whose regime put into effect several years apart two different centralizing constitutions, replete with undemocratic implications and clearly inspired by the corporate states of Italy and Portugal. The post–World War II Constitution, which came in the wake of the bloodless coup that deposed Vargas, established in effect a centralized republic which styles itself federal.

Next to Argentina's, the longest-enduring constitution of Latin America was Chile's Constitution of 1833. Destined to stand until 1925, that instrument provided for a president and two houses of congress to be elected by an indirect vote, the president for a five-year term, with the privilege of being re-elected for one more term. This highly centralized model restricted suffrage to males over twenty-five who could read and write and owned a prescribed amount of property, but it was liberalized in 1920.

True, the Latin American jurists and constitution-makers quite often looked to the United States, just as the Argentinians under the leadership of the writer, educator, and later president Domingo Faustino Sarmiento looked to the United States for leadership in educational methods. Not only was the United States a model to be imitated, but a rival to be equaled if not surpassed.[29] If imitation is the

28. José de P. Rodrigues Alves, *Génesis da idéa republicana no Brasil* (Santiago, 1933).

29. Thomas F. McGann, *Argentina, the United States, and the Inter-American System* (Cambridge, Mass., 1957), pp. 60–62; W. Stewart and W. M. Frencky, "The Influence of Horace Mann in the Educational Ideas

highest form of flattery, then the United States need take little gratification in the result. What happened was that the Latin-American countries, a compound of Indian, mestizo, Negro, and European cultures, were totally unprepared to accept the responsibilities of constitutionalism, and the very idea was honored in the breach. Instead, what the Latin-American nations practiced was government by military dictatorship, the rule of the caudillo.

All this was shrewdly forecast by General Pozzo di Borges, Russia's ambassador to France, who wrote to Nesselrode in 1817 to point out important differences between the people of the United States during the American Revolution and the rebellious colonists of New Spain. Should the Spanish-American rebels win, he warned, they might only clear the path for "barbarous and ferocious tyrants."[30] Francis Baylies, United States chargé d'affaires in Buenos Aires, wrote of Rosas to Secretary of State Edward Livingston in July, 1832, "the tremendous power with which he is clothed would transform a patriot into a Tyrant and an angel into a demon." Describing the summary executions and deportations which characterized Rosas' regime, Baylies added, "Such, Sir, is the happy condition of society in this *Sister Republic* of ours, whose free and liberal principles and hatred of despotism have so often been themes for the panegyrics of our mistaken, romantic and imaginative politicians. I think one week's residence here would cure them of this hallucination."[31]

of Domingo Sarmiento," *Hispanic American Historical Review*, XX (1940), 12–31.

30. A. Polovstoff, *Correspondance diplomatique . . . Russie en France . . . , 1814–30* (St. Petersburg, 1902), II, 230.

31. Francis Baylies to Edward Livingston, July, 1832, in W. R. Manning, ed., *Diplomatic Correspondence of the United States: Inter-American Affairs* (Washington, 1932), I, 132–133.

What the American observer might have added was that the Latin-American revolutions may have been indebted to the North American example for their wars of decolonization and their stirrings of nationalism, but that they chose the models of dictatorship offered them more immediately by Simón Bolívar and at second hand by Napoleon Bonaparte.

Why did this happen in South America, and why did the two continents basically diverge in pursuing their revolutions? To answer one must contrast the Thirteen Colonies with their relative homogeneity, the relatively high degree of literacy of their populations, the widespread ownership of property, the long experience of the colonial settlers in self-government, and their popular commitment to ideas of rational liberty and constitutionalism with the Spanish colonies so lacking in all these characteristics. Over that vast, tropical, and jungle-covered territory, the Spaniards had fixed a paternalistic colonial rule upon a native Indian population—poor, illiterate, superstitious, suppressed, and exploited. Spread over this enormous territory was a Creole white or semi-white population which was to seize the mantle of government from the Spanish ruling class. In place of a paternalistic rule there came feuding oligarchies largely indifferent to the welfare of the earth-bound peasantry. Ideas of nationality, independence, secularism, democracy, and freedom burst upon this medieval world with startling suddenness and were not easily digested. It was as though the Creoles were to experience, and at the same time, the Reformation and the Counter-Reformation, the American and French Revolutions, adding, as C. Northcote Parkinson remarks, "some scenes borrowed from the War of the Roses and others from the America of Buffalo Bill. Theirs was a history in which Saint Dominic, Don Quixote, Garibaldi, John of Gaunt, and Al Capone were all contemporaries and at variance with each other."[32] This confusion of ideas was compounded by the tragic costs of the fourteen-year-long wars of liberation, which left three million Creoles impoverished, exhausted, and largely devoid of experience in governance.

Out of the confused story of the Latin American Wars of Liberation one great reputation emerges, that of Simón Bolívar. Dubious of the durable nature of the republics, Bolívar reminded the delegates to the congress assembled at Angostura that while "nature endows us with the desire for freedom at our birth, yet men, whether from apathy or inborn inclinations, suffer the chains laid upon them." The presidency under the new constitution endowed Bolívar with supreme military power. When he returned to Colombia to find it torn by intrigues, some factions wanting him as king, others wishing to have him deposed, he replied publicly: "The voice of the nation has forced supreme power on me." Bolívar denied that he had aspirations for a throne, and insisted that he had accepted these powers in order "to safeguard the rights of the people." In time Bolívar came to see that a dictatorship was needed and that, if necessary, the constitution must be ignored. "The dictatorship must bring a total reform with it," he wrote. He found dictatorship "in vogue" and predicted that it would be "popular" since the soldiers wanted "coercion" and the people "provincial independence." In such a confusion, "a dictator unites the whole."

Yet Bolívar, haunted by the specter of Napoleon and holding ever before him the example of Washington, repeatedly declined the throne and opposed setting up a

32. C. Northcote Parkinson, *The Evolution of Political Thought* (Boston, 1958), pp. 251–254. See also Richard M. Morse, "The Heritage of Latin America," in *The Founding of New Societies* (New York, 1964), pp. 160, 161.

monarchy. A disillusioned man, he resigned office in 1830. Dying shortly thereafter, he summed up his career in these words, "There have been three great fools in history: Jesus, Don Quixote, and I," and his tragic disillusionment in the famous observation, "For us America is ungovernable. He who serves a revolution ploughs the seas."[33]

Save for Alexander Hamilton, who at the twilight of his career was despondent about the future of democracy,[34] none of the leading Founding Fathers gave voice to such cynicism and despair. Contrariwise, we can find many utterances of affirmation in the future of the American nation among its original Patriots. Dying six years after Bolívar, James Madison, chief architect of the American Constitution, left among his papers a note entitled "Advice to my Country," which concluded as follows: "The advice nearest to my heart and deepest in my convictions is, that the Union of the states be cherished and perpetuated. Let the open enemy of it be regarded as a Pandora with her box opened, and the disguised one as the serpent creeping with his deadly wiles into paradise."

After Bolívar ensued a prolonged period of political instability, from which Latin America has not yet completely emerged. Between cleric and secularist, landowner and peasant, oligarch and half-breed, country and town, sierra and seacoast, and military and civil establishments, hostilities long remained entrenched and have by no means been eliminated in our own time. Such instability was the spawn-

---

33. Simón Bolívar, *Obras Completas*, ed. by Vicente Lecuna and Esther Barret de Nazaris (2 vols., Havana, 1947), I, 168.

34. In a dispirited mood following the killing of his eldest son Philip in a duel, Hamilton referred to the Constitution as "a frail and worthless fabric," adding, "Every day proves to me more and more, that this American world was not made for me." Hamilton to Gouverneur Morris, draft in Hamilton's hand. Hamilton Papers, 1st Ser., Library of Congress. R. B. Morris, ed., *The Basic Ideas of Alexander Hamilton* (New York, 1957), p. 440.

ing ground for the caudillo or military leader, few of whom possessed anything like Bolívar's political scruples.

A fitting contrast to the reflective and liberal-minded Bolívar was that father of Mexican independence, General Antonio López de Santa Anna, who gained his laurels as liberator by exiling the dictator Iturbide. Fancying himself another Napoleon, Iturbide had reigned briefly as Agustín I, first Emperor of Mexico. Then for over thirty years Santa Anna, that curious savior-on-horseback, held sway over Mexico. A Creole of inherited wealth and position, Santa Anna gained his military experience in the royal army of New Spain. His boyhood hero was the great Bonaparte, and he never outgrew the ambition to be the Napoleon of the West. A supreme egotist, he has been characterized by Hubert Herring as having "made vanity a profession, bombast a fine art, treachery a specialty." He betrayed Spain for service with Iturbide; he betrayed Iturbide for his own ends; he betrayed the Liberals who gave him power, then betrayed the Conservatives who used him. Later he betrayed Mexico to the United States and, after taking money from the American government, betrayed his Northern friends for his own profit at home. "His vices were shabby and gross," a leading authority has observed. "He indulged his passion for cockfighting even in the national palace. For almost thirty years, Mexico, for lack of political maturity and a literate citizenry, was the victim of this fellow who made and unmade presidents, seized the top office for himself time and again, mismanaged his country's pathetic wars, and stole the savings of the peasants and the church."[35] Santa Anna announced that he had once "thrown up his cap for liberty" with great ardor, but that he "very soon found the folly of it." "A hundred years to come my people will not be fit for

35. Hubert Herring, *A History of Latin America* (2nd ed., New York, 1961), p. 307.

liberty." Only a despotism suited them, but he saw no reason "why it should not be a wise and virtuous one." Needless to say, despot Santa Anna lacked both wisdom and virtue.

Thus a bitterly poor country, an amalgam of Indian, mestizo, and European, was ill-served by its liberator and was destined to remain hungry. There is no need to emphasize the contrast between this caliber of revolutionary leadership and that offered the North Americans in 1776. Instead of dedication by their leaders to the cause of independence and union, the Mexicans and other Latin-American peoples were constantly led down the road to shabby betrayal.

The results were political instability and almost constant revolutions. As compared with the United States, which experienced one serious, bloody, but unsuccessful revolt, that of 1861–65, the Latin Americans have been confronted with overturn after overturn, with coups from the left, the right, and the center. Bolivia enjoyed sixty revolts and ten constitutions, and saw six presidents assassinated between 1826 and 1898. In about the same length of time Peru experienced forty revolts and fifteen constitutions. Ecuador had twenty-three dictators in about eighty years, while Venezuela had fifty-two uprisings in seventy years.[36]

Only during the regimes of the more effective dictators was some sort of stability achieved, and at a price. Thus, Rosas governed Argentina for twenty-three years, Francia ruled Paraguay for twenty-nine years, Gómez ruled Venezuela for twenty-seven years, and Díaz ruled Mexico for thirty-four. Some, like Cárdenas and Juárez, ruled well; others, badly; but the only alternative seemed anarchy. The one exception was Brazil where a monarchy was established in 1825 under the ruling Portuguese house of Braganza, and

36. Francisco García Calderón, Latin America: Its Rise and Progress, trans. by B. Miall (London, 1919), p. 103 et seq.

remained in power until 1889. Then a bloodless revolution led to the establishment of a republic in 1891. Ultimately Brazil, too, came under the rule of a dictatorship, that of Vargas, whose regime covered the eventful years 1930–45.

Into that simmering caldron of revolt and political instability the relatively staid United States of America, mindful both of its revolutionary tradition and its national interest, tossed a few ingredients of its own. Most immediately its explosive ingredient was doctrinal, but expansion, intervention, and economic penetration all contributed to bringing the pot to a boil from time to time.

It was no more possible to seal off the decaying Spanish empire from contacts with Yankees than from the contagion of American libertarian ideas. Thus, when Captain Josiah Roberts, of the Massachusetts sealer *Jefferson*, put in at Valparaiso, Chile, in 1792, he had many interesting discussions with the Chilean Captain-General Bernardo O'Higgins, son of a Creole mother and the Irish first governor of Chile, and himself destined to play a leading role in achieving independence for Chile. Referring to a United States passport, O'Higgins noted that it bore "the signature of His Excellency George Washington, whose immortal name I have had infinite satisfaction to see stamped for the first time by his own hand."[37] Meantime, despite the vigilance of Spanish customs inspectors who seized all subversive materials they could locate, including copies of the American Declaration of Independence and the United States Constitution, or even matches, pendants, and snuffboxes which might bear a message or a symbol of liberty, Americans succeeded in introducing revolutionary literature into Latin America. Young Richard Cleveland of Massachusetts and William Shaler of Connecticut, undertaking an extensive voy-

37. Harry Bernstein, *Origins of Inter-American Interest* (Philadelphia, 1945), pp. 77–81.

age along the coasts of Latin America, anchored at Valparaiso where they learned from some Chileans who took them into their confidence that they "resented their state of vassalage," and dared express the hope that "emancipation was not far distant." The New Englanders came well equipped as propagandists, carrying among their wares a copy of the federal Constitution and a Spanish translation of the Declaration of Independence.[38] Philadelphia merchants dispatched revolutionary literature into Cuba and American newspapers to Buenos Aires, while Americans then resident in Latin America came under surveillance by the Spanish viceroys who considered them agents of subversion.

While American enthusiasts as individuals helped fan the flames of revolution in Latin America, their government, involved in an apparently irreconcilable maritime conflict with Great Britain, felt disinclined to commit itself too deeply in Latin America and pursued the course of prudent contacts. Jefferson privately expressed sympathy with the Mexican and Cuban liberation movements, and indicated as early as 1811 that all European influence should be excluded from the Western Hemisphere.[39] President Madison dispatched special agents and consuls to Latin America and permitted Latin-American patriots resident in the United States to purchase arms for revolutionary ends, but he was cautious about extending recognition. Even a resolution of 1811 reported by the House Committee on the Spanish-American colonies, headed by the physician-scientist Samuel Latham Mitchill, did little more than voice "friendly interest" and favored amicable relations and commercial intercourse.[40]

38. Richard J. Cleveland, *A Narrative of Voyages and Commercial Enterprises* (2nd ed., Cambridge, Mass., 1843), p. 174.

39. Arthur P. Whitaker, *The Western Hemisphere Idea: Its Rise and Decline* (Ithaca, N.Y., 1954), pp. 28–29.

40. *Abridgment of Debates in Congress*, IV, 436.

Time seemed to work against the Latin-American revolutionaries, for as chaos expanded in Spanish America even the most rabid friends of Spanish-American independence preferred to sit on the sidelines. "The struggle for liberty in South America," John Randolph of Roanoke warned Congress in 1816, "will turn out in the end something like French liberty, a detestable despotism. You cannot make liberty out of Spanish matter—you might as well try to build a seventy-four out of saplings."[41] In contrast with Randolph's disillusionment were the sentiments of that incorrigible enthusiast, Matthew Lyon, formerly Congressman from Vermont, who wrote in the same year 1816 to President Monroe proposing the "Anglo Americanizing of the South," or at least incorporating everything from northern South America to New Orleans under the American government.[42] Few were prepared to follow Lyon at this time, certainly not New York's Senator Rufus King. In apparent repudiation of his erstwhile conspiratorial role in the patriot Miranda's ill-fated venture to liberate the Southern Hemisphere, King remarked in 1818 that whether the United States should acknowledge the independence of any of these colonies should be determined by its interests alone. Denying that he had in fact changed his former opinions, King declared it would be "an unfortunate decision" if America, considering the state of world affairs, should plunge into a war for the deliverance of these colonies, whose incapacity to manage their own affairs must for a time be a cause of great confusion and disorder.[43]

Others, bitten by that Pan-American mystique which has colored the relations of the United States and Latin-Ameri-

41. *Annals of Congress,* 14th Cong., 1st Sess., p. 727.

42. Matthew Lyon to Monroe, March 5, 1816, Monroe Papers, New York Public Library.

43. King to Christopher Gore, January 18, 1818, Rufus King Papers, New-York Historical Society, cited by Bernstein, *Origins,* p. 94.

can nations from almost the beginning, favored a more positive role for the United States. For example, Henry M. Brackenridge, Secretary to the United States mission to Buenos Aires, argued for a show of solidarity among all Western Hemisphere nations against trans-Atlantic monarchy, and urged the United States in 1817 "to be the first to acknowledge the independence of South America or any part of it, whenever it may be achieved now or ten years hence."[44] In Congress Joel Poinsett, who had served the United States for several years in Buenos Aires and Chile, came by 1822 to advocate recognition on the ground that it would prove a fillip to American commerce.[45] Poinsett's information and arguments profoundly influenced Henry Clay, that perennial presidential hopeful. "I consider the release of any part of America from the dominion of the Old World as adding to the general security of the new," Clay declared. In a widely publicized address delivered at Lexington, Kentucky, in 1821, Clay urged the recognition of the new republics as well as support by the United States "by all means short of actual war." Significantly, he proposed that the two Americas be "a sort of counterpoise" to the Holy Alliance "on behalf of independence and liberty," to operate "by the force of example and moral influence."[46]

Such a challenge to the government by a foremost Opposition leader could not long remain unanswered. Less than two months later, on July 4, Secretary of State John Quincy Adams, who had previously chided Clay for having "already

44. Henry M. Brackenridge, *South America: A Letter on the Present State of that Country to James Monroe, President of the United States* (Washington, 1817).

45. *Annals of Congress*, 17th Cong., 1st Sess., pp. 1395–1402. See also J. F. Rippy, *Joel R. Poinsett, Versatile American* (Durham, N.C., 1935).

46. *Argus of Western America* (Frankfurt, Kentucky), June 7, 1821.

mounted his South American great horse,"[47] enunciated two
seemingly contradictory principles. First he asserted that
"colonial establishments cannot fulfill the great objects of
government in the just purposes of civil society," and, second, he expressed doubts about the wisdom of allowing the
United States to become embroiled in wars between other
countries, even in the defense of liberty and its own
principles of government. Wary of the English, who were
casting long glances at Latin America, particularly Cuba,
Adams hoped to stem the European reactionary tide by
spreading liberal propaganda among Europe's colonial subjects. Thus, he felt that by putting America's own struggle
for independence on new and solid ground, he was strength-
ening the case for the independence of Latin America, despite
doubts that would not down about her fitness to enjoy
liberty. As Adams later explained, he deemed intervention
in foreign wars, even "wars for freedom," as changing the
very foundations of our government from *liberty* to *power*."[48]

Adams' Fourth of July oration laid the groundwork for his
own perhaps belated recognition that, though the movement
for independence in Spanish America may have been forced
upon the people of Latin America by external events, it was
a development of the great principles of the American Revolution.[49] That oration also heralded the forthcoming recognition by the United States of the Latin-American republics
and contained a number of seeds that sprouted full-grown in
the Monroe Doctrine.

On the score of the Monroe Doctrine, its promptings, its

47. C. F. Adams, ed., *Memoirs of John Quincy Adams* (12 vols., Philadelphia, 1874–77), IV, 28.

48. For a full discussion of this address, see A. P. Whitaker, *The United
States and the Independence of Latin America, 1800–1830* (New York,
1964), pp. 344–369.

49. J. Q. Adams, *Writings,* pp. 442–443, 466.

meaning, and its long-range significance, so much has been said that we need not tarry long over details. The issue of Latin-American recognition and intervention came to a head late in 1822 when, at the Congress of Verona, the Holy Alliance comprising France, Austria, Russia, and Prussia agreed to take steps to restore the authority of Ferdinand VII of Spain, who in 1820 had been forced to accept a constitutional monarchy. Richard Rush, the American minister to London, explored with George Canning, the British Foreign Secretary, the possibility of joint Anglo-American action against intervention in the New World on the part of the Holy Alliance. But President Monroe, responding to the advice of John Quincy Adams, decided to assert America's strength and independence by acting alone, even though this meant differing with two venerated Republican ex-Presidents, Jefferson and Madison. The Monroe Doctrine postulated an "American system" as opposed to a "European system." While offering a pledge that the United States would not involve itself in Europe's internal affairs, Monroe warned Europe to keep her hands off the New World and to cease all further efforts at colonization in the Western Hemisphere. On its face a declaration of withdrawal from European affairs, the Monroe Doctrine was really a commitment to leadership in world politics, certainly to Western Hemisphere politics, a bold and far-reaching commitment, modified in the course of time and extended to meet changing circumstances.

How did the powers dedicated to the principle of legitimacy feel about the Monroe Doctrine? We need only quote the Austrian chancellor Metternich, architect of Europe's counterrevolution. In a letter to his Russian colleague Nesselrode, dated January 19, 1824, Metternich gave voice to his irritation in these words:

These United States of America which we have seen arise and grow, and which during their too short youth already meditated projects which they dared not then avow, have suddenly left a sphere too narrow for their ambition, and have astonished Europe by a new act of revolt, more unprovoked, fully as audacious, and no less dangerous than the former. They have distinctly and clearly announced their intention to set not only power against power, but, to express it more exactly, altar against altar. In their indecent declarations they have cast blame and scorn on the institutions of Europe most worthy of respect, on the principles of its greatest sovereigns, on the whole of those measures which a sacred duty no less than an evident necessity has forced our governments to adopt to frustrate plans most criminal. In permitting themselves these unprovoked attacks, in fostering revolutions wherever they show themselves, in regretting those which have failed, in extending a helping hand to those which seem to prosper, they lend new strength to the apostles of sedition, and reanimate the courage of every conspirator. If this flood of evil doctrines and pernicious examples should extend over the whole of America, what would become of our religious and political institutions, of the moral force of our governments, and of that conservative system which has saved Europe from complete dissolution?[50]

If one views the American Revolution as primarily a war of decolonization, political independence, and the fulfillment of nationhood, one must share with John Quincy Adams a sense of the identity of purpose between the American war for liberation from British rule and the Latin American wars for independence from Spanish rule. Adams was

50. Dexter Perkins, *A History of the Monroe Doctrine* (Boston, 1963), pp. 27, 56–57. The subject of the Monroe Doctrine has also been thoroughly explored in Perkins, *The Monroe Doctrine, 1823–1826* (Cambridge, 1927); in S. F. Bemis, *John Quincy Adams and the Foundations of American Foreign Policy* (New York, 1849); and in A. P. Whitaker, *The Western Hemisphere Idea: Its Rise and Decline.*

not the last statesman to note that interrelationship. In rhetoric suitable to the Fourth of July oration he was delivering, Luis Muñoz Marín, Puerto Rico's pre-eminent statesman, declared on the eve of World War II:

> When the hour of midnight strikes tonight, the Fourth of July, symbol of the North, shall meet the Fifth of July, the date on which the liberation of the South was commenced in Venezuela; and it shall be as if those two dates should strike their hands, and the heart of the one should be close to the heart of the other, and that it should be as only one date. It is the date of America and around it there are grouped also other dates that belong to the whole of America: the 25th of May of the Argentine; the 7th of September of Brazil, the 20th of May of Cuba, the 27th of September of Santo Domingo, the 16th of September of Mexico, the 1st of July in Canada, the 1st of January of Haiti, the 15th of September of the whole of Central America—with all the other symbolic dates of America as a whole.
>
> All those dates, different in the calendar, are only one in the spirit and the purpose of America. In all those dates the word of democratic responsibility should be heard throughout America as a word of unity in the defense of the realizations and potentialities of democracy.[51]

The twentieth century has proved a testing-ground for that common revolutionary tradition of the two continents. Suddenly, in 1898, America found herself a colonial power. Imperialists, convinced of the importance of naval power and fortified by spurious Social Darwinism, justified Anglo-Saxon domination over "underdeveloped" nations by equating the "fittest" with the young, vigorous, and expansive American nation. Imperialists might rejoice over the Carib-

51. "Fourth of July Address." Broadcast by Luis Muñoz Marín, President of the Senate of Puerto Rico, July 4, 1941. Text supplied by the courtesy of the Honorable Luis Muñoz Marín.

bean and Far Eastern acquisitions of the United States and express the conviction that the American revolutionary tradition was not for export beyond the continental United States. So rabid an imperialist as Senator Albert J. Beveridge, in advocating the annexation by the United States of Cuba and Puerto Rico, might snort, "The proposition of the opposition makes the Declaration of Independence preposterous, like the reading of Job's lamentations would be at a wedding."[52]

The American conscience, however, would not easily be reconciled to accepting the role of permanent colonial rulers. Thus, when Congress on April 19, 1898, adopted its joint resolution for intervening in Cuba, it attached thereto the Teller Amendment. Sponsored by Senator Henry M. Teller of Colorado, it disclaimed any intention by the United States to "exercise sovereignty, jurisdiction, or control over said island, except for the pacification thereof," and pledged that the government and control of Cuba would be left to its people. Approved without a single dissenting vote, the Teller Amendment epitomized that naive and oversimplified comprehension of the uses of power with which the American people went to war with Spain. Many Americans saw in Cuba's resistance a parallel to their own struggle for independence from Great Britain. Regardless of intentions, that "splendid little war," as John Hay adjudged it, touched off an annexationist surge that gathered momentum as the war progressed. On July 7 President McKinley signed a joint congressional resolution annexing Hawaii to the United States, privately remarking, "We need Hawaii just as much and a good deal more than we did California. It is Manifest Destiny." The peace treaty with Spain, by which the United

52. Claude G. Bowers, *Beveridge and the Progressive Era* (Boston, 1932), pp. 73–76.

States acquired the Philippines and Puerto Rico, among other territories, touched off a scorching debate. Anti-annexationists denounced the conquest of alien lands and populations as a repudiation of the principles embodied in the Declaration of Independence and could summon to their side an array of special interest groups, trade-union leaders, American sugar, hemp, and tobacco growers who feared competition from duty-free products from the newly acquired islands, as well as intellectuals, like William James, who observed that if "the Anglo-Saxon race would drop its sniveling cant it would have a good deal less of a 'burden' to carry."

The administration of an overseas empire extending from the Caribbean to the Philippine Sea forced the American people to square their own traditions of self-government with their new role as governors of colonial dependencies. On the formulation of judicial rulings the United States built a colonial system in response to expediency, recognizing the power of Congress to apply or withhold basic guarantees as it saw fit in governing the newly acquired territories, and drastically revising the American concept of the equality of all parts of the Union, a tradition dating from the Northwest Territory Ordinance of 1787, as regards overseas territory which was not incorporated in the United States.

This American ambivalence toward other people's revolutions and toward the occupying of noncontiguous territories affected America's relations with Cuba. Despite the pledge of the Teller Amendment, the United States withheld granting Cuba immediate independence. A constitution drawn up in Cuba and based on the American model was rejected by the War Department because no provision was made therein for future relations between Cuba and the United States. Only when Cuba agreed to embody in her constitution the Platt Amendment, making that island a quasi-protectorate of the United States and assuring the acquisition by grant or lease of naval bases or coaling stations, were American troops pulled out of the island, a withdrawal which came as a stunning surprise to the rest of the world. The Platt Amendment was abrogated in 1934, but other U.S.-Cuban ties, notably in the form of trade agreements and American investments, survived for a generation longer, finally to succumb to Castro's revolution.

If Cuban-American relations have proved a standing challenge to America's pacific intentions toward the peoples of the Caribbean, the Panama Canal touched off a wave of anti-Yankee feeling in Latin America which still fuels provocative incidents. To secure the rights to build an Isthmian canal, Theodore Roosevelt supported a Wall Street–inspired Panamanian revolution from Colombia timed to coincide with the latter's rejection of a treaty granting rights to the United States to construct such a canal. The evidence is still circumstantial, but no one doubts that the timely arrival of the American naval force in Panama's waters was no mere happenstance, especially as their presence barred the way to Colombian troops dispatched to put down the almost bloodless revolution. There is a story that T.R. defended at a cabinet meeting his big-stick policy toward Colombia. Turning to his Secretary of War Elihu Root, he asserted, "Well, have I answered the charges? Have I defended myself?" "You certainly have, Mr. President," Root reputedly replied. "You have shown that you were accused of seduction and you have conclusively proved that you were guilty of rape."[53]

Roosevelt's determination to construct the Canal transformed the Caribbean into an American lake whose defense was vital to the security of the United States. When uprisings or internal deterioration threatened American interests

53. Quoted in Philip C. Jessup, *Elihu Root* (2 vols., New York, 1938), I, 404–405.

it was the Roosevelt-Taft-Wilson policy to land marines to maintain security and forestall revolution. Although the last contingent of marines was pulled out of Nicaragua in 1933, recent intervention in Santo Domingo, and, more controversially, in Guatemala, suggest that the "Colossus of the North" has not abandoned the "big stick," even though it is now wielded with a rubber casing.

It was Puerto Rico which was to provide that testing-ground of America's intentions toward a newly acquired colonial possession differing in language, cultural tradition, and ethnic background from the people of the United States. There the question was not on what terms America would depart but on what conditions America would remain. When U.S. troops landed on the island in 1898, their commander, General Nelson A. Miles, told the islanders that the Americans had come "to bring protection," "to promote prosperity," and to bestow "the blessings of the liberal institutions of our government." In effect, by the Foraker Act passed in 1900 Congress set up a civil government for Puerto Rico resembling a British Crown colony—a governor and council (or upper house) appointed by the President, and the lower house of the legislature elected by the people. Native reformers, pressing for an elective upper house and American citizenship, secured both demands from Congress in the Jones Act of 1917.

Although Puerto Rico had been granted a measure of self-government, economic benefits arising from association with the United States did not quickly materialize. Instead, it seemed rooted in the poverty and filth which had been its lot for generations. A major socioeconomic grievance stemmed from the failure of the United States to enforce a provision in the Foraker Act, repeated in the Jones Act, forbidding the ownership of more than five hundred acres of land in Puerto Rico. In point of fact most of the best land was operated by large-scale corporate enterprises, partly owned and partly leased by the operating companies.

An apostle of the "Good Neighbor" policy, Franklin Delano Roosevelt promptly put an end to unilateral intervention in Latin America by the United States. He believed profoundly in Western Hemisphere cooperation both for economic and defense ends. Concerned as he was with the entire Caribbean area, with the necessity for effecting social and economic changes in the British Crown colonies as well as in Puerto Rico,[54] Roosevelt initiated in the 1940's a program of reform in Puerto Rico which has not run its course. The territorial government began the condemnation and purchasing of landholdings in excess of five hundred acres, redistributing land to independent farmers and landless farm workers. Most significant was the program called "Operation Bootstrap," by which the government encouraged new industries by granting tax exemptions. "Operation Bootstrap" made Puerto Rico a model for the industrialization of underdeveloped nations. Finally, Puerto Rico was lifted from territorial status to the status of a commonwealth associated with the United States by its own desire and consent emphatically recorded in election after election. The commonwealth formula proved a neat solution of objections to taxation without representation. Although Puerto Ricans do not have a vote in Congress (where they are represented by an elected Resident Commissioner), they do not have to pay any federal taxes. Furthermore, all customs and excise taxes collected in Puerto Rico by the United States are turned over to the Puerto Rican treasury.

To date Puerto Rico's commonwealth status has survived the onslaughts of the *independistas,* the champions of statehood, and Castroite infiltration. Its success to date is a

54. See Rexford G. Tugwell, *The Stricken Land* (Garden City, N.Y., 1947), pp. 128–132 *et seq.,* 322.

tribute to the inventive and flexible approach which has more recently characterized America's relations with its overseas dominions.

Puerto Rico, if not the Philippines as well, proves that Americans are not comfortable in the role of colonial rulers. Although they have consistently renounced the intent to suppress and exploit,[55] their critics view their massive overseas investments as neo-imperialism and their humanitarian concern with raising the living standards of less fortunate nations as "welfare imperialism." Granted that the role of imperialist ruler is antipathetical to her own revolutionary traditions which stubbornly persist, it must be conceded that America has proven less tolerant of Latin-American revolutions which endanger her security as the United States chooses to define it. As a result, time after time America's own revolutionary traditions have been placed in seeming juxtaposition to the more thoroughgoing social revolutions carried out by a few Latin-American states in the twentieth century. These Latin-American revolutions have taken two forms—the Mexican and the Cuban on the one hand (there are those who would take exception to pairing the two)—and the Chilean and Venezuelan on the other. In all of them the United States has played a formidable role, not always constructive, but one which must be considered if only briefly.

That basic social reforms have been a crying need in Latin America in modern times no one can deny. Land monopoly, inequitable taxation, enormous poverty, and widespread corruption provide the seedbeds of social revolt. Back in 1758 Voltaire had Candide remark, "So you have already been to Paraguay?" "Indeed I have," replied Cacambo. "It's a wonderful system they have. . . . The people own nothing."

55. See Whitney T. Perkins, *Denial of Empire: The United States and Its Dependencies* (Leyden, 1962).

Perhaps the first Latin-American country in the twentieth century to do something about this basic inequality and poverty was Uruguay. Under that remarkable statesman José Batlle y Ordóñez, Uruguay in the ten or a dozen years following 1905 became a welfare state, vying with the Scandinavian nations. Widespread social security and retirement plans, nationalization of utilities, along with the maintenance of private capitalistic enterprises were and still are its landmarks, although its administration of these policies of state paternalism with its curious pluralistic presidency (inspired by the Swiss example), only recently supplanted by a single head of state, runs far short of perfection.[56]

Uruguay's welfare state antedated by several years the Mexican Revolution, but it is the latter that has been the more highly publicized and has pointed the direction for other Latin-American states. Mexico's revolution broke out in November, 1910, when the democratic reformer, Francisco I. Madero, the "Apostle of the Mexican Revolution," led a movement which by May of the following year had forced the dictator Díaz to resign and brought about the establishment of a liberal government. One might argue that the revolution was long overdue since the great movement of the *Reforma* in Mexico of the mid-nineteenth century had failed to bring about a real redistribution of property. In fact, by the end of the Díaz regime the landed estate had swallowed the landowning village and the landless were more numerous than ever before.[57] An advocate of democracy and an opponent of strong-arm rule of past days, Madero confessed that he derived inspiration from Washington and Jefferson, from Andrew Jackson and John Quincy

56. Frederick Pike, ed., *Freedom and Reform in Latin America* (South Bend, Ind., 1959), Ch. VI.

57. Humphreys, *Tradition and Revolt*, pp. 15, 16; G. M. McBride, *The Land System of Mexico* (New York, 1923), p. 155.

Adams. If there was a "spirit of '76" at any time in Mexico's history, it was manifested in the year 1910 when Madero rallied the people against Díaz. The administration of President Taft quickly recognized Madero's government, but, tragically, Madero was assassinated by agents of that saturnine alcoholic, the reactionary General Victoriano Huerta, who seized power and held it amid revolutionary upheaval. Although European powers recognized Huerta, President Taft, despite pressure by American business interests, and his successor Woodrow Wilson both refused. Wilson quickly outlined a policy of cooperating with only such governments as rested upon the undoubted consent of the governed. Thus, from the best of motives and with the aim of promoting a true revolution Wilson initiated a practice of judging other people's revolutions and military coups by North American standards—a holier-than-thou attitude appropriate to a people who assume that America is not only the arsenal of democracy but the chosen guardian of moral values. This point of view was to get America into difficulties at Versailles in 1919, and countless other times in the years thereafter. Meantime, as a result of our provocative intervention, whether to punish Huerta or to chase Pancho Villa, Carranza's enemy, we only succeeded in arousing the antagonism of most Mexicans and even of Carranza himself. Finally, with war with Germany looming, we withdrew from Mexico and recognized the constitutional regime set up under the new Mexican Constitution proclaimed on February 5, 1917.

The date of that Mexican Constitution is significant because some choose to discover the hand of the Bolsheviks in Mexico's social revolution. In fact, the Kerensky government did not take office in Russia until May, 1917, and the Bolsheviks only as a result of the famous "October Revolution." Thus, on any count the Mexican Revolution takes precedence over the Russian. Regardless of foreign influence, the Mexicans in their new Constitution of 1917 assured the state a positive, active role in social and economic spheres. That charter provided for universal suffrage, the curbing of foreign ownership of lands, mines, and oil fields; it restricted the power and property of the Church and monastic orders and established the eight-hour day, a minimum wage, and the breakup of large estates, with compensation by the government to the owners, and redistribution to the landless. It is to be noted that the economic reforms kept Mexico within the capitalist framework. Instead of embracing collectivism, the reforms served to extend the benefits of the ownership of private property by means of a vast redistribution program. Aside from such innovations, the Mexican Constitution paid deference to the American in its reaffirmation of the principles of representative government, in continuing the classic division of powers, in guarantees to the individual and his property, and in its federalism, which even in subsequent constitutions is closely modeled upon the United States example.[58] Finally, the earlier revolution was implemented by the reforms that were instituted by Cárdenas who, on assuming office in December, 1934, pressed a Six-Year Plan of land reform and expropriated the properties of foreign oil companies. His regime represented the apogee of radical reformism.[59] By the time the Mexican

58. J. L. Mecham, "The Origins of Federalism in Mexico," in *Hispanic American Historical Review*, XVIII (1938), 164–182.

59. For studies of the Mexican Revolution see Anita Brenner and George Leighton, *The Wind that Swept Mexico* (New York, 1943); J. Lloyd Mecham, "An Appraisal of the Mexican Revolution," in A. Curtis Wilgus, ed., *The Caribbean at Mid-Century* (Gainesville, Fla., 1951), pp. 170–201; Howard Cline, *The United States and Mexico* (Cambridge, 1953); *Mexico, Revolution to Evolution, 1940–1960* (New York, 1963); Frank Tannenbaum, *Mexico, The Struggle for Peace and Bread* (New York, 1956); Jesus S. Herzog, "Un ensayo sobre la revolución mejicanas," in Benjamin Keen, ed., *Readings in Latin American Civilization* (Boston, 1955), p. 364; John Womack, Jr., *Zapata and the Mexican Revolution* (New York, 1968).

Revolution had spent its force the standing order had been completely uprooted.

Compared to Mexico's, Cuba's recent social revolution seems far more tumultuous and the involvement of the United States far more controversial. That revolution quickly destroyed the old military apparatus and eliminated the island as a base for foreign (which was chiefly American) capital investment. The evidence is still not in as to whether its program for land redistribution has been moving at a more rapid pace than Mexico's, as to the extent to which the state has both in law and in fact supplanted the foreign plantation owners. Of Fidel Castro's philosophy we now have a rather full record, because of all recent revolutionaries he is the most tediously verbose. His Marxist-Leninist leanings were suspected but not proven prior to his achieving power, but today we can have no doubts.

What united Cubans of various political views behind Castro was his uninhibited hatred of the United States, an anti-Americanism whose roots can be traced to the Cuban patriot José Martí and the Spanish-American War. Hard indeed is the fate of a liberator, a truism brought home to Americans by more massive and more recent involvements. While Cuban nationalism may have had indigenous roots, with Castro's advent, and especially after the Bay of Pigs, positive models for the new Cuba were sought in Soviet theory and practice or in the collectivization of Mao's revolutionary China. Beyond and above this, Fidel's Cuba has now chosen for itself a place of leadership in the "national liberation movement," and it now has a new martyr in the person of Che Guevara. Whether this turning of a basically anti-American reform movement into a full-blown Communist, Soviet-oriented revolution was inevitable or the result of errors of American policy can be endlessly debated. Castro certainly is not of the "spirit of '76" but rather an assembly-line model of Russia's Bolshevik Revolution, with an authentic mixture of class war, the suppression of all opposition, expropriation without compensation, and revolutionary evangelism, the last of which has moved Cuba closer to Red China and Albania than to Moscow.[60]

To those who regard Cuba as conclusive proof that the formalistic shell of America's democratic institutions is no longer exportable to Latin America, one might suggest a look at Chile, which has managed to create a social revolution while at the same time holding out some safeguards to private property as well as inducements to foreign capital. For a country that came close to voting itself Communist in 1964, the only hemisphere republic ever to do so, that nation has managed to evolve such a formula under Eduardo Frei Montalva, who won the presidency by defeating an avowed Marxist candidate. Frei, a modest, dedicated intellectual in the F.D.R. tradition of reform, or more directly deriving his ideas from the liberal European Catholic movement, stands today as the principal exponent in South America of the hypothesis that reform by the moderate Left is the best means of forestalling extremist revolution. Building on the genuine progress achieved under the Alessandri regime in such areas as tax and land reform, Frei has made his program distinctive by the Chileanization (or partial nationalization) of copper—really a partnership between the Chilean government and the powerful North American copper companies. As the Anaconda agreement of 1969 reveals, such a partnership means in fact progressive nationalization with-

60. See Robert F. Smith, *The United States and Cuba: Business and Diplomacy, 1917–60* (New York, 1960); Richard H. Fagan, "Mass Mobilization in Cuba," *Journal of International Affairs*, XX (1966), 254 *et seq.*; Theodore Draper, *Castroism: Theory and Practice* (New York, 1965); C. Wright Mills, *Listen Yankee: The Revolution in Cuba* (New York, 1960); Maurice Zeitlin, *Revolutionary Politics and the Cuban Working Class* (Princeton, N.J., 1961).

out the sting of outright expropriation and confiscation. In addition, Frei has pressed ahead with land and tax reform, and formulated a new labor code, including the unionization of rural workers.[61] Whether Frei's middle-of-the-road program will survive the onslaughts of a revivified leftist opposition is problematical, but a stable and prosperous Chile embarked on a revolution by gradualism offers the best alternative to Castroism. Similarly, in Venezuela the proponents of democratic revolution have demonstrated the inherent virtues of their program. There Rómulo Betancourt, who as an exile in Puerto Rico sat at the feet of Muñoz Marín, instituted planned economic development and social reforms, in the face of guerrilla terror from the Left and army pressures from the Right. Not only did the Betancourt program vitalize democracy, but it held out more assurance for economic development than the extremist solutions recently adopted in Peru or Bolivia.[62]

If the underdeveloped nations of the Western Hemisphere are to be transformed through a revolution by gradualism in preference to the Soviet or Maoist models, then these nations, in collaboration with the United States, must utilize the tools at hand. Such tools have been offered by the Alliance for Progress, a proposal to lift an entire continent into the modern age. First advanced by Brazil's Kubitschek in 1958, the conception was eloquently restated three years later by President John F. Kennedy.[63]

The Alliance for Progress is rooted in the conviction that, as Kennedy put it, "political freedom must be accompanied

61. Leonard Gross, *The Last Best Hope: Eduardo Frei and Chilean Democracy* (New York, 1967).

62. Keith Botsford, "Venezuela: Revolution and Counter-revolution," in Irving Howe, ed., *A Dissenter's Guide to Foreign Policy* (New York, 1968), pp. 314–330.

63. *Department of State Bulletin*, April 3, 1961.

by social change." That there has been profound disillusionment with the progress of the Alliance has recently been brought home to North Americans by the outburst of *La Violencia* and anti-Yankeeism triggered by Governor Nelson Rockefeller's fact-finding mission to Latin America. That such disillusionment may be put down in part to the overambitious scope of the *Alianza* and the euphoric expectations it aroused, must be conceded in all fairness. Nonetheless, those who are dedicated to democratic solutions recognize that the *Alianza* must not be permitted to fail. To assure both democracy and political stability in Latin America, population controls must be instituted, equitable taxation enacted and enforced (a difficult task in the light of the resistance of the "haves" to acceptance of even modest tax burdens), land must be redistributed without reducing holdings to tiny uneconomical plots ("Haitianization"), or the income of rural workers stepped up by the unionization of farm workers (an achievement which has boosted Hawaii's farm workers to enviable wage levels). Moreover, despite evidence of recent domestic capital formation, private capital is still needed and must find continuing inducements to maintain its invested position in Latin America, even though the rewards must necessarily be more circumscribed than in the past, and aid must go directly to the people, not primarily to the governments.[64]

Despite recent progressive innovation and reforms and a challenging program of collective action on paper, Latin America's socioeconomic problems remain pervasive and frustrating. Their resolution by prompt and peaceful reform poses the only alternative to violent change in an authoritarian direction. For its own problems Latin America cannot evade its central responsibility by finding a convenient whip-

64. See Robert F. Kennedy, *To Seek a Newer World* (Garden City, N.Y., 1967), pp. 64–67, 76–77.

ping boy in the much-caricatured Uncle Sam. The breach that exists, as Colombia's President Carlos Lleras Restrepo has perceptively observed, is one between the industrialized and the less-developed countries. All the industrialized nations must assume their share of the burden to promote development in Latin America and other undeveloped nations, not the United States alone. If capital is needed to fill that breach, Latin America must manage to hold out inducements to capital comparable to those offered by Puerto Rico in "Operation Bootstrap," inducements buttressed by more durable and less capricious governmental systems. The regional common markets that it is in the process of setting up deserve expansion and implementation. In turn, as the Rockefeller Report has recommended, the industrial nations should join the United States in granting preferential tariffs to all developing countries and dollar debt payments may well be deferred to the extent that the underdeveloped nations are prepared to expend comparable amounts of their own currency for social and economic development. Finally, at a time of burgeoning nationalism in Latin America, with strident anti–North American overtones, it is important for the United States to demonstrate by example as well as by reminder that it shares with other nations of the Western Hemisphere a revolutionary and an anticolonial tradition, and that its concern is less with its own security than with improving the quality of life of all the peoples of this hemisphere.

Most exposed to the contagion of the American revolutionary spirit and the American way of life through daily contacts, movies, television, periodicals, books, and enormous economic penetration lies the neighbor on the United States' northern flank. Yet Canada alone, of all the nations of the New World, has managed to avoid a revolution to date.

In seeking an answer to what seems the riddle of the hemisphere, we might first of all pay obeisance to those prudent American peace commissioners who declined to press upon England Benjamin Franklin's and Congress's original demand for Canada. America settled for less and preserved national unity. Had Canada been joined to the United States, we would have had a conglomerate state of two cultures—one Anglo-Protestant and anticlerical, and the other French Catholic, with values largely inimical to those cherished by the majority. We would have had dangerous sectionalism in our midst before we had the chance to establish national unity. To compound our difficulties, we would have inherited a group of Loyalist refugees, implacable in their hatred of the American Revolution and dedicated to the proposition that all men were not born equal nor were they endowed by their creator with the unalienable rights to life, liberty, and the pursuit of happiness. In other words, we would have started the nation lacking a political or cultural consensus. Such ominous beginnings might well have doomed the entire experiment to failure.

Instead, a people less intolerant of economic inequality or social stratification, a people whose tradition is not of a glorious revolution but rather of a little revolt in 1837 that was quickly snuffed out, have found a certain unity in their traditional anti-Americanism. The roots of that anti-Americanism can be traced not to the French habitants, who remained sullenly neutral during the American Revolution,[65] but to the thousands of fiery British Loyalist immigrants who went into Upper Canada, Nova Scotia, and New Bruns-

---

65. See, most recently, Gustave Lanctot, *Canada and the American Revolution, 1774–1783*, trans. by Margaret M. Cameron (Cambridge, Mass., 1967). For intrigues of the French Revolutionary government to arouse the French-Canadians to revolt, see T. S. Webster, "A New Yorker in the Era of the French Revolution," New-York Historical Society, *Quarterly*, LIII (1969), 251–272.

wick. On this more hospitable soil these emigrés sought to erect a conservative social edifice that they had failed to maintain in the rebellious states from which they had fled.[66] To the residents of Upper Canada, mindful of American expansionism at the time of the War of 1812, the American and French Revolutions were regarded as "masks for oppression," and America's revolutionary evangelism foreboded the subversion of legitimate authority in the name of liberty.

The American Civil War proved a catalyst to Canadian confederation of the discordant provinces of Upper and Lower Canada. What brought them together was the awareness of the military might of the Union armies. "Look around you to the valley of Virginia," exhorted the Irish-Canadian patriot Thomas D'Arcy McGee in 1864, "look around you to the mountains of Georgia, and you will find reason enough."[67]

Even as late as the twentieth century Canadians were fearful that the United States was "waiting to gobble us up." In 1909 Oliver Asselin reminded his Canadian readers that "the amiable Nation of Pirates which stole Texas, Cuba, Puerto Rico, and the Philippines cannot be depended on to act justly towards a weaker nation."[68] What exercised the Canadians most about America was not its expansionism, however, but the nature of its democratic society, with its

66. Seymour Martin Lipset, *Revolution and Counter-Revolution—The United States and Canada*, reprinted in Thomas R. Ford, ed., *The Revolutionary Theme in Contemporary America* (Lexington, Ky., 1955), pp. 38–42.

67. Quoted in Peter B. Waite, *The Life and Times of Confederation, 1864–1867* (Toronto, 1962), p. 28. For differences in constitutional structure between Canada and the U.S., see J. A. Williams, "Canada and the Civil War," in H. Hyman, ed., *Heard Round the World* (New York, 1969), pp. 284–289.

68. Oliver Asselin, *A Quebec View of Canadian Nationalism* (Montreal, 1909), p. 19. For a recent review of Canadian attitudes, see S. F. Wise and Robert C. Brown, *Canada Views the United States* (Seattle, 1967).

strident party politics, its sectionalism, mobbism, and whole-
sale acceptance of hordes of non-English immigrants from
Continental Europe.

There is another side to the coin in Canada, however improbable it might seem. As Gustave Lanctot, a most recent
specialist on French Canada has noted, the Canadian population during the American Revolution was exposed to an
"American indoctrination" which "taught the Canadians
their political alphabet and gave them their first lesson in
constitutional law." That lesson was not forgotten. The constitutional reformers of the 1830's admired the technique
exemplified by the provisions in American state constitutions
for constitutional revision. In Upper Canada William Lyon
Mackenzie recognized the merits of the example of the
United States to those like himself who wished to modify
colonial rule in Canada. Although the armed outbreak of
December, 1837, against colonial rule was easily suppressed,
the insurrectionaries found a good deal of support on the
United States side of the border, notably in New York and
Vermont. It was Congress which clamped down by blocking
up holes in the neutrality law, but the American people were
on the side of the rebellion. In the aftermath of the rebellion
a good deal of sentiment for annexation to the United States
appeared in the 40's among certain elements of both the
English-speaking and the French population of Canada.

The United States Constitution was carefully scrutinized
by the members of the Quebec Constitutional Conference of
1864. The American Civil War served to discredit states'
rights advocates in Canada and buttressed the case of the
Hamiltonian-minded nationalists.[69] Indeed, the confederation plan embodied in the British North America Act bore a

---

69. Joseph Pope, ed., *Confederation: Being a Series of Hitherto Unpublished Documents Bearing on the British North America Act* (Toronto,
1895), pp. 86–87.

striking resemblance to the suggestions submitted by Hamilton to the Philadelphia Convention on June 18, 1787. Among Hamilton's proposals which the Convention rejected but the Canadians copied were the grant of residual powers to the federal government rather than the other way around, life terms for senators, a federal veto over state laws, and the appointment of state executives by the federal government.[70]

That century-old Canadian unity, Hamiltonian in inspiration, is now strangely troubled by the threat posed by a romantic French nationalism, a manifestation of sturdy cultural independence founded on solid socioeconomic grievances and yet conveying political overtones quite anachronistic in our Nuclear Space Age and not in tune to the economic realities of eastern Canada.[71] Tied to separatism, with its strong cultural roots, is a rising demand for a republican system.

Republicanism and radical reformism among French Canadians have long lain dormant, only occasionally to surface under unusual provocation. One such catalyst was the American Revolution. Disaffected both from their *seigneurs* and from the British government, the *habitants* seemed ready to rise. But the failure of the American invasion of Canada snuffed out the sparks of revolutionary ardor. Again, under the stimulus of the European Revolutions of 1848, French-Canadian radicalism in the form of the Rouge movement—combining notions of political democracy, nationalism, and anticlericalism—gained ground for a decade or so, and then went into eclipse. Radical republicanism, with some tradi-

70. See William P. M. Kennedy, *The Constitution of Canada, 1534–1937* (London, 1938), p. 414; Lynn H. Parsons, "Federalism, the British Empire and Alexander Hamilton," *New-York Historical Society Quarterly,* LII (1968), 65–69.

71. See Seymour Martin Lipset, *The First New Nation* (New York, 1967), pp. 286, 287.

tional American overtones, is one element in the French Canadian ferment of the present day, which finds antimonarchists in the ranks of both Quebec separatists and federationists, while Quebec Liberals have put themselves on record in favor of the republican system.[72] Perhaps at long last those French Canadians whose ancestors Congress wooed assiduously but ineffectively back in 1775 have come to recognize the enduring political values of the American Revolutionary tradition, which they have distrusted for so long.

Whether or not republicanism holds the answer to Canada's difficulties, American federalism has special relevance.[73] What Canada seems to require is a system that will confer upon the Canadian federal government power adequate to cope with ever growing national problems while reserving to the provinces the autonomy that Canada's bicultural society and Quebec's unique situation demand. Obviously English centralization, which has proved ineffective in the mother country in coping with the burgeoning nationalism of Scot and Welshman, does not provide the solution.

72. See Kenneth D. McRae, "The Structure of Canadian History," in Louis Hartz, ed., *The Founding of New Societies: Studies in the History of the United States, Latin America, South Africa, and Australia* (New York, 1964), pp. 235–238.

73. It provided precedents, for example, for the Australian federal system. See Carl J. Friedrich, *The Impact of American Constitutionalism Abroad* (Boston, 1967), p. 61.

V

THE AMERICAN REVOLUTION
AND THE EMERGING NATIONS
OF AFRICA AND ASIA

IT IS ONE of the ironies of our time that the nation which achieved its independence in the first great anticolonial revolution of the modern world should now be castigated by its critics for assuming the mantle of colonialism so abruptly dropped by other Western powers. If the American presence in Africa and Asia today prompts such charges, it should be remembered by those who would set the balance true that America can boast both an anticolonial tradition and an equally strong expansionist and imperialist streak. The imperialist urge was a late manifestation, however. There was little evidence of it in the early days of the republic.

The Revolutionary Patriots, especially those who were concerned about the palpable injustice of the institution of Negro slavery, had little sympathy with the exercise of colonial rule over native peoples by the European powers. While the first American merchant ship in the Chinese trade was preparing to return from Canton to New York, John Jay, one month from formally taking up his duties as Secretary for Foreign Affairs, was turning his thoughts to the condition of the exploited natives of India. He advised his liberal-minded Anglo-American friend Benjamin Vaughan that "the India business never appeared to me a difficult one. Do justice, and all is easy; cease to treat those unhappy nations as slaves, and be content to trade with them as with other independent Kingdoms. On such an event advantageous tho' fair treaties might be made with them." Jay added, "Your tribute, indeed, would be at an end, but it ought not to have had a beginning; and I wish it may ever prove a curse to those who impose and exact it in any country."[1] Thus, at the very moment when the British were entrapping India into serving as the foundation of a Second British Empire to replace the American they had just lost, one Revolutionary Patriot served notice that some Americans would never be reconciled to colonialism in Asia.

Indeed, some Americans never were. On the eve of the decision of the Monroe administration to recognize the new states of Spanish America, Secretary of State John Quincy Adams stated in a letter to Edward Everett, the editor of the influential *North American Review,* that the anticolonial principle that he had expounded looked forward to the downfall of the British Empire in India. Adams went on to denounce colonial establishments as incompatible with America's political institutions, and to urge upon the human family the duty to abolish colonial establishments as it was already abolishing the slave trade.[2] In enunciating these novel principles, Adams put the United States squarely behind the aspirations of all colonial peoples everywhere.

John Quincy Adams had some grand impulses, expansive, humanitarian, and liberal, and it has taken the rest of his countrymen more than a century to catch up with him. Once the United States entered World War II President Franklin Delano Roosevelt urged Winston Churchill to establish an

1. John Jay to Benjamin Vaughan, November 30, 1784. Jay Papers, Special Collections, Columbia University Libraries.
2. John Quincy Adams, *Writings,* ed. by C. F. Adams, VII, 200.

independent, federated India. More than that, Roosevelt unilaterally proclaimed that the principles of the Atlantic Charter extended also to the Pacific and Indian Oceans and everywhere else on earth. Churchill bided his time. Then with the turning point of the war, following in quick succession El Alamein, the stand of the Red Army at Stalingrad, and the smashing naval victory of the United States at Guadalcanal, Churchill declared on November 9, 1942: "Let me, however, make this clear, in case there should be any mistake about it in any quarter. We mean to hold our own. I have not become the King's First Minister in order to preside over the liquidation of the British Empire."[3]

Churchill might hurl defiance right and left, but the winds of change were already sweeping the world, and an American President had given a great psychological lift to the forces of decolonization. Another Secretary of State, John Foster Dulles, speaking to the nation during the Indochina crisis on May 7, 1954, reaffirmed Adams' support for colonial liberation everywhere when he declared, "The United States, as the first colony in modern history to win independence for itself, instinctively shares the aspirations for liberty of all dependent and colonial peoples. We want to help and not hinder the spread of liberty. We do not seek to perpetuate Western colonialism." Administrations come and administrations go, but it is safe to predict that no American administration in the foreseeable future is likely to repudiate Dulles' anticolonial professions. What in fact does the historic record show?

First of all, despite America's long tradition of anticolonialism, despite the wave of sympathy that swept the United States in behalf of the African and Asian liberation movements which mounted in full fury in the years since World War II, Americans have managed to put a checkrein on their

---

3. Robert E. Sherwood, *Roosevelt and Hopkins* (New York, 1948), p. 656.

instinctive libertarian feelings. They did so, first, out of consideration for some of America's NATO allies, whose colonial empires were so rapidly dismembered, and, secondly, in calculated assessment of the new balance of colonial power which might well tip the scale in the Cold War. If our immediate concern was less with liberty than with winning the emergent states over to the Free World side, Americans are perhaps no whit different today than in 1823, when they stood foursquare behind a Monroe Doctrine which put national interest ahead of all other considerations.

In the eyes of the African, America stands as the classic symbol of a land of freedom rather than as an activist force for the liberation of native peoples. Kwame Nkrumah touchingly evoked the memory of America to Africans. As he was leaving the United States in 1945 after ten years of study and hardship, and as his ship passed the Statue of Liberty, Nkrumah vowed through misty eyes, "I shall never rest until I have carried your message to Africa." Now, opinions may differ as to the kind of liberty the *Osagyefo*, or Redeemer, brought to Ghana. His totalitarian, one-party regime, with its censorship, deportations, and prolonged imprisonment without trial for political opponents may have been an exemplification of "scientific socialism," but it certainly was not bourgeois American democracy. In his enforced exile in Guinea, Nkrumah has plenty of time to meditate on the semantic meanings of "liberty."

Africa has always lain on the conscience of America, but like other matters that trouble one's conscience, it is more comfortable to push them back into the furthermost recesses of one's mind. Until 1808, Americans had been the beneficiaries of the execrable slave trade, and some Americans continued for years thereafter to profit from the illegal barter in human beings from Africa. Men of conscience from New England and Quaker merchants from Philadelphia had long vied with English businessmen in plying the lucrative slave trade, upon which Southern plantation prosperity came to be so perilously amassed. Indeed, it is a conventional viewpoint to consider the early Americans as Anglo-Americans, or at least transplanted Europeans, while in fact more than a fifth of the population that made up the rebellious Thirteen Colonies were either unwilling immigrants from the west coast of Africa or claimed African origin.

Men of good will sought to end the slave system, but what to do with the ex-slaves was a moot point. In the belief that Africans could not adapt to the American way of life, a serious colonization movement, supported by a number of American Presidents, was launched. Sponsored by the American Colonization Society, the movement won enthusiastic support. For a time everyone was for it, save, with few exceptions, the Negroes themselves.

The colonization movement is less important for the results it achieved than for the negative attitude toward racial integration in America which it exemplified and for its thinly concealed imperialist notions. Dreamers like Jehudi Ashmun, the agent of the American Colonization Society in Africa, envisaged an American colonial empire stretching for a vast distance along Africa's west coast. John H. B. Latrobe, who devoted many years to the colonization project, made no secret of his conviction that time was on the side of the United States in supplanting European rivals in Africa because America could pour thousands upon thousands of "pilgrims" upon the African continent, where the climate was as congenial as was New England for the earlier Pilgrims.[4]

Any danger that the colonization movement might at the start have established an American colonial empire in Africa

4. *African Repository*, III, 331.

was quickly scotched by John Quincy Adams, that stalwart humanitarian and anti-imperialist. It was unconstitutional for the United States to build and own colonies, Secretary of State Adams instructed the cabinet of President Monroe. For the government to purchase African territory was to take a step toward "engrafting" a "colonial establishment" on the Constitution.[5] Oddly enough, ex-President Jefferson, whose views on the strict construction of the Constitution stood out in sharp contrast to those of the nationalist President John Quincy Adams, was sympathetic to disbursing money for African colonization out of public land sales. If necessary, he would have settled the issue by constitutional amendment. In fact, the proposal to buttress the shaky fortunes of the American Colonization Society with federal funds appealed to a wide sector of public opinion. Nevertheless, congressional representatives from the cotton states, deeming colonization to pose an inherent threat both to the survival as well as to the extension of slavery, managed to block all such appropriation bills. To compound the difficulties of the Society, the rising abolitionist movement attacked colonization as a snare and deception designed to perpetuate the institution of slavery in America by drawing off free Negroes from the population.

Attacked by the enemies of slavery as well as by its defenders, lacking adequate funds, the colonization movement shriveled, and then was in effect abandoned. It could boast one accomplishment—the establishment of the state of Liberia, the only example of the direct transplantation of American institutions to Africa. Originally Liberia was merely a colony of the American Colonization Society, which scraped up enough funds to purchase a tract on the

5. C. F. Adams, ed., *Memoirs of John Quincy Adams* (Philadelphia, 1875), IV, 292–294.

west coast of Africa, and managed by the eve of the Civil War to colonize therein some fifteen thousand free Negroes, at the unimpressive rate of five hundred a year.[6] Thereafter, American colonizing efforts were directed to futile attempts to export the freedmen to Central America and the islands of the Caribbean, and the cause of African colonization perished. With its demise vanished the twin dreams of an African empire for America as well as an all-white America.

However stirred the American imagination may have been by Stanley's discovery of missionary-explorer Livingstone, it should be remembered that it was Leopold of Belgium, not an American President, who exploited that knowledge. However fascinated American readers may have been by the stirring stories of Paul Du Chaillu, the French explorer who was to become an American citizen, it was France, not America, which acted on and profited by his information. And it remained for British statesmen and businessmen to exploit the activities of Cecil Rhodes. The United States showed its concern for the African people, along with its interest in maintaining an open door for American commerce in Africa, by participating in the Berlin Conference of 1884–85, which laid down ground rules for the scramble by imperial powers for Africa, but President Cleveland declined to submit the Final Act of this Conference to the Senate because, as Secretary of State Bayard remarked, the United States was unprepared to accept political engagements "in so remote and undefined a region as that of the Congo Basin."[7] The United States also participated in the two conferences dealing with Morocco, held in Madrid in 1880 and in Al-

6. See the perceptive account in P. J. Staudenraus, *The African Colonization Movement, 1816–1865* (New York, 1961).

7. Gorge L. Beer, *The African Question at the Paris Peace Conference* (New York, 1923), p. 264.

geciras in 1906, but avoiding lasting engagements.[8] In short, America pretty consistently abstained from the imperialism business in Africa, private investment notwithstanding.

Poverty-stricken and neglected, Liberia drifted from colonial status to independence, although not without conforming to the ritualism laid down by the American Revolution. Under the leadership of its early patriot, Virginia-born Hilary Teague, Liberia issued a Declaration of Independence in 1847. It was, however, unlike Jefferson's in two respects. It came after, not before, the adoption of the American-style Constitution, drawn up by the American Colonization Society but duly adopted by a ratifying convention elected in Liberia. It was not concerned with proclaiming the right of revolution against tyranny, but rather with itemizing the reasons why the Negroes felt impelled to leave America, the land of their persecution.

The Liberian Declaration of Independence proved especially revealing about the attitude of these newly-settled "Liberians" toward the indigenous Africans, whose grievances are nowhere discussed. The Constitution implied that citizenship would not automatically be granted to the natives, that the objective of the colony was to benefit the immigrant Negro-American. For the native African, Liberia was to afford an inferior political status, with citizenship in effect open only to those who as children had been bound out to settlers for apprenticeship training.[9]

For Liberian leaders like Teague and Alexander Crummell, only the standards of the West could assure the success and prosperity of the people of West Africa. The settlers from America were to be the forerunners of a great imperial

8. See Rupert Emerson, *Africa and United States Policy* (Englewood Cliffs, N.J., 1967), p. 16.

9. For an illuminating account, see Robert W. July, *The Origins of Modern African Thought* (New York, 1967), pp. 93–100.

dream of introducing both Western civilization and Christianity among the native Africans. Only in the most limited sense can one say that the dream ever materialized. Today its chief beneficiaries are the twenty thousand Liberians claiming descent from the original colonizers from America. Forming a ruling elite, they constitute some 3 to 5 percent of the entire population, and their chief of state is that colorful Afro-American President William Vacanarat Shadrach Tubman. In Liberia, America seems omnipresent. Not only was the nation settled by Americans, but its capital, Monrovia, was named for President Monroe; it has another town called Philadelphia, a county called Maryland, American rubber and mining interests heavily concerned in its economy, a Liberian Frontier Force trained by American officers, and, to top it all, it has chosen for its national symbol a United States flag with one star only, and for its national currency the United States dollar. However, even though Liberia's Constitution is patterned closely on that of the United States and drawn up by a dean of the Harvard Law School and its laws were codified by Cornell professors, its government comes woefully short of achieving democracy. It has been aptly remarked that its tradition of one-party minority rule seems closer to that of White Mississippi than to the revolutionary tradition of the Founding Fathers.[10]

It is perhaps ironical that the only other colony of Afro-Americans on the west coast of Africa should have been settled by those who had adhered to a counterrevolutionary tradition. I am referring to the black Tory refugees who settled Sierra Leone. It was Britain's growing interest in the worldwide problem of slavery that culminated in the founding of the Sierra Leone refuge in 1787, a generation before the founding of Liberia. Originally settled by London's

10. See Raymond Leslie Buell, *Liberia: A Century of Survival* (Philadelphia, 1947); George Dalton, "History, Politics, and Economic Development in Liberia," *Journal of Economic History*, XXV (1965), 569–591.

black poor, the frail colony was quickly replenished by former slaves from the American colonies, who had escaped during the War for Independence and joined the British forces fighting in America. Instead of being returned to their owners as stipulated in the Treaty of Peace of 1783, they were mustered out and given free passage to Nova Scotia. There they found good farm land scarce, and the choicest pre-empted by the white Loyalists. Resented by the white community and reduced to the status of tenancy or landlessness, the Nova Scotia Negroes found a spokesman in Thomas Peters, who arranged with the philanthropist Granville Sharp for the emigration of some twelve hundred blacks from Halifax to Sierra Leone in January, 1792. Finding that their claims to land ownership were withheld and that they were being thrust back to a condition akin to the slavery that had once oppressed them, the Nova Scotians staged a short-lived rebellion against the government of Sierra Leone. How much the issues which precipitated the American Revolution had rubbed off on these black Tories is difficult, if not impossible, to determine, but they could hardly have been unaware of the parallel between the American issue of no taxation without representation and their own situation. In the long run it was British nineteenth-century bourgeois values which were to be cherished in Sierra Leone, and the American Revolution remained at best a dimly-remembered tradition.[11]

Otherwise, America's revolutionary traditions have been brought to Africa either directly by American Negroes, by African leaders educated in the United States, or more recently by the dedicated Peace Corps men and women who have put up their blackboards in remote hamlets from

11. See G. Halliburton, "The Nova Scotia Settlers of 1792," *Sierra Leone Studies*, N.S., No. 9 (December, 1957), pp. 16–25; Anthony Kirk-Greene, "David George: The Nova Scotia Experience," *loc. cit.*, No. 14 (December, 1960), pp. 93–120; July, *Modern African Thought*, pp. 48–66.

Upper Volta to Kenya, and whose more durable contribution it is doubtless too early to appraise.

In the generation prior to World War I, interest in Africa burgeoned among American Negroes, and it has today perhaps reached its highest point, with black Americans studying Swahili and pressing for the introduction in American educational institutions of a variety of courses in Afro-American history. Carter G. Woodson's *Journal of Negro History* made pioneer contributions to tying together the strands of African and American Negro cultural history. But it remained for Marcus Garvey to dramatize the Negro nationalist movement and its relation with Mother Africa. "We believe in the freedom of Africa for the Negro people of the world." "We also demand Africa for the Africans at home and abroad," he declared. Although Garvey's African colonization plans bogged down and he himself never set foot in Africa, he had a real impact on African and American Negro intellectuals. Kwame Nkrumah confessed that "the book that did more than any other to fire" his enthusiasm was *Philosophy and Opinions of Marcus Garvey,* published in 1923. One source credits Garvey with personally converting Jomo Kenyatta to the philosophy of Africa for the Africans.

Immeasurably important in quickening African nationalism were the efforts of the American Negro scholar and founder of the N.A.A.C.P., William E. B. Du Bois, who perhaps more than any other single individual contributed to sustaining the concept of Pan-Africanism until its maturation after World War II. Without credentials, Du Bois took it upon himself to have the voice of Africa expressed at the Versailles Peace Conference. In 1919 he convened a Pan-African Conference in Paris, attended by fifty-seven delegates from fifteen countries, including a dozen from nine African countries. The Congress issued a call for self-determination, "as fast as . . . development permits." Pan-African Congresses, American in conception, continued to meet abroad, and in New York, but it was the Manchester Conference of 1945, in which Du Bois was once more the moving spirit and at which Makonnen, Nkrumah, Jomo Kenyatta, and other prominent African intellectuals were present, that revealed the Marxist orientation of this movement.

Aside from Garveyism and leaders like Du Bois, an increasing number of Africans came to America to be educated. Kwame Nkrumah studied at Lincoln University, and later lectured there in philosophy, receiving graduate degrees both from Lincoln and the University of Pennsylvania. He then continued his studies in England, where he was recruited to serve as secretary of the United Gold Coast Convention, which sought independence by constitutional means. Secondly, he founded the Convention People's Party, with its catchy slogan, "Independence Now!" Another famous Lincoln University alumnus is Dr. Nnamdi Azikiwe, known more affectionately as "Zik." He and Nkrumah and other Africans had suffered from discrimination and poverty in the United States, but still retained their admiration for this country. In an address at Lincoln University in 1954 Zik remarked, "Claude McKay said that although the United States fed him with bread of bitterness and sank into his flesh its tiger's tooth, yet he loved this 'cultural hell.' Many times I have often felt that way too, but I have faith in this country as a bastion of democracy." He professed his faith both in the American democratic experiment and in the libertarian values held by Abraham Lincoln. Zik offered an ingenious explanation of why the outside world seems so critical of the shortcomings of American democracy. "Because of the universal respect in which America is held and its high esteem," he explained, "the outside world expects the United States, like Caesar's wife, to be beyond reproach, so far as respect for human dignity is concerned, bearing in mind 'the spirit of '76.'" The constitutional struggles and victories in which the N.A.A.C.P. has been involved, according to Zik, "have given the United States a fair chance of reconciling the theory of democracy with its practice in America. It has also fired the imagination of the sleeping African giant, who is now waking up and taking his rightful place in the comity of Nations. What a glorious victory for the American Negro!" That leading African intellectual, French-educated Leopold Sedar Senghor, was inspired by New York to write his poem, "To New York," which may be considered a manifestation of "negritude."

If in a general sense these critical new leaders of sub-Saharan Africa continued to look, as did Zik, to the "Spirit of '76," they also looked to the October Revolution, to Rousseau, John Stuart Mill, and a congeries of miscellaneous reformers and revolutionaries. There are still resemblances in the young African nations to the young American nation in the generation after 1776. There is a search for tradition, for symbols. African leaders have resurrected the glories of old. They have sought to instill in their nations a proud tradition of early nations and tribal leadership, of the medieval kingdoms of Ghana, Mali, and Songha, of nineteenth-century heroes such as the Basuto chief Moshesh and the Zulu conqueror Chaka, and to inculcate national pride in such commemorative events as the Fanti Confederation of 1871.[12]

African leaders started their movements of subversion as young men, young like most of the leaders of the American Revolution. As time has passed, these original leaders, the heroes of their revolutionary movements, find themselves

12. See Immanuel Wallerstein, *The Road to Independence: Ghana and the Ivory Coast* (The Hague, 1964), p. 156.

opposed by still younger post-independence leaders whose ideological commitments have reflected new goals.[13] An analogous ideological conflict between young and old has been uncovered among the American Federalist leaders themselves by a recent investigation.[14]

Secondly, while the New African state-builders generally have chosen the parliamentary system instead of the presidential system as found in our Constitution, they have paid more than lipservice to one of the essential features of that Constitution, which is federalism. It was tried in Nigeria, beginning with Sir Arthur Richards' Constitution of 1947 and the two more recent Constitutions.[15] It was believed that only a federal system could hold the discordant sections together and even that has tragically broken down as Ibo-speaking easterners have seceded and set up their own state of Biafra. Nevertheless, federalism may still be the only viable solution to separatist trends. Although it has temporarily failed in Nigeria, federalism still offers the best hope for the Congo, if that strife-torn state can manage to win back the allegiance of its dissident provinces.

Thirdly, they have drawn upon the experience of the United States in organizing a common market. Already three East African nations have established a common market, and three more are about to join.

Fourthly, they have built a one-party democracy not unlike that in the United States prior to the rise of the two-party system, although some of the new states make their one-party system explicit, while this country for a time side-

13. See Victor T. Le Vine, *Political Leadership in Africa* (Stanford, 1967).

14. David H. Fischer, *The Revolution of American Conservatism* (New York, 1965).

15. K. Onwuka Dike, *One Hundred Years of British Rule in Nigeria, 1851–1951* (Lagos, 1957), p. 43; Michael Crowder, *A Short History of Nigeria* (rev. ed., New York, 1966), pp. 273–288.

stepped the issue. Their essential aim has been to establish a national consensus through authoritarian methods, and it is hoped that democratic instincts will prevent them from moving down the road to totalitarianism.[16] Since 1965 a rash of military coups have resulted in supplanting, exiling, or even executing leaders of parties that had been in power since independence. In some cases this enforced change of leadership might well have taken place had there been a free electoral system and the opportunity to choose an alternative party. With neither option available, change when it comes is not likely to take place peacefully.[17]

The case for one-party democracy has been succinctly stated in the *Conscience Africaine* Manifesto. "Above all we do not want parties at present because what characterizes parties is conflict, while what we want is Union."[18] Could President Washington have put the matter more explicitly?

Fifthly, their notion of nonalignment is little different from the idea of neutrality which Hamilton voiced in the *Federalist* and which Washington expounded in the Farewell Address. The United States played off England against France and Spain with as blatant a display of self-interest as the new nations are playing the non-Communist bloc off against the Communists.

Finally, they are basically egalitarian and reject the separate-but-equal notions of the accommodation of the races which the Supreme Court of our own country has now held to be unacceptable. Indeed, the demand for racial equality is the most conspicuous attribute of African nation-

16. See Julius K. Nyerere, *Freedom and Unity* (London, 1967), pp. 195–203, 260–263; Wallerstein, *Road to Independence*, pp. 161, 162.

17. See L. Gray Cowan, *The Dilemmas of African Independence* (rev. ed., New York, 1968), pp. 11, 12, 19–24.

18. A. P. Merriam, *Congo: Background of Conflict* (Evanston, Ill., 1961), p. 328.

alism. The *Conscience Africaine* declared, "We reject with vehemence the principle of equal but separate. It is deeply offensive to us."[19]

If the United States' Constitution does not seem to have been the conscious model in most cases, it may be put down to the fact that so little was known about it in Tropical Africa, whose present-day leaders received much of their education under English or French colonial tutelage. And it must be conceded at the start that the British, much more than the French or the Belgians, and certainly the Portuguese, pursued a policy of training their Africans (at least their West Africans) for eventual self-government within the Commonwealth. One might argue that they would not have been so overflowing with disinterested magnanimity had they known that so many of the newborn states would quickly opt "out" of that same Commonwealth.

While leaders in sub-Saharan Africa have so frequently paid tribute to the "spirit of '76," if not to the letter of the constitutional system which emerged from the American Revolution, that spirit has proven entirely uncongenial to the strange and anachronistic world of South Africa. That republic, dedicated to the principle of *separate* but *unequal*, considers the American federal system and the American federal judiciary to be not only unsuitable but downright subversive. Instead, a unitary Constitution was adopted in 1910. Only in this way could the Boer faction be sure of supremacy over both the English and the nonwhite, a supremacy which they have managed to maintain to this day. Hence, there are no separate states, and no Supreme Court with the power to apply "due process" to the task of lifting the natives to their rightful place in South African life. For white supremacists, whether of the South African or the

19. *Ibid.*, p. 322.

American extremist brand, the Declaration of Independence and the American constitutional system are threatening instruments.[20] A strange exception to that rule is Rhodesia, whose present spokesmen consider the fight for self-determination and independence from Great Britain directly analogous to that fought by the Patriots of '76. That the people of the United States, or at least the majority, consider the American Revolution to be a continuous commitment to the notion of equality spelled out so eloquently in Jefferson's great Declaration, seems to be overlooked by Rhodesia's Prime Minister and the white minority which backs him.

The Moslem world of North Africa and the Middle East, to which freedom and independence have turned out at times to be self-destructive weapons, has in the past looked to the United States for something more than oil revenues, vast and indiscriminate though these dubious blessings have proven. The familiar tune "To the Shores of Tripoli" evokes memories of resolute operations in the years 1803–04, by America's young navy against the Tripolitan corsairs who had been preying upon American shipping in the Mediterranean, and again, by an American expedition in 1815, against piratical Algiers. An American squadron remaining in the Mediterranean for a time assured the safety of American commerce. More peaceful contacts with the Middle East were soon initiated by American archaeologists, whose contribution to the unearthing and interpreting of the region's priceless ancient treasures bolstered the pride of the states of the Middle East. Mission and educational operations conducted by Americans at American-run institutions like Robert College in Constantinople and the Syrian Protestant College (now the American University in Beirut)—both founded over a century ago—served to propagate West-

20. See C. W. de Kiewiet, "The Frontier and the Constitution of South Africa," in Conyers Read, ed., *The Constitution Reconsidered* (New York, 1938), pp. 336–338.

ern notions of freedom and independence. And how fruitful their teachings have been! It was Lebanese and Syrian Christians, trained at the American University, who introduced the Western seed of nationalism to Egypt, a seed which sprouted in Middle Eastern sands as Pan-Arabism.[21] Fragmented into separate nationalisms, Pan-Arabism achieved a new if dubious cohesion and an ever-dangerous belligerency with the emergence of the state of Israel. Exploited by the Soviet Union for its own objectives, Pan-Arabism has swept the Middle East from end to end since World War II. If a onetime American ambassador to Egpyt felt the diplomatic need to hail the Egyptian Revolution as an Oriental counterpart of the Spirit of '76, most Americans are not convinced that a Gamal Abdel Nasser is cut of the same piece of cloth as a Thomas Jefferson.[22]

In short, its anticolonial and nationalist manifestations notwithstanding, Pan-Arabism finds little relevance in the American Revolutionary tradition, but one of its offshoots, the Algerian nationalist movement, was not only heartened by America's anticolonial stance in World War II (as were other African independence movements) but offers some tantalizing analogies to the peace negotiations which led to American independence. Let us consider a few of these analogies.

Long and protracted were the parleys between the insurgent Americans and the British, as were those some years back between the French government and the Algerian rebels. The American commissioners, it must be remembered, sought not only independence but territorial integrity

21. E. A. Speiser, *The United States and the Near East* (Cambridge, Mass., 1950), pp. 238–239; and, most recently, James A. Field, Jr., *America and the Mediterranean World* (Princeton, N.J., 1969).

22. See Philip K. Hitti, *Islam and the West* (Princeton, N.J., 1962), pp. 91, 92; George E. Kirk, *A Short History of the Middle East* (7th rev. ed., New York, 1964), pp. 282, 283, 306–307.

and elbow room. One might compare their insistence upon the inclusion of the transappalachian West with the demands pressed by the Algerian nationalists to the French Sahara. America's case was perhaps no stronger, either juridically or morally, for it rested its claims to the West upon vague charter provisions conferred by the English Crown which it had repudiated, and these claims, like the Algerian, were not bolstered by effective military occupation. It must be borne in mind that the bulk of the territory George Rogers Clark had conquered in the Northwest had largely slipped away from America's grip by the close of the war. All the Great Powers opposed America's obtaining the West, and indubitably the claims of both Spain and England to that region were strong ones. But after a partition of the American continent, desired by everyone but America, the new republic would not have been left with a durable fragment. Similarly, the partition of Algeria according to the myriad of plans that were put forth, would not have assured the FLN a viable state, nor would the secession of Katanga or Oriental provinces have allowed the Congo the wherewithal to survive and prosper.

The Algerian negotiations suggest a still further analogy to the American Revolutionary settlement. In both sets of negotiations the Loyalists posed a thorny problem. The former comprised the American Tories, the latter the large European community in Algeria, contemptuously referred to by Frenchmen as *"pieds noires"*—the black feet. In both cases the rights and grievances of this substantial segment of the population loyal to the mother country threatened to prevent any agreement. Neither settlement effectively protected the Loyalists in fact, and both were followed by mass Loyalist emigration. The differences, however, are still more striking. The exodus of the Tories gave America a chance to build a nation on the basis of consensus, while the constant threat to the stability of the new Algerian government suggests that among the Arabs themselves there exists no real consensus as to what kind of government they do want. Furthermore, the departure of the European settler in Algeria left a vacuum both in professional and administrative skills and in technical competence that it will take at least a generation to fill.[23] That was not true of the North American Revolution, whose Tories possessed no monopoly of either wealth or talent. Unlike Algeria, which seems to have merely switched military guardians from France to the Soviet Union by winning its independence, the United States managed to free itself from Britain without leaving the back door open to any other foreign power.

One could properly challenge as strained the analogy between Mustafa Kemal's "Turkish Revolution" and its American predecessor. Regardless of its immediate inspiration, the Turkish Revolution accomplished in short order much that had been initiated long before in both the United States and France. It swept out the ruling dynasty, established a republic, separated church and state, abolished religious qualifications for voting and holding office, ended polygamy, and elevated the status of women. This extraordinary transformation, occurring within a relatively brief span of years,[24] stands as dramatic testimony to the impact upon Turkey of Western-style revolutionary goals.

And what, may we ask, of the American Revolutionary tradition in Israel? Like America, Israel, to which the United States has always had a special relationship, owed its

23. See Joseph Kraft, *The Struggle for Algeria* (Garden City, N.Y., 1961). For the impact of America's anticolonialism upon Ferhat Abbas, see Edgar O'Ballance, *The Algerian Insurrection, 1954–62* (Hamden, Conn., 1967), pp. 31, 32; upon West Africa, Michael Crowder, *West Africa under Colonial Rule* (Evanston, 1968), pp. 483, 484.

24. See Lewis V. Thomas and Richard N. Frye, *The United States and Turkey and Iran* (Cambridge, Mass., 1951). The models used were European rather than American—the Italian penal code, the Swiss civil code, and German commercial law.

origins to actions initiated in Great Britain, and like America, Israel was obliged to resort to force to terminate British control. Nonetheless, it should be borne in mind that in its origins, the state of Israel was conceived by Zionists like Herzl and Weizmann who admired the British constitutional system. Since the idea of a Jewish national home was spelled out in the Balfour Declaration of 1917, and since England operated the Palestine Mandate, the English models rather than the American might be expected to persevere. Ethical and social concepts from Bible and Talmud, from Enlightenment sources as well as socialist thought, contributed to the Jewish effort to build a life based on work, freedom, equality, and cooperation. When it was clear that the prospect of a Jewish national home held out by the Balfour Declaration was basically repudiated by the British White Paper of 1939, underground groups like the Irgut Zvai Leumi, and the Sternists—as well as the Haganah, the military arm of the Jewish Agency—found in the American and Irish revolutionary tradition encouragement for their revolt against British rule. Israel carried on its own War of Independence against both the British and the Arab states, and on May 14, 1948, issued its own Declaration of Independence. Its senior statesmen, impressed by Britain's constitutional experience, have governed without a formal written constitution or a bill of rights. However, within the democratic parliamentary republic of Israel a younger generation of politicians and political scientists are pressing demands for a written Constitution along the American model.[25] The religious issue, along with the tense military situation, have conspired to postpone for Israel her day of constitutionalism. The common

25. The United States by joint congressional resolution of June 30, 1922, endorsed the policy of the Jewish National Home; President Truman in 1945 voiced American public opinion in favor of settling Jewish refugees in Palestine, and recognized the Republic of Israel immediately upon learning that the new state had been launched.

interest of Israel and the United States in achieving a stabilized peace in the Middle East is calculated for the foreseeable future to tighten the bonds between the two peoples. In turn, this relationship may direct constitutional thinking in Israel toward the American constitutional experience and away from the British.

Since the establishment of the American nation there has always been an American presence in Asia, whether as trader, missionary, explorer, or diplomat. Americans have made their impact felt as benefactors and humanitarians, as businessmen, as conquerors and as liberators. But America's greatest impact has been reserved for the twentieth century, when, for a variety of reasons, the United States has played a central role in the reconstruction of five Asian states—the Philippines, Japan, Korea, Taiwan, and Vietnam, although the American Revolutionary tradition has not passed unnoticed elsewhere.

The first American presence, however, was relatively pacific and noninterventionist. Samuel Shaw, a Revolutionary artilleryman and merchant, sailed as supercargo on the *Empress of China* in 1784–85, and sent back to John Jay, Secretary for Foreign Affairs, an illuminating as well as amusing account of affairs in the port of Canton. Even before the first American ship arrived, the Chinese had learned from other sources the general facts of the American Revolution, which soon was a subject for the decorative arts on porcelain and wallpaper. There is no evidence that they regarded the advent of the "new nation" as specially relevant to them or perceived the dangers inherent in its revolutionary ideology.[26]

26. See Samuel Shaw to John Jay, May 19, 1785; Robert Morris to John Jay, May 19, 1785, Jay Papers, Columbia University Libraries, Special Collections. See also George H. Danton, *The Cultural Contacts of the United States and China* (New York, 1931).

Long before Americans had penetrated the bamboo curtain the Japanese had learned by way of the Dutch about the American Revolution. They also learned from a special report of 1809 to a Nagasaki high official how independence came about in America. It seems, according to the account, "a military official named Washington, and a civil official named Franklin promptly stood up [in their assembly] and declared, 'We must not lose this heaven-given opportunity. We must sever relations with the English forever.'" Then the account goes on to say that at a "general meeting in Philadelphia" Washington aspired to become the "highest official for a term of four years," which was renewed. It explains how the "sagacious" Hancock assisted Washington "in governing" and what equality meant in American society. According to this quaint account,

in the new Country there is no distinction of ruler and subject; only the difference between noble and base, high and low. The heads of the national, state, and county governments are different men, but they are all sovereigns in their respective positions. Now, their homes, their doings, their food and drink, and their clothing are not different from those of the common people. Of course, when they assume office they become clothed with authority, so the masses regard them with respectful fear. But this is only for a period of four years. Then, again, the officials are not designated from above, but are chosen, according to their ability, by ballot-casting among the people, those receiving many ballots being named to office.[27]

Contacts with Asia continued. In 1838 Lieutenant Wilkes headed a scientific expedition for the United States Navy which explored Pacific waters and reached Antarctica. By

27. Shunzo Sakamaki, *Japan and the United States, 1790–1853* (Tokyo, 1940), pp. 122, 133–134, 140–145.

the middle of the nineteenth century the march of Manifest Destiny had brought America to the western shores of the Pacific and had converted her into a Pacific power. Following a visit to Japan of Commodore Matthew Perry in 1853, His Imperial Highness made a treaty with the United States granting trade rights at two ports. At long last the bamboo curtain had been lifted.

Asians also saw a less pacific and less attractive side of the United States. In 1864 the United States made a token appearance with nine British, four Dutch, and three French warships in bombarding the Japanese city of Shimonoseki to reopen Japan to the West. America joined with Germany and England in carving up Samoa, but unlike Maria Theresa who reputedly wept when she accepted her share of Poland, we shed no tears. The United States seemed hell-bent for expansion. In the fateful year 1898, Americans engineered a revolution on the Hawaiian Islands which were then annexed to the United States; the Philippines, after an easy conquest from Spain, staged a revolt against her new conqueror, only to be subdued after several years of search-and-destroy operations. If America's new imperial ambitions seemed in contrast with its early national traditions, the fact was not lost on many notable dissenters. In any event, the new expansionism that seemed to be turning the Pacific into an American lake, coupled with a racist policy at home toward Chinese and Japanese immigrants and their descendants, were in combination poorly calculated to sell the American Revolutionary tradition abroad.

Some Asiatics were prepared to overlook the predatory posture of Uncle Sam, with its racist overtones, and to find in America's libertarian traditions and its constitutional system inspiring lessons for reshaping their own nations. In China constitutional reformers like K'ang Yu-wei sought a constitutional monarchy to serve as a transition from autocracy to democracy. While admiring the prosperity and contentment he found in the United States, K'ang rejected the United States' republican political system as unsuited to the Chinese people.[28] Contrariwise, revolutionaries like Sun Yat-sen felt more enthusiasm for the American example. Father of the Republic of China, Sun Yat-sen began preaching his gospel of national revolution as far back as 1885. Deeply immersed in the revolutionary traditions of England under Cromwell, of America under Washington, and of the French Revolution, he was in theory committed to democracy. Speaking of liberty, Sun Yat-sen remarked:

> In their wars Westerners extolled liberty to the skies and made it sacred; they even made a saying like "Give me liberty or give me death" their battle cry. Chinese students, in translating Western theories have introduced these words into China; they have upheld liberty and determined to fight for it.

Realistically, Sun Yat-sen added that "liberty develops as the power of the people develops," and that while the intellectuals had a Western enthusiasm for liberty, the mass of the people had little understanding of its meaning. Instead of the slogan, "Liberty, Equality, Fraternity," he preferred as the watchword of the Chinese Revolution, "People's Nationalism, People's Sovereignty, People's Livelihood," rather cynically observing as regards the last that "if we should propose making fortunes, all the people would welcome the call." In short, the liberty that Sun Yat-sen sought was to be secured for the nation rather than the individual, a marked difference from the ends of the American Revolution.

To the Chinese Communists the revolution that Sun Yat-sen instituted in 1911 had analogies to the American, in that

28. Kung-Chi'üan Hsiaio, *The Case for Constitutional Monarchy: K'ang Yu-Wei's Plan for the Democratization of China*, Institute of Pacific Relations China Council Series, No. 1 (Chungking, China, 1945).

they consider it a liberal-democratic bourgeois revolution, but Sun Yat-sen himself entertained certain reservations about the American Revolution as he did about Wilsonian idealism. Both had raised false hopes, he maintained. He was critical of the failure of the equality clause of the Declaration of Independence to be applied to the Negro. He then epitomized "the first American war" as "a war of the people for their own independence and equality," while he saw the Civil War as waged for the "equality of Negroes." Thus, in the long run, he found American history to be "a story of struggle for equality" and constituting "a shining page in the history of the world." Showing a considerable knowledge both of the history of the United States, the framing of the Constitution, and the party struggles of Jeffersonians and Hamiltonians, Sun Yat-sen regarded the American federal principle as inapplicable to China.[29]

If Sun Yat-sen was not prepared to reject the entire American example out of hand, his successor Yüan Shih-k'ai, as president of the phantom Chinese republic, was urged to reject the model of the American republic by one of his principal advisers, an American named Dr. Frank Goodnow. When, back in 1914, the Chinese republic was framing its constitutional system, Dr. Goodnow prepared a memorandum in which he insisted that the monarchical system was better suited to China than the republican, and that China was in fact ready only for a dictatorship.[30] His views at that time did not go unchallenged. The noted Chinese scholar, Liang Ch'i-chao, sought desperately to establish a republic.[31]

29. Sun Yat-sen, *San Min Chu I: The Three Principles of the People,* trans. into English by Frank W. Price (Shanghai, 1928), pp. 11, 121–179, *passim;* 189–193, *passim;* 201–216, *passim;* 226–234.

30. B. L. Putnam Weale, *The Fight for the Republic of China,* Ch. X.

31. Harold M. Vinacke, *A History of the Far East in Modern Times* (New York, 1946), pp. 241, 242.

As Sun Yat-sen's political heir and disciple, Chiang Kai-shek showed himself well informed about America's revolutionary traditions. To the American and French Revolutions he attributed the currents of the new era that brought democracy to the West and nationalism and independence (by which is meant opposition to Western colonialism) in the East.[32] Contrariwise, his adversary Mao Tse-tung, who finally brought about Chiang's expulsion from the Chinese mainland, used the American Revolutionary example for quite different ends. As a youth he was tremendously impressed by the duration of Washington's struggle for independence. "Victory and independence only came to the United States after eight years of fighting under Washington," he said to his friend Hsiao San, who had lent him a book on the subject, "eight long, bitter years." For expediency during World War II, Mao made polite, even friendly references to the United States. His party not only referred to America as a democracy, but drew a parallel between America's War for Independence in the eighteenth century and China's war for independence in the twentieth. It was then the party line to depict Washington as leading the struggle for democracy against the "big landowners and big merchants," and even as late as July 4, 1944, to praise Franklin D. Roosevelt and Vice President Wallace as worthy heirs of Washington, Jefferson, and Lincoln.

All that inspiration from the history books went down the drain once it appeared that American policy had veered toward support of Chiang Kai-shek against the Communists. Then the United States duly took its place as an imperialist warmonger, and the Leninist basis of Mao's thinking, his anti-imperialism, his notion of an alliance between the prole-

32. Chiang Chung-cheng (Chiang Kai-shek), *Soviet Russia in China: A Summing Up at Seventy* (New York, 1958), pp. 3–4, 211–212.

tariat and the peasantry as the form of state power during the "democratic" (presocialist) phase of the revolution gained naked exposure. From Stalin also he borrowed the concept of the "four-class bloc" which lies at the heart of his theory of the "people's democratic dictatorship," but he himself has given an original Chinese turn to Marxist-Leninism.

The kind of revolution which the American people conducted back in 1776, with its insistence on conformity to law, with its obeisance to standards of international behavior, would in fact be much too decorous a model for the revolutionary leaders of the new China. "A revolution is not a dinner party," Mao reminds us, "or writing an essay, or painting a picture, or doing embroidery; it cannot be so refined, so leisurely and gentle, so temperate, kind, courteous, restrained and magnanimous. A revolution is an insurrection, an act of violence by which one class overthrows another."[33] Mao's cultural revolution, which has mounted a terrible civil war virtually continental in scope, testifies to the strength of his convictions. Not only is the American Revolution a rejected model for Red China, but in fact the Chinese people are endlessly reminded that America is not a revolutionary, but a counterrevolutionary power, and the chief enemy of the "peoples and nations all over the world that want to make revolutions and liberate themselves."[34]

America's determination to sustain and defend Taiwan springs from the traumatic experience she suffered in the "loss" of China to the Communists after emerging victorious in World War II. That reaction affords a curious contrast to

33. "Report on an Investigation of the Peasant Movement in Hunan" (March, 1927), Mao Tse-tung, *Selected Works*, I, 28.

34. Chou En-lai, "Report to the National Peoples Congress," quoted in speech of Senator Ernest F. Hollings (September 20, 1968), *Congressional Record*, 90th Cong., 2nd Sess.

the response of Americans to the losses suffered in the Cold War in Eastern Europe and to the futile gestures made by the United States to hearten the "captive peoples" behind the Iron Curtain.

Although a ward of the United States, Taiwan is no carbon copy of American-style democracy. Its constitutional system combines features drawn from Sun Yat-sen's theories of governmental powers, from the American presidential system, and from European parliamentary governments. Elected by the National Assembly rather than directly by the people, the president is constitutionally prohibited from serving a third term, a restriction that was lifted to permit Chiang Kai-shek to continue in office. Instead of the American tripartite division of powers, the Republic of China has established five branches known as yuans. The president or premier of the Executive Yuan, or cabinet, must, according to the constitution, resign if an important government bill is rejected by the Legislative Yuan and his request for reconsideration overruled by two-thirds of the attending members, in analogy to the two-thirds vote required under the United States Constitution to override a veto. In addition, there is a Judicial Yuan, or highest court, a Control Yuan with censorial and impeachment powers, and an Examination Yuan with appointing powers. Civil liberties, though guaranteed by the constitution, have been suspended on the ground of national emergency, and, while on paper Taiwan has a multi-party system, in fact the Kuomintang is dominant and the two opposition parties quite minuscule. Guarded by the Seventh Fleet, its security guaranteed by a joint resolution adopted by the American Congress in 1955, the Republic of China has up to now not only warded off noisy blasts from its mainland adversary but, thanks to massive American aid, rapid industrialization, and sweeping land reforms, it has succeeded in placing its people on a footing of relative prosperity.

It was the Filipinos, however, rather than the Chinese, who would provide the sternest test of America's intentions toward the people of Asia. The Philippines came to the United States by accident, one might say, rather than as a result of long-range plotting, and the Treaty of Paris of 1898 by which Spain ceded those islands to the United States was ratified in the United States Senate by a paper-thin margin, so strong was the opposition by stalwart anti-imperialists in this country.[35] The United States took over an archipelago with a long-standing tradition of resistance to conquerors. Ferdinand Magellan, the Portuguese navigator who claimed the Philippines for Spain, was killed on the island of Mactan by a Filipino chieftain. Aspirations for independence, fanned by the successful revolts of the Latin American colonies from the Spanish Empire, came to a climax with an open rebellion in 1896. The fate of the nationalist movement was by no means settled when the United States arrived on the scene. The Filipino insurrectionaries, counting on an alleged promise from Admiral Dewey to help in establishing an independent Philippines,[36] declared the Philippines independent and adopted a liberal and democratic constitution, reflecting ideas drawn from the Enlightenment and the American Revolution, including a provision separating church and state.

However much the Anglophile foreign policy elite may have emulated British liberal imperialist notions or have

35. See, most recently, Robert L. Beisner, *Twelve Against Empire: The Anti-Imperialists, 1898–1900* (New York, 1968).

36. See Emilio Aguinaldo and Vincente Albano Pacis, *A Second Look at America* (New York, 1957), pp. 49–66. For the American testimony on this alleged deal, see Henry F. Graff, *American Imperialism and the Philippine Insurrection* (Boston, 1969), pp. 1–34.

become captive to the dream of an Anglo-American world order,[37] however much some Americans may have wanted to keep the Philippines in permanent colonial subjection— and there is grave doubt that such an objective was entertained seriously or for long—there were simply too many domestic opponents to such a policy to make it a politically prudent one. Committed by our own Revolutionary traditions to the doctrine of government by consent of the governed as well as to anticolonialism and antimilitarism, badgered incessantly by anti-imperialists on the one side, and by a combination of beet-sugar, labor, and other economic interests unenthusiastic about Philippines' competition on the other, the United States moved by gradual stages from constituting the Philippine Islands an unorganized territory in 1902, to granting the islands commonwealth status under the Tydings-McDuffie Act of 1934. Cutting loose the Philippines, an event which was scheduled to take place ten years after the establishment of a commonwealth government, meant subjecting all Philippine products to the full United States tariff rates on foreign goods, while at the same time retaining for the United States the right to maintain military bases after independence. From the worst features of the Tydings-McDuffie Act both the Philippines and the United States were saved by the cruel accident of Japanese occupation during World War II. Finally, on July 4,

37. These themes are developed by Ernest R. May, *American Imperialism: A Speculative Essay* (New York, 1968). Revisionist historians insist that American imperialism between the 1870's and 1898 took the form of commercial expansion to counter the threat of domestic underconsumption of industrial goods. In their view the United States, while not seeking a formal empire on the European model, attempted to secure the open door for American goods in other nation's empires. See William Appleton Williams, *The Tragedy of American Diplomacy* (rev. and enlarged ed., New York, 1962); Walter LaFeber, *The New Empire: An Interpretation of American Expansion, 1860–1890* (Ithaca, N.Y., 1963).

1946, the Filipinos celebrated their independence amid the ruins of war.[38]

In retrospect, it must be said that the United States, in its administration of the Philippines, not only abjured the permanent role of imperial ruler but pretty consistently supported the main objectives of the Filipinos' own revolution—political independence. It transplanted to the islands American constitutional doctrines, the notion of separation of church and state, and the secularization of education. It opened up all careers to Filipinos, improved public health, promoted the development of the economy, and eventually laid the groundwork for an American-style Constitution, which departs from the American example notably in its rejection of federalism, its preference for centralization, and its more extensive Bill of Rights (twenty-three articles in length). On the debit side of the ledger, the evils of land monopoly and debt peonage inherited from Spanish rule were in essence but little alleviated after a half century of control by the United States. It remained for Ramón Magsaysay, called in the Philippines "Our Abraham Lincoln," to introduce thoroughgoing reforms in these areas.[39] In sum, despite persistent problems growing out of economic interrelationships and the continued American presence on military bases, problems not lightly resolved, the Philippines has by free choice committed itself to binding alliances with the United States and aligned itself with the Free World.

The commonwealth status and ultimate independence for the Philippines may have proven to be the delayed response

38. See Grayson Kirk, *Philippine Independence* (New York, 1936); George E. Taylor, *The Philippines and the United States: Problems of Partnership* (New York, 1964); Robert A. Smith, *Philippine Freedom, 1946–1958* (New York, 1958), pp. 325–327.

39. G. A. Grunder and W. E. Livesey, *The Philippines and the United States* (Norman, Okla., 1951).

of America's conscience to its uncongenial posture as governor of alien peoples against their will. Japan, on the other hand, stands as the most extraordinary example of America's determination to exercise moral responsibility for reshaping an aggressor nation according to notions derived from American democracy. Long before World War II America's revolutionary and constitutional experience had left its impress on Japanese constitutional thinking. Even at the time of Commodore Perry's arrival in Japan in 1853, the governing class was familiar, via China, with such documents as the Declaration of Independence and the United States Constitution. Later on, that Japanese enlightenment leader, Fukuzawa Yūkichi, had an American history book put into Chinese. The American struggle for freedom inspired the Japanese novel and influenced educators of the stature of Okuma Shigenobu, the founder of Waseda University and an aficionado of Jefferson. However, once the Meiji Constitution was promulgated in 1889, America's influence appeared on the wane, a decline accelerated by the conflicting expansionist drives of the two nations, compounded by America's discriminatory immigration policy. The reactionary military clique that seized control in prewar Japan destroyed all vestiges of liberalism found in the Meiji Constitution. Japan's crushing defeat in World War II stripped the military of its influence and created a power vacuum which the American occupation presence proceeded to fill. And what an extraordinary timetable for democratic reform was now set in operation!

Between August 27, 1945, when American naval units entered Sagami Bay, and April 28, 1952, when, with the effectuation of the Treaty of San Francisco, Japan regained her status as a sovereign nation, Japan was an occupied country, and the occupier was the United States. By directions of the Joint Chiefs of Staff the American government spelled out to General Douglas MacArthur, Supreme Com-

mander for the Allied Powers, America's evangelical belief
in the superiority of democratic institutions. With extraordinary vigor MacArthur and his staff set about the task of
reshaping virtually every sector of Japanese life. There is no
other instance on record where so much power, control, and
initiative were exercised by a *single* democratic power, for
one must bear in mind that the occupations of Germany and
Austria were multinational.[40]

The old Meiji Constitution, theoretically granted to the
people by the Emperor, provided for a theocratic, patri-
archal constitutional system. In contrast, the so-called Mac-
Arthur Constitution audaciously expressed notions of popular sovereignty completely alien to Japanese thought. The
preamble of the 1947 Constitution declares:

> Government is a sacred trust of the people, the authority
> for which is derived from the people, the powers of which
> are exercised by the representatives of the people, and the
> benefits of which are enjoyed by the people. This is a uni-
> versal principle of mankind upon which this Constitution is
> founded.

After this affirmation of Lincolnesque doctrine, the Constitution affirms the peoples' "right to life, liberty, and the
pursuit of happiness." Then, leaving Jefferson, Madison's
basic bill of rights is included, with some interesting addi-
tions, including a guarantee of academic freedom, of the
"equal rights" of husband and wife in a marriage to be
"based only on the mutual consent of both sexes," and of the
right of collective bargaining, of assembly and association.

40. Robert E. Ward, ed., *Political Development in Modern Japan* (Prince-
ton, N.J., 1968), pp. 481–484. For early democratic memorials, see W. W.
McLaren, ed., "Japanese Government Documents," Asiatic Society, *Transac-
tions*, XLII (Tokyo, 1914), 427–433. For the earlier years, see also Sir
George Sansom, *The Western World and Japan* (New York, 1950); Herbert
Passin, ed., *The United States and Japan* (New York, 1966), pp. 6–18.

These rights of labor were further spelled out in 1947 in the original Trade Union Law which fostered labor organization and collective bargaining, even though General MacArthur soon found it expedient to place the lid on general strikes and augment the power of the government over work stoppages. The Constitution confers on a two-house Diet the powers stripped from the Emperor, with executive power lodged in the cabinet, a Supreme Court and an explicit provision for American-style judicial review.

If there is much in the MacArthur Constitution that sounds bizarre to Japanese ears, much that turns out to be close paraphrasing or direct plagiarism from the Constitution of the United States and the several American states, there is no gainsaying the fact that democratic rights were buttressed therein, even though the results at times fell short of expectations. For instance, the encouragement of trade-unionism led to the setting up of a giant labor federation which promptly became the leading opponent of the security treaty and has fought it ever since, while the antitrust, or anti-*zaibatsu*, program never fulfilled the intentions of the American economic advisers. On the other hand, the American Occupation might properly take pride in the success of its program for democratizing landholdings, with profound benefits to the peasant population. There are those who feel that middle-class America, with its capitalist ideology, cannot speak on the same wave length with Oriental peasants. This achievement in land reform, American-inspired, may prove embarrassing to reconcile with the preconceptions of such critics.[41] In short, more than anywhere else in Asia, the

41. Kazuo Kawaii, *Japan's American Interlude* (Chicago, 1960), pp. 56–58, 98–105, 143, 147–148, 160–173; Jerome B. Cohen, *Japan's Postwar Economy* (Bloomington, Ind., 1958); T. A. Bisson, *Zaibatsu Dissolution in Japan* (Berkeley and Los Angeles, 1954); Warren S. Hunsberger, *Japan and the United States in World Trade* (New York, 1964); Ardath W. Burke, *The Government of Japan* (2nd ed., New York, 1964), pp. 17–25, 184–186.

United States, drawing on the Great Declaration, the Constitution, and the New and Fair Deals, set up for Japan the
guideposts for a dynamic alternative to Communism.

Korea, that erstwhile if reluctant member of Japan's colonial empire, has also felt the impact of the American democratic tradition, brought home to that nation both by its
intellectuals and by the American occupation forces. Korea's
revolutionary nationalism attained full-blown proportions
under Japanese rule and was expounded not only clandes-
tinely within the peninsula but propagandized by Korean
exiles overseas. In keeping the torch of independence lit, one
revolutionary, Syngman Rhee, played a major role. While
imprisoned in Korea at the turn of the century, Rhee wrote a
lengthy treatise entitled *The Spirit of Independence: Korea,*
in which he treated both the American and the French
Revolutions. Rhee expressed his admiration for the oratory
of Patrick Henry and inserted Henry's portrait in his volume.
He studied American history at Princeton, wrote a dissertation on neutrality as influenced by the United States, and,
though professing himself a liberal Jeffersonian, he was
persuaded by Dean Edward Elliott to advocate the center-
ing of power in the executive and to oppose the notion of
separation of powers.

Rhee embarrassed America's ally of World War I, the
Japanese, by applying Wilson's Fourteen Points as his yard-
stick and demanding independence for Korea.[42] In fact, a
group of thirty-three Korean patriots issued a formal Declaration of Independence on March 1, 1919. Once Korea's
independence was achieved by America's victory over
Japan, Rhee continued to proclaim his faith in democracy as
"the only form of government" and his unswerving alle-

42. For a critical account of Rhee, see Kwang Il Koh, "In Quest of National
Unity and Power: Political Ideas and Practices of Syngman Rhee," Ph.D.
dissertation, Rutgers University, 1962.

giance to "the fundamental freedom of individuals." Liberation in 1945 also brought the bitter fruit of partition to the
Korean people. In the southern portion of Korea, which
United States troops occupied until 1949 (only to return not
long thereafter to protect South Korea's independence
against aggression), the concepts of popular government
were introduced and civil rights proclaimed. It did not take
long for the people of South Korea to discover that Rhee's
affirmations did not always square with his acts. As president of the postwar Republic of Korea, immediately concerned with establishing national unity, he closed down
dissenting newspapers and jailed opposition leaders. Rhee's
philosophy, embodied in his *Il Min Chu I* ("One Principle of
the People"), was modeled after Sun Yat-sen's "Three Principles of the People." Therein he emphasized the "will of the
people" to achieve his goal of national unity and unification,
and to eliminate class distinctions, factionalism, and the
inequality of the sexes. Originally favoring nonparty rule,
Rhee found it expedient to establish a party to achieve his
own re-election, but felt less cordially disposed to the opposition party. In April, 1960, the Rhee regime was finally
toppled. Its successor, the Second Republic, with its constitutional prejudices against a strong executive, was quickly
superseded by the military regime of General Chung Hee
Park, who, claiming that his coup was aimed at overthrow-
ing "the antidemocratic system" of the Second Republic,
restored and invigorated the presidential system.

The Constitution of 1948, as amended numerous times up
to now, provides presently for the presidential system patterned after that of the United States. On the other hand, it
permits the almost total suspension of civil liberties under a
state of siege as well as substantial restrictions even without
a declaration of a state of emergency. The Constitution
holds out to Koreans the ideal of equality, but neither social
nor economic equality have in fact been achieved as yet by

peasants and workers. In fairness it should be added that the tragic Korean civil war, from whose wounds South Korea is only just recovering, is still too close to us for any objective appraisal of the extent to which Western democratic and egalitarian ideas can successfully be implanted on the soil of the Asiatic mainland.[43]

There are few common strands linking Peiping and Delhi, Karachi and Tokyo, and in that vast subcontinent of Asia, with its teeming hundreds of millions confronting incessantly the pangs of hunger, the American presence has been less consequential than in the Far East. True, the American response has traditionally been generous, whether through missionary sources, philanthropic foundations, or under the auspices of the United States government. More recently, under the Point Four program, substantial technical assistance has been rendered to the emerging nations in this area to enable them to meet their planned goals for economic stability. Cynics have charged America with using foreign aid as a tool in the fight against Communism, and it must be conceded that the governments in underdeveloped lands have a talent for discovering quickly that if there is no actual Communist threat to their countries they had better create one if they wish to qualify for American aid.[44]

As regards India, one might argue that, despite the inspiration that the Indian nationalist leaders derived from America's War for Independence and the example of the United States as a powerful and prosperous democracy,[45]

43. See John Kie-Chang Oh, *Korea, Democracy on Trial* (Ithaca, N.Y., 1968), pp. 65–68, 72, 73, 105, 133, 158.

44. Merle Curti, *American Philanthropy Abroad* (New Brunswick, N.J., 1963), pp. 135, 136, 467, 589, 610–611, 613; S. Chandrasekha, *American Aid and India's Economic Development* (New York, 1965).

45. Nehru, for example, follows Charles and Mary Beard's *The Rise of American Civilization*, in his interpretation of the American Revolution as inaugurating a "real intellectual, economic, and social revolution." Jawaharlal Nehru, *The Discovery of India*, ed. by Robert I. Crane (New York, 1959), p. 104; *Visit to America* (Allahabad, 1935).

political theory has run a two-way course, and of late Americans may have derived more from recent Indian political thought than they have from us. Mohandas Gandhi confessed that he took from Tolstoi the notion of noncooperation and from that American dissenter, Henry David Thoreau, his doctrine of civil disobedience.[46] The Thoreau-Tolstoi-Gandhi doctrine has added a totally new dimension to the American principle of government by consent of the governed and has proved a formidable weapon not only in the fight to achieve decolonization but in the battle for civil rights for peoples throughout the world, including the United States, peoples so long discriminated against by reason of color.

Otherwise, Indian leaders, trained in England and brought up to admire the British Constitution, cast their glances more often toward England's liberals and to European nationalists like Mazzini than to American Revolutionary statesmen for their models. The admiration for France and the French Revolution of Rammohun Roy, called the father of modern India, has often been remarked.[47] Examples, to be sure, can be found reflecting American constitutional thinking in the democratic federal constitution adopted under the guidance of the Congress party once India had secured her independence.[48] In fact, no new nation in Asia has succeeded in completely ignoring the

46. See, M. K. Gandhi, *Satyagraha in Gandhiji's Own Words* (Allahabad, 1935), pp. 8–10.

47. Eric J. Hobsbawm, *The Age of Revolution, 1789–1848* (New York, 1962), pp. 76–77.

48. M. K. Gandhi, *An Autobiography: The Story of My Experiments with Truth* (Boston, 1957), p. 172; Bruce T. McCully, *English Education and the Origins of Indian Nationalism* (New York, 1960), pp. 388–391, 396. In Mar.-Apr. 1942 F.D.R. urged on Churchill a temporary national government for India similar to the Articles of Confederation, to be followed by a permanent constitution after the war. *Foreign Relations of the United States, 1942,* I (Washington, 1964), 604–634.

ritual of the American Revolution. Even neutralist Burma, with its Marxist slant, found it expedient to issue a Declaration of Independence on January 4, 1948, in which it proclaimed: "As a free people, we shall discharge the duties that the free peoples of the world's free nations discharge."[49]

It is one of the ironic paradoxes of our time that the United States, which helped trigger the nationalist revolutions of Southeast Asia, should have subsequently been cast in the ill-fitting role of an imperialist warmonger seeking to supplant the French as the colonial masters of old Indochina. It is indeed ironic, when one bears in mind that, hardly had World War II moved into full stream, when President Franklin Delano Roosevelt expressed positive views in favor of independence for various colonial peoples. In January, 1943, shortly after the Anglo-American landings in Morocco, the American President privately assured the Sultan of Morocco of America's hopes for Moroccan freedom. Aside from the dramatic impact of F.D.R.'s anticolonial stance on the African independence movements, it should be noted that Roosevelt seemed entirely clear in his own mind about the future of Southeast Asia. As Secretary of State Hull noted in 1943, F.D.R. took strong exception to France's according military facilities to the Japanese in Indochina. While en route to the Casablanca Conference, F.D.R. told his son Elliott: "The native Indochinese have been so flagrantly downtrodden that they thought to themselves: Anything must be better than to live under French colonial rule." "Don't think for a moment," he added, "that Americans would be dying tonight, if it had not been for the shortsighted greed of the French, the British, and the Dutch."

Having decided that France had misruled Indochina, the President then aimed to prevent France from reasserting her

49. U Nu, *The People Win Through* (New York, 1957), pp. 39–40.

sovereignty over the area. At a White House conference on March 27, 1943, the President proposed to British Foreign Secretary Anthony Eden that a trusteeship be established for Indochina. He may have had in mind, according to General Joseph W. Stilwell, the U.S. Commander in the China theater, a trusteeship under three commissioners, an American, a Chinese, and a Briton. The recently published secret documents on the Cairo and Teheran Conferences reveal that F.D.R. sought to convert Stalin to his own views on Indochina in order to outvote a weary Churchill. Agreeing with Stalin about the evils of French colonial rule and about having the French "pay for their criminal collaboration with Germany," Roosevelt observed that "after one hundred years of French rule the inhabitants were worse off than they had been before." When Churchill interposed an objection, F.D.R., according to the State Department record, cut him off with a curt: "Now look, Winston, you are outvoted three to one." The third vote was that of Chiang Kaishek who was present at Cairo but not at Teheran. When the proposal for a trusteeship council for Indochina was brought up at Yalta in February, 1945, Churchill vetoed it. Needing Churchill's support on seemingly more urgent matters, F.D.R. let the issue be tabled. On his return to the United States aboard the cruiser *Quincy*, the President vented to journalists his disappointment at having been thwarted. "Stalin liked the idea. China liked the idea. The British don't like it. It might bust up their empire." In short, according to F.D.R.'s son Elliott, the President held these views about Indochina almost to his dying day, and kept insisting that Indochina, "liberated in main part by American arms and American troops, should never simply be handed back to the French, to be milked by their imperialists."[50]

Thus, if any single person is to be hailed as the liberator of

50. Most recently these quotations from F.D.R. have been assembled in Bernard B. Fall, *Last Reflections on War* (New York, 1967), pp. 126–130.

the Dutch and French empires of Southeast Asia, it should be neither Sukarno nor Ho Chi Minh, but Franklin Delano Roosevelt. The President had a wonderful talent for over-simplifying complex issues and for sweeping historical generalizations which were comforting to him but often lacked scrupulous accuracy. We have it on no less an authority than Edwin O. Reischauer that F.D.R. did not stand alone, for there was a group of Asia specialists in the State Department who felt that the United States should not support the restoration of colonial regimes that had been swept away by Japanese conquest. Such a move, it was felt, would violate America's traditional belief in self-determination as well as her sporadically cherished anticolonial sentiment stemming in no small part from her own anticolonial origins.[51]

The coming of the Cold War clarified or warped one's vision depending on one's point of view, and F.D.R.'s vision of emancipating the Indo-Chinese from the colonial yoke of France died with him.[52] In the eyes of Western statesmen, Indochina could not safely be turned over to Ho Chi Minh, Vietnam's foremost anticolonial leader, who had spent twenty years in the service of the Communist International. Instead, the West propped up the playboy regime of Bao Dai, then that of the ill-fated Diem. Perhaps the big decision was made when, following France's defeat at Dienbienphu, the United States, along with the South Vietnamese, refused to sign the Geneva agreement of 1954. The resultant truncated state became the tragic and costly responsibility of the United States.

Vietnam has since then been the cross that Americans have borne. Whether this terrible burden is carried out of a determination to contain the Communists, as America man-

51. Edwin O. Reischauer, *Beyond Vietnam: The United States and Asia* (New York, 1968), pp. 20, 21.

52. Arthur M. Schlesinger, Jr., *The Bitter Heritage: Vietnam and American Democracy* (New York, 1967), p. 11.

aged to do in Greece and Turkey, out of a conviction of the validity of the "falling domino" theory, whether because Americans have impliedly committed themselves to a new Monroe Doctrine for Southeast Asia or have sunk into the quagmire as a result of earlier and ill-conceived policies, Americans in overwhelming numbers and of both parties agree that somehow a path to peace must be marked out.

Whatever the ending of this tragically misconceived war, the United States needs desperately to rebuild its image as a supporter of government by consent of the governed, to recapture the anticolonial stance of a John Jay or a John Quincy Adams or a Franklin Delano Roosevelt, and once more to resume its honored place in the front ranks of the nations founded on revolutionary principles.

"All men are created equal." These were Jefferson's words in 1776. They were also Ho Chi Minh's in 1945, in the opening sentences of the Declaration of Independence of the Democratic Republic of Vietnam. His use of them was open and intended. American members of the O.S.S. mission parachuted to Ho in the summer of 1945 recall his efforts to obtain either a copy of the Declaration or an approximation of its essential passages.[53] Whether Ho meant them in the way Jefferson did—and one would have to be a fuzzy-minded ideologue to believe so—his resort to the Great Declaration demonstrates that it is no longer the exclusive property of America but belongs to the world. If the peasant Left chooses to think of Americans as rich reactionaries concerned only with counter-insurgency operations, it is so much more America's need to remind the underdeveloped nations of her own revolutionary traditions, and that her deep concern with their achieving independence and freedom is matched only by her disinterested commitment to

53. Bernard B. Fall, ed., *Ho Chi Minh, On Revolution* (New York, 1967), p. 143.

help them fight their battles to escape the twin perils of overpopulation and famine.

Without entering into a dispute as to how effective the American military presence has been in Asia in preventing a take-over by Communism, we must now recognize from the lessons of Vietnam that naked force alone is not the answer to Communism's power and appeal, nor our dollars however wisely spent. America must contest Communism in the market place of ideas and be prepared to find our notions of democracy somewhat transmuted when applied by Latin-American, Asian, or African customers.[54] We must be prepared to find, first, that the path toward democracy in the arc from Pakistan to Taiwan is strewn with obstacles. Secondly, we must recognize that the new nations will continue to seek African or Asian solutions to their problems rather than American or Russian. This might well involve accepting what President Senghor of Senegal has called "a middle course, for a *democratic socialism*."[55] Thirdly, Americans must be reconciled to a good many more revolutions and governmental take-overs among the underdeveloped nations in the foreseeable future. How to channel this revolutionary energy into a constructive course should be the main concern of the democratic West rather than how to crush insurgency.[56] Finally, America must by consistent behavior at home correct the image of racism which, perhaps unfairly, has been fastened on to the American people by the underdeveloped states, an image which detracts from the appeal of American democracy to an Asian or African.[57]

54. See Edwin O. Reischauer, *Wanted: An Asian Policy* (Cambridge, Mass., 1955).

55. Leopold Sedar Senghor, *On African Socialism*, trans. by Mercer Cook (New York, 1964), p. xi.

56. See C. E. Black, *The Dynamics of Modernization* (New York, 1968).

57 See, e.g., Mao's "Statement Supporting the American Negroes in Their Just Struggle Against Racial Discrimination by U.S. Imperialism," in *Quotations from Chairman Mao Tse-Tung* (New York, 1967), p. 6.

These are revolutionary times—politically, socially, scientifically. Those who lead revolutions are in both temperament and goals significantly different from the Patriots of 1776. But so are the Americans as a people. The colonists seemed weak and exploited by a powerful empire. Today America is powerful and affluent. Americans, too, have indeed changed, but they must recapture the most precious of all values derived from our Revolutionary experience—that tolerance of change. In renewing her role as an anticolonial democratic nation America must show a toleration for other people's governments which are neither popular nor democratic in our present sense.

For emerging nations to achieve a developmental breakthrough, a massive collective effort comparable to the American Moon Shot may be required.[58] As with the Apollo Project, such an effort may by its very dimension have to be in its initial stage[59] state-directed rather than left to individual enterprise. That the means some emerging nations may adopt to achieve economic growth may well prove distasteful to American traditions seems predictable, but it might also be expected that Americans who have adapted themselves to both a political and a technological revolution in their own nation should cooperate with others in achieving ends needed to bring tranquillity to this disturbed planet.

Back in 1851, President Millard Fillmore declared the American mission was not to "impose upon other countries

58. The debate over whether a democratic emerging nation can achieve modernization has recently been waged by Robert L. Heilbroner and Dennis H. Wrong in *A Dissenter's Guide to Foreign Policy,* ed. by Irving Howe (New York, 1968), pp. 241–282.

59. Milovan Djilas argues that when an underdeveloped nation emerges out of the industrial stage into the era of automation and electronic controls a more mobile and diversified structure of ownership needs to be, and is being, devised, and cites Jugoslavia as an example. *The Unperfect Society,* trans. by Dorian Cooke (New York, 1969), pp. 188–190.

our form of government by artifice or force, but to teach by example and show by our success." Translating Fillmore's advice to our own times, one might propose that, in place of a war of counter-insurgency America must offer a more positive program, a more appealing war, one to be waged against illiteracy, disease, prejudice, and overpopulation. Marshaling the talents of the Free World in such a war, and fortified by a renewed faith in the principles of her own great Revolution, America need not shrink from the task or retreat into a new isolation. Instead, Americans must be prepared to continue to play that leading role in reshaping the world into a more rational and a more peaceful planet, that their strength, resources, technical competence, and humanitarian impulses have marked out for them.

INDEX

Adams, John, 16, 42, 52, 70, 75, 99, 101, 136; *A Defence of the Constitutions of Government of the United States,* 44, 90, 95; on Franklin and Voltaire, 44–45; propagandist of revolution in Holland, 46; Calkoen letters, 47; on revolutionary Jacobinism, 71; on effects of American Revolution in Europe, 89

Adams, John Quincy, 99, 156, 157, 165, 166, 180, 220; on Monroe Doctrine, 98; on foreign intervention, 154–155; on anticolonialism, 179, 183

Adams, Samuel, 16, 59

Affaires de l'Angleterre et de l'Amérique, 41

Africa, 178–194; and United States, 183–185; emerging nations compared with Revolutionary America, 190–193; slave trade in, 181–182; colonization of, 182–186. *See also* African nations.

El Alamein, 180

Albania, 169

Alberdi, Juan Bautista, 142, 143

Alessandri, Arturo, 169

Alfieri, Vittorio, on American Revolution, 116

Alfred, King, 14

Algeria, 195–197

Alliance for Progress, 170–171

Amaru, Tupuc, 130, 133

American Colonization Society, 182, 183, 185

American Revolution, 3, 12, 18–20, 29, 34, 35, 75, 90, 99–101, 131, 132, 140, 144–146, 155, 169, 201, 202, 204, 213, 215, 217, 222, 223; ritual in, 125; as model, 9, 19, 29, 32–34, 43, 44, 48, 53, 75, 87, 89, 91, 96, 123–125; Battles of, 3, 8, 65, 66, 83, 109; influence in France, 38–40, 53; and French Revolution compared, 55, 57–61, 63; influence on European enlisted men, 43; negative impact in Latin America, 132; unadaptable to Venezuela, 138–139; influence in

Canada, 173–176; and Africa, 190–193; rejected as model in China, 203, 205

Anticolonialism. *See* Colonialism, Imperialism

Anti-Imperialism. *See* Imperialism, Colonialism

Aranda, Pedro Pablo Abarca de Bolea, Conde de, on Spanish possessions in Western Hemisphere, 131–132

Argentina, 130, 141, 142, 144, 145, 152, 154, 158; Constitution, 142–143

Arieli, Yehoshua, American nationalism and political consensus, 10–11 *n*

Aristocracy, 21, 126

Arnold, Oliver, 65

d'Artois, Charles Philippe, Comte, 62

Articles of Confederation, and Belgium, 91; and Russia, 106; and Germany, 122; proposed for India, 216 *n;* Confederacy, 104

Asselin, Oliver, on United States, 174

Ashmun, Jehudi, 182

Asia, 199–223; and United States, 199–204; American Revolution as example, 222–223. *See also* Asian nations

Atlantic Charter, 120

Austria, 123, 124

Azikiwe, Nnamdi, on American democracy, 189, 190

Babeuf, Gracchus, 45, 108

Bakunin, Michael, *Federalism, Socialism, and Anti-Theologism,* 104–105; on American social problems, 105

Balfour Declaration, 198

Bancroft, Edward, 84, 85

Bancroft, George, on North German Constitution, 113

Barbé-Marbois, F., 29

Barbosa, Ruy, and Brazil's 1891 Constitution, 144

Bayard, Thomas F., 184

Baylies, Francis, on Rosas regime, 145

Beethoven, Ludwig van, 93

Belgium, and America, 90–91; Constitution, 92–93

Belmont, August, on European republicanism, 115–116

Beneš, Eduard, on America as model, 126–127

Betancourt, Rómulo, and Venezuelan reforms, 170

Beveridge, Albert J., 159

Biafra, 191

Bill of Rights, United States, 17, 18, 22, 70, 126; and religious liberty, 87–88; proposed amendments to, 88; in: France, 56; Germany, 112–113; Italy, 88; Philippines, 209; Japan, 211, 212. *See also* Massachusetts, Pennsylvania, Virginia

Bismarck, Otto von, 109, 113

Blake, William, 79, 81

Bolívar, Simón, 136, 146, 148, 149; sketch, 138–139; on America, 139; on government, 139–140; on Washington, 141; on dictatorship, 147

Bolivia, 130, 150, 170

Bolkhovitinov, N. N., on American Revolution and Russia, 100

Borges, Pozzo di, on Latin American rebels, 145

Boston Massacre, 63

Botta, Carlo, 117

Brackenridge, Henry M., on Latin American recognition, 154

Braganza, House of, 150, 151
Brazil, 131, 132, 142, 158; and Declaration of Independence, 141; and federalism, 143–144; dictatorship and monarchy in, 150–151
Bright, John, on American Civil War, 119
Brinton, Crane, 58
Brown, John, 4
Brown, Moses, 4
Bryant, William Cullen, 3
Burke, Aedanus, 22, 31
Burke, Edmund, 34, 35; on Ireland, 85
Burma, 2, 217
Burns, Robert, 81

Ça Ira, 46, 62, 71, 72
Calkoen, Hendrick, 47
Calonne, Charles Alexandre de, 54
Calura, Bernardo Maria, 117
Canada, 158; and United States, 172–176; and radical republicanism, 176, 177; Loyalists in Nova Scotia, 187
Canning, George, 129, 156
Canton, 178, 199
Capellen, Joan Derk van der, 47
Cárdenas, Lázaro, 150, 167
Carolinas, the, frontier eruptions, 4
Carr, Benjamin, 72
Carranza, Venustiano, 166
Cartwright, Major John, 81
Castiglione, Luigi, 116
Castro, Fidel, 11, 45, 167, 170; and Cuban revolution, 168–169
Catherine II, Empress of Russia, 49, 76, 102; and revolutions, 99
Cavour, Count Camillo, 118
Charles III, King of Spain, 76, 77, 131
Chastellux, François-Jean, Marquis de, 10, 42

Chateaubriand, Vicomte de, 58
Chernyshevski, Nicholas, 105–106
Chiang Kai-shek, 204, 206
Chile, 25, 41, 131, 151, 154, 164; Constitution of 1833, 144; and reform, 169–170
China, 201–205, 210, 218; leaders' views on America, 201–205; American model rejected, 203, 205
China, People's Republic of, 11, 168, 169, 205
China, Republic of, 199, 205, 206, 207, 221; structure of government, 206
Churchill, Winston, 179, 180, 216 n, 218
Cincinnati, Society of, 22
Civil disobedience, 3, 216
Civil liberties, and Jews in Europe, 87; in American state constitutions, 102; in Soviet Union, 108; in Republic of China, 206; in South Korea, 214; in India, 216
Civil War, of United States, 104, 118, 119, 206, 219; Russian views on, 107; and U.S. traditions, 118; and Canada, 174, 175; Sun Yat-sen on, 203
Clark, George Rogers, 196
Clay, Henry, 154
Cleveland, Grover, 184
Cleveland, Richard, 151
Cobden, Richard, 119
Code Napoléon, 88, 89
Cold War, 206, 219; new states' exploitation of, 8
Coleridge, Samuel Taylor, 81
Colombia, 139, 147, 161
Colonialism, U.S., 18, 201, 207, 208, 208 n; opposition to, 32–33, 178–180, 183–185, 208, 219; U.S. and Africa, 182–184, 186; European conferences on, 184–185. Anti-

colonialism, 107, 146, 157, 179, 183; in Algeria, 195. Neocolonialism, 195

Common market, U.S., 32–34; Europe: 34; *Zollverein*, 111; Latin America, 152; Africa, 191

Commonwealth, British, 193; Puerto Rico, 163; Philippines, 208

Communism, 192, 215, 219–221

Condorcet, Marquis de, 43, 45, 75; "The Influence of the American Revolution in Europe," 52, 53

Confiscation, 25–26

Congo, 184, 191, 196

Connecticut, 15, 31

Conscience Africaine Manifesto, 192

Constitution, United States, 9, 10, 12, 13, 14, 17, 18, 22, 35, 56, 70, 72, 131, 139–141, 148, 151, 152, 167, 175, 183, 203, 209, 210, 213, 216; British, 7, 14, 17, 216; French, 41, 55, 56; Belgian, 92–93; Swedish, 95; Norwegian, 95; 1848 and Frankfurt Assembly, 112–114; Weimar, 121–122; Argentine, 142–143; Chilean, 144; Mexican, 166–167; Liberian, 185; in Africa, 191; Philippines, 209; Japanese, 211–212; Korean, 214. *See also* State constitutions

Constitutionalism, 75, 78, 102, 191; United States model, 19; in Russia, 103; French foundation in, 55; in Germany, 109, 112–114; in Latin America, 131, 169

Continental Congress, 15, 58, 79

Cook, Captain James, 49

Cooper, James Fenimore, 103

Coray, Adamantios, 98

Cornwallis, Charles, 2nd Earl, 66

Corny, Ethis de, 36

Corsica, 77

Costillo, Hidalgo y, revolt of, 137

Creoles, in Latin America, 131–132, 135–137, 146

Crèvecoeur, Michel-Guillaume Jean de, 29, 30

Crummell, Alexander, 185

Cuba, 23, 27–28, 131, 152, 155, 158, 159, 164, 168, 169, 174; annexation of, 159–160; U.S.-Cuban ties, 160, and Castro, 168–169

Czechoslovakia, and self-determination, 123–127; and United States tradition, 125; and Soviet invasion of, 127–128

Dai, Bao, 219

Danton, Georges Jacques, 60

Dawes, Thomas, 16

Deane, Silas, 51, 52

Debtors, treatment of, 26–27

Decembrists, 102

Declaration of Independence, United States, 17, 21, 30, 32, 99, 101, 128, 151, 152, 159, 160, 194, 203, 210, 213; as model, 3; and legitimacy, 8; and Germany, 112, 114, 120; France, 41, 55, 58; Belgium, 91; Russia, 106; Czechoslovakia, 125; Latin America, 141; Liberia, 185; Israel, 198; Burma, 217; Vietnam, 220

Declaration of the Rights of Man and Citizen, 56

Decolonization, 157, 216; Latin American insurrections, 130, 147; in Haiti, 135, U.S. sympathy for Afro-Asian, 180–181, 183; Rhodesia, 194

Delacroix, Jean François, 69

Démeunier, Jean-Nicolas, 42

Democracy, 15, 53, 148, 221; upthrust in England, 82; in Latin America, 138

Denmark, 96

Dewey, Adm. George, 207
Díaz, Porfirio, 150, 165, 166
Dickinson, John, 82
Dictatorship, 13, 22; military, in France, 61; in Latin America, 142–150
Diem, Ngo Dinh, 219
Dienbienphu, 219
Diplomacy, 134, 213, 215, 217; United States, 8, 12, 48; "new," 51
Djilas, Milovan, 222 n
Dolfin, Daniel, 116
Dominican Republic, 133
Du Bois, William E. B., and Pan-Africanism, 188, 189
Du Chaillu, Paul, 184
Dulles, John Foster, on anticolonialism, 180
Dumas, Charles William Frederic, 47
Dumouriez, Charles François, 42
Du Pont, Pierre Samuel, 43

East Africa, 34
Ebeling, Christopher Daniel, on American Revolution, 110
Ecuador, 150
Eden, Anthony, 218
Education, 10; U.S. model for Argentina, 144; of African leaders, 186, 189
Egypt, 195
Eisenhower, Dwight D., 115
Elliot, Edward, 213
Emancipation, of Jews in France, 88, 89. See also Negroes, Religious Liberty, Slavery
Emancipation Proclamation, 119, 120
Empress of China, 199
Enlightenment, in France, 40, 41, 76; in Germany, 110; in Czecho-slovakia, 126; in Latin America, 131, 137, 138; in Israel, 198; in Philippines, 207
Equality, 20, 21, 24; in Germany, 110; in Africa, 192, 193
Everett, Edward, 98, 179
Executive power, 15, 206

Fair Deal, 213
Falsen, C. M., 95
Fanti Confederation, 190
Federalism, 34, 75, 78, 96; U.S., 19–20; and Belgium, 91; and Russia, 102, 104, 105; in Germany, 113–114, 122; in Venezuela, 139; in Brazil, 143–144; in Canada, 177; in Africa, 191, 193; in Asia, 203. Antifederalism, 9
Federalist, The, 20, 28, 35, 192
Federalists, 68, 72–73
Federal Overture, 72
Ferdinand VII, King of Spain, 137, 156
Filangeri, Gaetano, 117
Fillmore, Millard, 222, 223
Fiske, John, 106
Foraker Act, 162
Forsyth, John, on U.S. foreign policy, 99
Founding Fathers, 11, 12, 17, 20, 21, 32, 35, 74, 109, 117, 142, 148, 186
"Four Freedoms," 120
Fourteen Points, 121, 123, 213
Fox, Charles James, 80
France, 22, 52, 192, 197, 217, 218; quasi war with U.S., 9; compared with U.S., 38–40, 43, 44, 46, 53–54; as colonial power, 219
Francia, José Gaspar Rodríguez de, 150
Frankfurt Assembly, aims, 109; and U.S. constitutionalism, 111–112; failure of, 113, 114

Franklin, Benjamin, 22, 41, 47, 48, 51, 52, 111, 112, 116–118, 173, 200; and *américanistes*, 43; and Voltaire, 44, 45; as propagandist of revolution, 45; literary hoaxes of, 45, 46; and *Ça Ira*, 46; diplomacy, 48–49; on neutral shipping, 50; on suffrage in England, 81; on Ireland, 84

Frederick II, the Great, 76, 77, 110

Frei Montalva, Eduardo, 169–170

French Revolution, 9, 11, 36, 37, 63, 67, 68, 70, 72, 76, 99, 146, 202, 204, 213; compared with American Revolution, 55, 57–61, 63, 67–68, 76; leadership of, 59–61; excesses of, 68, 70, 72; primacy of, 76; emancipation of Jews, 88, 89; influence of, 93, 94; and Belgium, 91; and Italian Constitution, 117; and Weimar Constitution, 122; and Latin America, 132, 133, 137

Gandhi, Mohandas K., doctrine, 216

Gardoqui, Don Diego de, 132

Garibaldi, Giuseppe, 115, 118, 146

Garvey, Marcus, 188

Gazette de Leyde, 47

Genêt, Edmond Charles, 68, 70, 71

George III, King of England, 31, 57, 107

Georgia, 17

Germany, 87, 94, 110, 121–122, 201; soldiers in American Revolution, 109; *Zollverein*, 111; Constitutions, 112–114

Ghana, 181, 190

Goethe, Johann Wolfgang von, 10, 75, 103

Goltz, Bernhard Wilhelm, Count von der, 112

Gómez, Juan Vicente, 150

"Good Neighbor" Policy, 163

Goodnow, Frank, memorandum on China, 203

Goodrich, Chauncey, 68

Gordon, Thomas, 13, 77

Grattan, Henry, 83

Graydon, Alexander, 58

Great Britain, 52, 94, 129–130, 192, 194, 196, 201; Constitution of, 7, 14, 17, 216; debt controversy with U.S., 27; Jay Treaty, 67–68; radicalism, 78, 81; reform, 80–82; on American Revolution, 78–80; and Latin America, 129, 134, 152, 159; and Sierra Leone, 186, 187; Commonwealth, 193; and Israel, 198; and India, 216

Greece, 220; American revolutionary example, 97–98; and United States response to, 98

Grenville, George, 54

Guadalcanal, 180

Guatemala, 162

Guevara, Che, 3, 168

Guerrilla Warfare, 3

Guinea, 181

Haerne, Désiré de, 92

Haiti, 132, 133, 158, 162

Hájek, J. S., 123 n

Hamilton, Alexander, 20, 25, 27, 34, 42, 138, 192; disavowal of Sears' raid, 5; political parties, 9; on French Revolution, 68; and Miranda, 135–136; on Louisiana and Floridas, 136; cynical about democracy, 148; influence in Canada, 176

Hancock, John, 4, 200

Harcourt, Sir William, 84

Hartley, David, 48, 49

Hawaii, 159, 201

Hay, John, 159

Hébert, Jacques René, 61

Henderson, Richard, 14
Henry, Patrick, 26, 213
Herring, Hubert, 149
Herzen, Alexander, 115; *William Penn*, 103; on American federalism, 104
Herzl, Theodor, 198
Hitler, Adolf, 109
Ho Chi Minh, 219, 220
Hobsbawm, Eric, 76
Holy Alliance, 154, 156
Hopkinson, Francis, 65
Howe, Samuel Gridley, 98
Hsiao San, 204
Huerta, Victoriano, 166
Hull, Cordell, 217
Humboldt, Alexander von, 135
Humor, Revolutionary, French cartoons, 61–62; American songs, 64–65
Hungary, 123; Revolution of 1848, 114–115
Hutchinson, Thomas, 5

Imperialism, U.S., 158–159, 178; in Caribbean, 159–160; in Philippines, 160; in Latin America, 161–164; and Cuba, 159, 160, 168; in Africa, 182–184, 186; in Asia, 201. European, 184, 185. Anti-Imperialism, of U.S., in Latin America, 164; anti-Americanism in Latin America, 161, 171. Neoimperialism, 164, 208 *n*
India, 11, 178, 179, 180
Indochina, 180; F. D. Roosevelt on, 217–218. *See also* Vietnam
Indonesia, 2
Intervention, by U.S., 120, 135; in Latin America, 133, 151, 161–164; in Haiti, 134, 135; by Argentina in provinces, 143

Ireland, 11, 78, 93, 117; discontent with Great Britain, 82; pro-American activities, 83; American Revolution as model, 82, 85–86; and autonomous Parliament, 85
Isolationism, U.S., 8. *See also* Neutrality
Israel, 11, 195, 197–199
Italy, and Virginia Bill for Religious Freedom, 88; admiration of U.S., 116–117; U.S. Constitutional system, 118; as example to Vargas, 144
Iturbide, Augustin de, 137, 149

Jackson, Andrew, 99, 165
James, William, 160
Japan, 199, 201, 213; and U.S., 200, 210; and U.S. occupation, 210–212; Constitution, 211, 212; reforms, 212
Jay, John, 10, 27, 32, 48, 49, 51, 199, 200; on mob rule, 5; Treaty, 67, 68; and Genêt, 68; critic of French Revolution, 72–73; and Aranda, 131; and Gardoqui, 132; on exploited natives of India, 178–179
Jefferson, Thomas, 3, 17, 19, 20, 24, 31, 33, 36, 38, 47, 67, 69, 71, 77, 107, 138, 141, 156, 165, 185, 194, 195, 204, 210, 211, 213, 220; on political parties, 9; and *américanistes*, 43; sympathetic to French Revolution, 69, 70, 72; on role of American Revolution, 74–75; bill for religious freedom, 88; and Greece, 97–98; and Santo Domingo, 134; sympathy with Latin American libertarian movements, 152; on African colonization, 183
Jews, and civil liberties, 87; attitude to American Revolution, 87; in celebrating Constitution, 88

Jones Act, 162
Joseph II, Emperor of Austria, 76, 112
Juárez, Benito, 150
Judicial Review, 122–123; U.S. model in Austria, 123; in Czechoslovakia, 126; in Japan, 212

K'ang Yu-wei, 201, 202
Kemal, Mustafa, 197
Kentucky, 154; Transylvania Colony, 14
Kennedy, John F., 170, 171
Kenya, 2, 188
Kenyatta, Jomo, 188, 189
Kesser, Hermann, 128
King, Rufus, 68; on Santo Domingo, 134; on Latin American independence, 135; and Miranda, 135; on Latin American intervention, 153
Korea, 199, 213; North, 48; South, 214–215
Kossuth, Louis, 114–115
Kubitschek, Juscelino, 170
Kuomintang, 206

Lafayette, Marquis de, 37, 42, 43, 60, 84, 116, 141
Lamb, John, 4
Lanctot, Gustave, 175
Lansing, Robert, 124
Latin America, 11, 25, 34, 97, 129–172, 179, 221. See also Latin American countries
Latrobe, John H. B., 182
Launay, Bernard Jordan de, 36
Laurens, Henry, 30, 31, 58
Lavrov, Peter, 106
Leadership, 9; American Revolutionary, 6, 14, 17, 28; U.S. and France compared, 11, 57–60; in

Latin America, 137, 149, 150; in Africa, 190, 191
Leclerc, Charles Victor Emmanuel, 133
Lee, Arthur, 59
Legality, American and French Revolutions rooted in, 55
Legislature, Bicameral, U.S., 17; in France, 56; in Belgium, 93; in Argentina, 140, 142
Legitimacy, 8, 156–157
Lenin, V. I., 34, 105, 107, 108, 121, 128, 168, 204, 205; "A Letter to American Workers," 106–107
Leopold II, King of Belgium, 184
Liang Ch'i-chao, 203
Liberalism, in France, 55; in England, 80–81; in Russia, 102–103; in India, 216
Liberia, 183–184; independence, 185; U.S. influences in, 185, 186
Liberty, 102, 104, 105, 116, 155, 157, 180–181, 184; individual, 75; Bakunin on, 104–105; in Germany, 110; Bolívar on, 139; Santa Anna on, 149; Sun Yat-sen on, 202
Lincoln, Abraham, 32, 120, 121, 125, 189, 204, 209, 211
Linguet, Simon-Nicolas-Henri, 91
Lipset, Seymour Martin, 7
List, Friedrich, 111
Livingston, Edward, 145
Livingston, William, 42
Livingstone, David, 184
Locke, John, 13, 78
Lolme, Jean, De, 44
Lomonosov, M. V., 101
Louis XVI, King of France, 36, 40, 62, 67
Loyalists (Tories), 9, 23, 24, 25, 28, 57, 87, 173, 187, 196, 197. See also Algeria
Lucas, Charles, 77, 82

Luzac, Jean, 47
Lyon, Matthew, 153

Mably, Abbé de, 42
MacArthur, Douglas, 210, 211, 212
McDougall, Alexander, 4
McGee, Thomas D'Arcy, 174
McKay, Claude, 189
McKinley, William, 159
Mackenzie, William Lyon, 175
Madero, Francisco I., 165, 166
Madison, James, 20, 28, 35, 69, 88, 156, 211; and neutrality, 51; "Advice to my Country," 148; and aid to Latin America, 152
Magellan, Ferdinand, 207
Magsaysay, Ramón, 209
Makonnen, Ras, 189
Mali, 190
Mamatey, Victor S., 124
"Manifest Destiny," 159, 201
Mansfield, William Murray, 1st Earl of, 79
Mao Tse-tung, 3, 168, 170; theories of, 204–205
Marat, Jean Paul, 60
Marcontoni, Antonio, 117
Maria Theresa, Empress, 201
Marie Antoinette, Queen of France, 62
Marion, Francis, 3
Marseillaise, 72
Martí, José, 168
Marx, Karl, 34; on Emancipation Proclamation, 119–120; followers, 168, 169, 189, 205, 217
Masaryk, Thomas G., 124–126
Mason, George, 17, 26, 56
Massachusetts, Constitutional Convention, 15–16, 21, 87; Constitution of 1780, 15
Maupeou, René Nicolas Charles Augustin, 76

Mazzei, Philip, 43, 47
Mazzini, Giuseppe, 115, 118, 216
Meiji Constitution, 210, 211
Mendelssohn, Moses, 89
Metternich, Prince von, on Napoleon, 93; on legitimacy, 156–157
Mexico, 23, 137, 149, 150, 152, 158, 164–168; and U.S., 166; Constitution, 166–167
Michelet, Jules, 104
Middle East, 194–199; and U.S., 194
Mignogna, Nicola, 118
Miles, Nelson A., 162
Miliukov, Paul N., 107
Mill, John Stuart, 190
Mirabeau, H. G. R., Comte de, 22, 43, 60
Miranda, Francisco de, 135, 136, 153
Mississippi River, navigation, 131, 132
Mitchill, Samuel Latham, 152
Mohl, Robert von, 112
Monarchy, 12, 22; fear of, in U.S., 70; San Martín on, 138; Bolívar opposition to, 147, 148; Constitutional, 102
Monroe Doctrine, 98, 155, 156, 181
Monroe, James, 153, 179, 183, 186, 220; on Greece, 98. See also Doctrine
Montesquieu, Charles de Secondat, Baron de, 140
Morellet, Abbé André, 47
Morocco, 184, 217
Morris, Gouverneur, 69
Morris, Robert, 24
Muñoz Marín, Luis, 157–158, 170
Muraviev, Nikita, 103

N.A.A.C.P., 188, 190
Napoleon Bonaparte, 11, 38, 93, 112,

117, 137, 146, 147, 149; as administrator, 93
Napoleon III, Emperor of the French, 108
Nasser, Gamal Abdel, 195
Nationalism, 10, 11, 125; in Latin America, 146; in British Empire, 177
Navigation Laws, 33
Necker, Jacques, 40, 53; and *compte rendu*, 54
Negroes, 185, 190, 203; and slavery, 19, 31–32; slave trade, 181, 182; and American Colonization Society, 182, 183, 184; in Nova Scotia, 187; U.S., and African nationalism, 188
Nehru, Jawaharlal, 9, 215 *n*
Neocolonialism. *See* Colonialism, Imperialism
Neo-Imperialism. *See* Imperialism, Colonialism
Nesselrode, Count Karl Robert, 145, 156
Netherlands, 200; and contraband trade, 46–47; revolt in, 89–90; and U.S. example, 89–90
Neutrality, U.S., 8, 19, 50, 67, 70; toward Canada, 175. *See also* Nonalignment
Neutrality, Proclamation of, 8, 67, 70
New Deal, 213
New England, 4, 22, 152; on slave trade, 181, 182
Newenham, Edward, 83
New Hampshire, boundary dispute, 15; Constitutional Convention, 16
New York, City, 4, 5, 15, 71, 190; State, 175
Nicaragua, 162
Nigeria, 2, 20, 191
Nkrumah, Kwame, 181, 188, 189

Noailles, Vicomte de, 42
Nonalignment, and independent nations, 9; in Africa, 192
North, Frederick, Lord North, ministry, 80, 85
Northwest Ordinance, 19, 160
Norway, 95
Nova Scotia, 187
Novikov, Nikolai I., 100–101

October Revolution, 107, 124, 128, 190; and Mexico, 166; and Cuba, 169
O'Higgins, Bernardo, 25, 151
"Operation Bootstrap," 163, 172
Ordóñez, José Batlle y, 165
Oswald, Richard, 48
Otis, James, 58, 59

Paine, Thomas, 17, 52; *Common Sense*, 8; *Crisis* letter, 11–12
Pakistan, 221
Palmer, R. R., 28, 40, 41, 47, 76
Panama, canal, 161; revolution, 161
Panama, Congress of, 140
Pan-Americanism, 153–154
Pan-Arabism, 195
Paoli, Pasquale, 77
Paraguay, 150, 164
Park, Chung Hee, 214
Parker, Sir Peter, 64
Parkinson, C. Northcote, 146, 147
Parliamentary system, reform in England, 80; in Africa, 191; in China, Republic of, 206
Parsons, Theophilus, 21
Peace Corps, 187, 188
Pedro I (Brazil), 141
Penal Code, 10; U.S. Quaker model and Russia, 102
Penn, Lady Juliana, 26
Penn, William, 97

Pennsylvania, 4, 31, 102; Declaration of Rights, 23; Constitution, 117; and aid to Santo Domingo, 133
Perry, Matthew, 201, 210
Peru, 130, 150, 170
Pestel, Pavel Ivanovich, 102
Peters, Thomas, 187
Philadelphia, 6, 65, 186, 200; and "Jacobins," 71; and Jews, 88; merchants in Latin America, 152; on slave trade, 181, 182
Philippines, 160, 164, 174, 199, 201; and U.S. administration, 207–209, 210
Pickens, Andrew, 3
Pickering, Timothy, 135
Pinckney, Charles, 29, 30, 69
Pitt, William, the Younger, 80
Platt Amendment, 161
Poinsett, Joel, 154
Poland, 47, 77, 90, 99, 123, 201
Political parties, one-party system, 9; in Germany, 122; in Africa, 191, 192; in Korea, 214
Polk, James K., 109
Portugal, 144
Presidency, 191; and Czechoslovakia, 126; U.S. system in Brazil, 144; pluralistic in Uruguay, 165; in Taiwan, 206; in South Korea, 214
Price, Richard, Observations on Civil Liberty and the Justice and Policy of the War with America, 79; on religious liberty in Ireland, 86–87
Propaganda, U.S., 41, 44, 49; in Latin America, 151, 152; on European enlisted men, 43; pro-American in England, 78–80
Puerto Rico, 131, 159, 160, 163, 164, 170, 174; as colonial possession, 162–163; reforms, 163

Pugachev Revolt, 99, 106
Puritanism, 13

Radicalism, 78–81, 102–108, 176, 177
Radishchev, A. N., Journey from St. Petersburg to Moscow, 101–102
Randolph, John, 153
Ransonnet, Jean-Pierre, 91
Raynal, Abbé Guillaume, Philosophical History of European Institutions, 40; Two Indies, 41
Rayneval, Joseph-Matthias Gérard de, 102
Reform, land, U.S., 24; in Latin America, 169, 171; in China, 206–207
Reischauer, Edwin O., 219
Religious liberty, 10, 40; in Ireland, 86–87; and German Jews, 87; in U.S., 87; in Argentine Constitution, 143
Republicanism, 12, 13, 20; in Germany, 122; in Latin America, 142; in Southern states, 143; in Canada, 176–177
Restrepo, Carlos Lleras, 172
Revolutions of 1848, 111, 115, 116, 117, 176; in France, 108; Constitutionalism, 109, 112; Hungary, 114. See also Frankfurt Assembly
Rhee, Syngman, 213, 214
Rhode Island, and slavery, 31
Rhodes, Cecil, 184
Rhodesia, 194
Ritual, American Revolution as, 125; in Latin America, 158; in Africa, 183, 185, 187, 188; in Asia, 217
Rivington, James, 5
Roberts, Josiah, 151
Robespierre, Maximilien de, 60, 108
Rochambeau, Comte de, 43

Rochefoucauld d'Anville, Louis-Alexandre, 43
Rockefeller, Nelson A., Report on Latin America, 171, 172
Rockingham, Marquess of, 80
Rolland, Romain, on Wilson, 121
Roosevelt, Franklin Delano, 80, 120, 169, 204, 220; on self-determination, 127; on Latin American intervention and Puerto Rican status, 163; on Indian independence, 179–180, 216 n; on Indochinese independence, 217–218, 219
Roosevelt, Theodore, 161, 162
Root, Elihu, 161
Rosas, Juan Manuel de, 142, 145, 150
Rousseau, Jean-Jacques, 13, 40, 59, 137, 190; *Emile*, 138
Roy, Rammohun, 216
Rush, Richard, 108, 109
Russia, on U.S., 99–108. See also Soviet Union

Saint Domingue, 132–134. See also Haiti
Saint-Just, Louis Antoine Léon de, 61
Samoa, 201
Sanders, George, 115
San Martín, José de, 138
San Francisco, Treaty of, 210
Santa Anna, Antonio López de, 149–150
Santo Domingo. See Dominican Republic
Sarmiento, Domingo Faustino, 144
Schurz, Carl, 111
Seamen, as revolutionaries, 4, 5
Sears, Isaac, 4, 6
Secularism, U.S., 89
Ségur, Philip Henri, Comte de, 42

Self-Determination, 89, 219; and Czechoslovakia, 123–125; and U.N. Declaration, 127
Senghor, Leopold Sedar, 190, 221
Serfdom, Russian, 102
Seven Years' War, 39
Shaler, William, 151
Sharp, Granville, 187
Shaw, Samuel, 199
Shays' Rebellion, 7, 70
Shelburne, William Petty (Fitzmaurice), 2nd Earl of, later 1st Marquess of Lansdowne, 47, 48, 79; and Franklin, 81; on Ireland, 83
Shigenobu, Okuma, 210
Short, William, 43
Sierra Leone, 186–187
Sieyès, Abbé, 140
Slavery, in U.S., 19, 30–32, 118, 178, 183; in Haiti, 132–136
Socialism, "Scientific," 181. See also Marx, Karl
Songha, 190
Sons of Liberty, 4, 58
South Africa, 193, 194
Southey, Robert, 81
Sovereignty, popular, 13, 16, 40, 75, 94, 120, 139, 211
Soviet Union, 11, 26, 27, 124, 169, 190, 195, 197; invasion of Czechoslovakia, 127–128
Spain, 77, 159, 192, 196, 201, 207; and Western Hemisphere possessions, 48, 78, 129–131; and U.S., 131, 132
Speech, freedom of, 18, 100
"Spirit of '76," 166, 168, 190, 193, 195
Staatslexicon, of Rotteck and Weeker, 112
Stalin, Joseph, 127, 205, 218
Stalingrad, 180
Stanley, Sir Henry Morton, 184

State Constitutions, U.S., 102, 175; and France, 41, 55, 56; and religious liberty, 87; and Belgium, 91, 92; and Norway, 95
Statehood, 19, 157
Stilwell, Joseph W., 218
Stowe, Harriet Beecher, 103, 119
Sucre, Antonio José de, 141
Suffrage, U.S., 19; Bakunin on universal, 105; in Chile, 144; Mexican universal, 167
Sukarno, Achmed, 219
Sumarakov, A. P., 101
Sumter, Thomas, 3
Sun Yat-sen, 204, 206, 214; on liberty, 202; on U.S. federalism, 203
Sweden, 76, 96; and U.S. model, 95

Taft, William Howard, 162, 166
Taiwan. See China, Republic of
Taxation, in France, 55; in Latin America, 130, 171
Teague, Hilary, 185
Tea Party, 5, 64
Teller, Henry M., Teller Amendment, 159
Tennis Court Oath, 55
Thoreau, Henry David, 216
Tiradentes, Conspiracy of, 131
Tocqueville, Alexis de, 75, 103, 105, 106
Tolstoi, Leo, 216
Tooke, John Horne, 78, 79
Toussaint L'Ouverture, Pierre Dominique, 133, 134, 137
Townshend, Thomas, later 1st Viscount Sydney, 54, 55
Treaty of 1783, 24, 26, 27, 187
Trenchard, John, 13, 77
Tubman, William Vacanarat Shadrach, 186
Turberville, George de, 39
Turgot, Anne Robert Jacques, 40, 42

Turkey, 220; Revolution, 197
Turner, Frederick Jackson, 105
Tydings-McDuffie Act, 208

United Nations, Declaration of, 127
United Provinces. See Netherlands
United States, diplomacy, 48–51; and revolutions abroad, 120, 134; and Haitian recognition, 135; and Israel, 197, 198 n, 199; and Asia, 199–201, 207–210, 215, 217
U Nu, 9
Upper Volta, 188
Uruguay, 165

Vargas, Getulio, 144, 151
Vattel, Emmerich von, 49
Vaughan, Benjamin, 50, 81, 179
Venezuela, 136, 139–141, 150, 158, 164; reforms, 170
Vergennes, Charles Gravier, Comte de, 39
Vergil, 41
Vermont, 17, 31; dispute with New York, 15; support to Canada, 175
Versailles, Peace Conference of, 166, 188
Vietnam, 11, 199, 219; U.S. intervention, 219, 220, 221. South, 219; Democratic Republic of, 48, 220
Villa, Pancho, 166
Vioménil, Baron de, 29
Virginia, Declaration of Rights, 17, 18, 20–21, 87, 211; Constitution, 24, 31, 56
Volkonsky, Sergei, 103
Voltaire, François Marie Arouet de, 44, 45, 164

Wallace, Henry A., 204
Walpole, Horace, on Ireland, 83

Washington, George, 10, 22, 27, 35, 37, 42, 46, 47, 61, 68, 69, 70, 71, 83, 85, 86, 95, 97, 101, 102, 103, 106, 116, 118, 121, 125, 136, 140, 141, 147, 151, 165, 200, 202, 204; Circular to the States, 35; Newburgh Address, 61; on Ireland, 86; on U.S. civil liberties, 88; Farewell Address, 192
Weber, Max, 121–122
Webster, Daniel, 114
Webster, Noah, 10
Weimar Constitution, 121–122
Weizmann, Chaim, 198
Wells, H. G., 121
Wilberforce, William, 72
Wilkes, Charles, 200
Wilkes, John, 78
Wilhelm II, German Kaiser, 109
Wilson, James, 6
Wilson, Woodrow, 48, 51, 120, 124, 128, 162, 203; Mobile speech, 51; war message, 120–121; Fourteen Points, 121, 123; and Germany, 121; "Peace without Victory," 123; and Czechoslovakia, 123–124; on recognition of states, 166
Wolcott, Oliver, Jr., 68
Woodson, Carter G., 188
Wordsworth, William, 81
Wyvill, Rev. Christopher, 80

Yalta Conference, 127, 218
"Young America" Movement, 115, 116
Ypsilanti, Demetrios, 98
Yüan Shih-k'ai, 203
Yugoslavia, 20, 125
Yūkichi, Fukuzawa, 210

Zenger Case, 18
Zollverein, 111